A POPULIST EXCEPTION?

THE 2017 NEW ZEALAND GENERAL ELECTION

A POPULIST EXCEPTION?

THE 2017 NEW ZEALAND GENERAL ELECTION

EDITED BY JACK VOWLES
AND JENNIFER CURTIN

Australian
National
University

PRESS

ANU PRESS

Published by ANU Press
The Australian National University
Acton ACT 2601, Australia
Email: anupress@anu.edu.au

Available to download for free at press.anu.edu.au

ISBN (print): 9781760463854
ISBN (online): 9781760463861

WorldCat (print): 1178915541
WorldCat (online): 1178915122

DOI: 10.22459/PE.2020

Cover design and layout by ANU Press

Cover photograph: Deputy Prime Minister Winston Peters, Prime Minister Jacinda Ardern and Green Party leader James Shaw standing in 'unity' at the stand up after the 'Next steps in Government's Plan for NZ' speech at AUT, Auckland. © Stuff Limited.

CONTENTS

LIST OF FIGURES AND TABLES

Figures

Tables

ACKNOWLEDGEMENTS

Jennifer Curtin and Jack Vowles

In 2019, Professor Robert Wade (London School of Economics) visited his homeland, New Zealand. He discussed the reasons why Trumpian-style politics could last for 30 years. Several months before his talk, a New Zealand Ministry of Foreign Affairs and Trade briefing reminded the government that, at the global level, economic and security issues had resulted in widespread populist sentiment: 'elected leaders, appealing to their political bases, are pursuing nativist and protectionist policies and rejecting globalisation and the institutions that support and enforce it' (Ministry of Foreign Affairs and Trade, 2019). This reference to populism was also flagged as a threat in a New Zealand Defence Force report, which argued that the increasing gap between rich and poor was fostering nationalist movements in the region and elsewhere.

New Zealand is evidently not immune to populism; however, the 2017 general election result suggested that the extent of discontent evident in jurisdictions elsewhere had yet to resonate with New Zealand voters. Through an analysis of survey data gathered through the New Zealand Election Study (NZES), this volume examines the question of whether, in 2017, New Zealand proved to be a 'populist exception'.

The NZES has a long tradition—the 2017 'wave' is the 10th since its first outing in 1990. The next study, for 2020, already in preparation, will mark 30 years of a continuous time series. The 2017 study was led by Jack Vowles at Victoria University and supported by a team of scholars from universities across New Zealand. As editors of this volume, we have benefited greatly from the insights of our colleagues Lara Greaves (University of Auckland), Janine Hayward (University of Otago) and Fiona Barker, Kate McMillan and Matthew Gibbons (Victoria University of Wellington). This volume has been a wholly collaborative effort.

No survey research can be completed without significant funding and much work. We greatly appreciate the generosity of the Victoria University of Wellington's Research Committee and Summer Scholar funds, the University of Auckland's Faculty Research Development and Summer Scholar funds, the New Zealand Electoral Commission and the University of Otago. Funding secured from the British Academy by Nick Vivyan and Patrick Kuhn (Durham University) enabled us to increase the sample size and, consequently, to provide data for their research on reporting of turnout.

The Centre of Methods and Policy Application in the Social Sciences (otherwise known as COMPASS) at the University of Auckland also provided wonderful service in the administration of the NZES. In particular, we must thank Lara Greaves, Martin von Randow, Barry Milne and the team of students and friends who systematically worked to ensure that the over 10,000 surveys were distributed in good time. Their efforts consumed several weekends; therefore, we acknowledge them here by name: Nidhi Aggarwal, Mo Anwar, Sarah Boyd, Bianca Brown, Lucy Cowie, Reuben Curtin Symes, Caitlyn Drinkwater, Sonali Dutt, Chris Garner, Laura Garner, Auguste Harrington, Hasith Kandaudahewa, Chooi-Wen Khoo, Tony Koson Sriamporn, Cinnamon Lindsay, Luke Oldfield, Camille Reid, Sophie Sills, Elizabeth Strickett and Irene Wu. Our thanks also go to the Public Policy Institute at the University of Auckland for sharing their space with us for this process and to Matthew Gibbons, Ruairi Cahill-Fleury, Joshua James, Correna Matika, Usman Shahid and Benjamin Yeung for their voter validation work across the country.

Charles Crothers at Auckland University of Technology provided very helpful insights and comments on the conceptual framework and several of the early chapters, as did the ANU Press Social Sciences Editorial Board. The board and the anonymous readers shared feedback on the full manuscript, challenging us to strengthen our arguments regarding New Zealand's 'style' of populism. Sue Osborne's editing skills were invaluable, as were those of Capstone Editing, while Frank Bongiorno, Emily Tinker and Richard Reid worked tirelessly with us in the final stages of publication. Finally, as was the case with our volume on the 2014 election (*A Bark but no Bite*, also published by ANU Press), our analysis was dependent on the generosity of our survey respondents. We hope they find this as interesting to read as we found it to write.

References

Ministry of Foreign Affairs and Trade (New Zealand). (2019). *Strategic intentions 2019–2023*. Retrieved from www.mfat.govt.nz/assets/About-us/MFAT-Strategic-Intentions-2019-2023.pdf

THE POPULIST EXCEPTION? THE 2017 NEW ZEALAND GENERAL ELECTION

Jack Vowles, Jennifer Curtin and Fiona Barker

The 2017 New Zealand general election (23 September) occurred at a time when the global political landscape was being profoundly shaped by growing ideological polarisation and volatility in electoral politics. Only a year had passed since the contentious Brexit referendum and the election of Donald Trump as President of the United States. In fact, New Zealand's general and Germany's federal elections were held on the same weekend. In Germany, the radical right *Alternative für Deutschland* made an electoral breakthrough, at the expense of the mainstream centre-left (Social Democratic Party of Germany) and centre-right (Christian Democratic Union/Christian Social Union) parties, although the vote shifts were not sufficient to significantly disrupt the party system. It is not surprising that many have been tempted to interpret New Zealand's election results both within this international political context and through the lens of the rise of right-wing and authoritarian populism. Indeed, the formation of a coalition government that includes a party widely described as populist—the New Zealand First Party—prompted one commentator to argue that the 'far-right' had 'seized power' in New Zealand (Mack, 2017).

It is not difficult to rebut a claim that New Zealand acts as a simple mirror of recent 'populist politics' patterns seen elsewhere. However, other assertions warrant more scrutiny. Some have posited the existence of a distinctive 'Antipodean' form of populism (Moffitt, 2017). Others have made the case that New Zealand is a 'populist exception', bucking the international trend in favour of some form of electorally moderate 'politics as usual'. However, there is also a sense that New Zealand's own history contains examples of populism, although past episodes have perhaps acted as some form of inoculation. Crucially, what is this phenomenon called populism—do we (and how do we) know it when we see it?

Using data from the 2017 New Zealand Election Study (NZES), this book seeks to answer those questions. The goals are twofold: (1) to situate New Zealand's 2017 election in a contemporary international context in which there is particular concern about the rise of so-called populist politics and (2) to analyse the political attitudes and preferences of New Zealanders in 2017 to identify and further interpret longer-term patterns in New Zealand politics that are made possible by this 10th iteration of the NZES. The former task is made possible by the Comparative Study of Electoral Systems (CSES), to which the NZES contributes data, and includes questions (designed to elicit populist attitudes) that have been asked of citizens by election studies in a range of advanced democracies (CSES, 2016). The chapters in this book explore and critique such questions on populism (and those theories that lie behind them), seeking to uncover the nature of populism and associated attitudinal dimensions in New Zealand.

New Zealand offers a relevant case to study because historians and political scientists broadly agree that the country's political culture contains strong traditions of both populism and authoritarianism. At first glance, New Zealand's exceptionalism might seem unexpected. International scholarship frequently identifies New Zealand First as the standard-bearer of populist politics in New Zealand; however, populist and authoritarian support for other parties is also observable. Meanwhile, the changing nature of New Zealand society complicates a simple application of populist theory, as exemplified by increasing recognition of the Treaty rights of the indigenous Māori population, the existence of designated Māori parliamentary representation[1] and the increasing diversity of the New Zealand population following recent high levels of net immigration.

The 2017 election provides an appropriate case to examine populism in New Zealand because, following coalition negotiations, the apparently populist New Zealand First Party entered into government with the

---

1   For the 2017 election, there were seven Māori seats of 71 electorate seats in parliament, the boundaries of which overlie the 'general' electorates. Persons of Māori descent can choose either the general or Māori roll—the number that choose the Māori option determines the number of seats assigned.

Labour Party. In a broader context, the 2017 election was both won and lost by the party defending its record in office since 2008—the centre-right New Zealand National Party (Vowles, 2018). National won the most votes; however, they lost the battle over government formation to a coalition comprised of the Labour and New Zealand First parties, with the support of the Green Party. The outcome was unexpected for several reasons. First, the Labour Party had been languishing in opinion polls, with only approximately 24 per cent support for several months prior to the election. Second, just over seven weeks before election day, on 1 August 2017, Labour unanimously voted to change its leader. Leadership changes so close to an election are unusual in New Zealand politics. Labour's new leader, Jacinda Ardern, was young, feminist and identified herself as a politically progressive social democrat. She rapidly acquired a high level of public popularity, taking Labour to a party vote of 37 per cent at the election and, therefore, the potential core of a coalition. The second surprise occurred on 19 October, when New Zealand First party leader Winston Peters announced that he would form a government with Labour, citing the need for capitalism to 'regain … its human face' as having influenced his approach to the negotiations (Peters, 2017). The Green Party provided the new government with support on confidence and supply. Jacinda Ardern became prime minister and Winston Peters her deputy. New Zealand First members of parliament took four seats in the 20-member Cabinet and the Greens received three ministerial positions outside of Cabinet. This was the first time in the history of the mixed member proportional system (since 1996) that a party with the second-most votes gained the position of leading a government.

Reactions to the new coalition arrangements were mixed. Some were shocked, believing that the centre-right had been robbed (Winston Peters settles for stardust, 2017). *The Australian* mocked the result with the headline 'Shock in New Zealand as losers take power'. The author of this article suggested that it was a 'vanilla election' ending with a 'bitter aftertaste', while decrying the 'rise of celebrity politicians, the fall of good governments and the terror of the populists' (Sheridan, 2017). Others claimed that a 'nicer, kinder and better NZ' could be expected and that having Ardern as prime minister would be 'profound' for young women (Radio New Zealand, 2017).

Jacinda Ardern was widely recognised as being of the same progressive mould as Canada's Justin Trudeau or France's Emmanuel Macron. However, unlike these two leaders, hers was not a single-party government; therefore, there arose inevitable predictions of the difficulties and potentially dire consequences that lay ahead. Both the Labour and Green parties were criticised for their willingness to work with New Zealand First, given its populist bent. However, this was not the first time that New Zealand First had served in government. The party had been in coalition with the National Party between 1996 and 1998 and had supported Helen Clark's Labour Government between 2005 and 2008. The key difference in 2017 was the breadth of ideologies and policy commitments folded into the new government's agenda and the extent to which New Zealand First was a key player.

While it might be natural to see New Zealand First's centrality to this outcome as an example of populism on the rise, we argue that the case of New Zealand reveals that populism need not be associated with authoritarianism, nor necessarily with the 'radical right'. Our examination of both the historical and contemporary contexts demonstrates that, at least in elite-level politics, both populism and authoritarianism are currently relatively weak in New Zealand. This does not render the country immune to populist rhetoric (both inclusive and exclusive); nor does it preclude the emergence of a cultural and generational backlash (Norris & Inglehart, 2019). Indeed, some commentators viewed the 2017 election as one fought along generational battle lines, on both material and post-material issues (Shadwell, 2017).

In this volume, we draw on original data from the NZES to examine the results of the 2017 election and the extent to which they support the claim that New Zealand is indeed a populist exception. In Chapter 1, we begin by revisiting international definitions of populism and examining their relevance to New Zealand. We conclude by identifying selected historical occurrences of populism in New Zealand's political system and political culture and discussing factors that complicate the application of populism to the case of New Zealand.

Chapter 2 probes more deeply into the background of the 2017 election, comparing the results with those of 2014 and examining the pattern of vote shifts between the two elections and the changes in issue salience that shaped the outcome. It compares the level of vote volatility and the size of the party system with data from other OECD democracies and examines the social and demographic correlates of vote choice.

Chapter 3 outlines how we have measured and operationalised the concept of populism in relation to public attitudes in New Zealand. Questions derived from the module of questions designed under the auspices of the CSES are discussed and critiqued. We construct alternative scales of populism and authoritarianism from a mixture of items from the CSES and NZES and then examine the extent to which these attitudinal sets are associated with a range of social and demographic variables, including generational age cohorts.

Drawing on the conceptualisation and operationalisation outlined in the early part of the book, Chapters 4–8 provide in-depth analyses of the ways in which populism and authoritarianism played out across various key issues and demographics in the 2017 election. In Chapter 4, we examine the language used by New Zealand's political parties and analyse how populist and authoritarian attitudes are associated with left–right ideological positions, vote choices and satisfaction and support for democracy.

Drawing on time series data, Chapter 5 compares public opinion regarding immigration in New Zealand to that of other countries with comparable immigration experiences. It identifies the specific characteristics of New Zealanders' concerns regarding immigration (by party preferences), asking how closely these opinions and preferences mirror the European and American experience with anti-immigrant populism.

Chapter 6 focuses on the 'gender factor' in the 2017 election, beginning with an examination of Jacinda Ardern's political rhetoric of hope and positivity, as opposed to fear and division, and the emotional and attitudinal effects that this generated. Further, it investigates the gender gap in vote choice and attitudes to feminist issues that, in a populist moment, possess the potential to result in a cultural backlash.

Chapter 7 discusses the election results among Māori, including analysis of the downfall of the Māori Party and political participation by Māori beyond turnout. It investigates populism and authoritarianism among Māori (compared to non-Māori) through an examination of opinions regarding the Māori electorates and reveals how these have changed over time as a result of the various attempts by conservative politicians to tap into anti-Māori sentiment.

Chapter 8 analyses preferences for either a Labour- or National-led coalition—these were marginally in favour of the latter, thereby creating issues of legitimacy. It also demonstrates that the coalition outcome was closer to the median voter than the centre-right alternatives. Confidence in the principle of coalition government and satisfaction with democracy were only slightly eroded, more among the older than younger population and among authoritarians already uncomfortable with coalitions. Populists, on the other hand, were (and remained) in favour of the principle of coalition government.

We draw the volume to a close by bringing together the substantive findings from each chapter to reinforce our key arguments—that distinguishing between exclusionary and inclusive forms of populism is necessary and invaluable to context-rich research. Through empirical analyses, we demonstrate that inclusive forms of populism can be pluralist in orientation if a leader's rhetorical approach recognises 'the people' as diverse and encompassing. This is not to deny that New Zealand has a history of authoritarian populism, nor do we suggest an absence of authoritarian values among the New Zealand voting public. However, in the 2017 New Zealand general election, the exclusionary populism observable in many parts of the globe was notably absent.

References

Comparative Study of Electoral Systems. (2016). *CSES Module 5: Democracy divided? People, politicians and the politics of populism.* Retrieved from www.cses.org/wp-content/uploads/2019/03/CSES5_ContentSubcommittee_Final Report.pdf

Mack, B. (2017). How the far right is poisoning New Zealand. *Washington Post.* Retrieved from www.washingtonpost.com/news/global-opinions/wp/2017/11/08/how-the-far-right-is-poisoning-new-zealand/

Moffitt, B. (2017). Populism in Australia and New Zealand. In C. R. Kaltwasser, P. Taggart, P. O. Espejo & P. Ostiguy (Eds.), *The Oxford handbook of populism* (pp. 121–139). Oxford, United Kingdom: Oxford University Press. doi.org/10.1093/oxfordhb/9780198803560.013.5

Norris, P. & Inglehart, R. (2019). *Cultural backlash. Trump, Brexit and the rise of authoritarian populism.* New York: Cambridge University Press. doi.org/10.1017/9781108595841

Peters, W. (2017). Post-election announcement speech. *Scoop*. Retrieved from www.scoop.co.nz/stories/PA1710/S00050/peters-post-election-announcement-speech.htm

Radio New Zealand. (2017). NZ's new PM. What is being said. *Radio New Zealand*. Retrieved from www.rnz.co.nz/news/political/341884/nz-s-new-pm-what-is-being-said

Shadwell, T. (2017). I used to report on Jacinda Ardern. This is why she is good for NZ. *The Independent*. Retrieved from www.independent.co.uk/voices/jacinda-arden-labour-jacindamania-new-zealand-elections-prime-minister-dj-a8009546.html

Sheridan, G. (2017). NZ shock: Losers take power. *The Australian*. Retrieved from www.theaustralian.com.au/nation/world/new-zealand-shock-losers-labour-and-nz-first-take-power/news-story/78dfb678806601e8387b2f6c1be3b3ac

Vowles, J. (2018). Surprise, surprise: The New Zealand general election of 2017. *Kōtuitui: New Zealand Journal of Social Sciences Online*. doi.org/10.1080/1177083X.2018.1443472

Winston Peters settles for stardust. (2017). *Otago Daily Times*. Retrieved from www.odt.co.nz/news/national/winston-peters-settles-stardust

1

POPULISM AND ELECTORAL POLITICS IN NEW ZEALAND

Fiona Barker and Jack Vowles

In 1848, Karl Marx wrote that 'a spectre stalks the land of Europe—the spectre of communism' (p. 14). In the early 21st century, 'populism' constitutes a new apparition that is feared by many, haunting the wider world of representative democracy (Albertazzi & McDonnell, 2008). Populism has been described as one of two 'deformations' of liberal democracy, as a response to the alternative deformation of elitism (Galston, 2018). To Cas Mudde (2015, n.p.), for example, populism is an 'illiberal democratic response to undemocratic liberalism'.

Much current discussion of populism frames the phenomenon pejoratively, as a disorder or affliction that threatens liberal democracy. Populism is said to be the antithesis of both pluralism and elitism. In this analysis of recent New Zealand politics, we challenge this construction of the concept, in both the New Zealand context and elsewhere. Some forms of populism may be anti-pluralist and, indeed, become anti-democratic, particularly when combined with authoritarianism. History has shown that apparently populist appeals to 'the people' may have a dark side, particularly when strong leaders become authoritarian and these appeals exclude some ethnic groups, immigrants or other minorities. However, other forms of populism accept difference, defining the core populist idea of 'the people' across ethnic and cultural distinctions to include everyone except a narrow elite, defined as those who exert excessive power based on concentrated wealth and influence. In ideological terms, populism exists on the left and on the right, overlapping with 'inclusionary' versus 'exclusionary' dimensions.

This chapter considers the coherence, validity and portability of various constructions of populism and their applicability to contemporary New Zealand politics. This will allow us to begin to assess if, how and why New Zealand may be an exception to a trend that, elsewhere, is not only populist but sometimes also authoritarian. Is there, as Moffitt (2017) argued, an 'Antipodean form of populism' that New Zealand shares with Australia? Of course, the meanings of words and concepts are not fixed. Within the broad framework of its discourse, populism may be defined however one likes. But to contribute value in political analysis, populism requires a minimal definition that all can understand and share.

Defining Populism: Existing Approaches

Populism has taken several forms in political discourse, so many that it has been described as offering a 'classic example' of what political scientists describe as a 'stretched concept, pulled out of shape by overuse and misuse' (Brett, 2013, p. 410). Scholars have failed to reach consensus on a single approach to defining and measuring populism. Indeed, the recently published *Oxford handbook of populism* features three alternative constructions: ideological, organisational/strategic and discursive/performative (Kaltwasser, Ostiguy, Espejo & Taggart, 2017, pp. 1–2). However, these three constructions do not exhaust the available options. The lack of a single, clear definition in the scholarly literature is compounded by the changing real-world politics of populism—namely, the entry of parties that are described as populist into government and the wildly varying, 'almost random', vernacular uses of the term, including both in the media and by politicians themselves (Bale, Taggart & van Kessel, 2011, p. 128).

The most straightforward application of the concept is a label used to classify political parties and movements as 'populist' or 'non-populist'— this was Mudde's (2007) starting point. Individual politicians may be similarly categorised. Notably, populism tends to be a label ascribed by others, but not necessarily embraced by the relevant parties or movements in question. A populist/non-populist dichotomy is a crude instrument.

Parties can be represented on a continuum or scale, as demonstrated by Norris (2020). Once the existence of degrees of populism or non-populism is admitted, the picture becomes more complex.

What does the label 'populist' connote? Mudde's ideational approach is the most widely applied. In his terms, populism is a 'thin ideology', able to be employed by parties and movements with varied objectives—for example, both neoliberal and anti-neoliberal. Its foundations are deeply moral, pitting a 'pure people' against a 'corrupt elite'. The people are capable of generating a 'general will' that expresses their purported common interests against the elite's special interests. Populism finds its opposite in both elitism and pluralism. Populism is anti-pluralist due to its emphasis on the general will. Mudde regarded this as 'a kind of vulgar Rousseauian argument' (2017, p. 8). Populists are strongly convinced of the intrinsic morality of their views; therefore, according to Mudde, they constitute a danger to democracy. While Mudde's approach has been applied widely, doubts exist concerning its ability to travel. It works best as an ideal-type applied to authoritarian and exclusionary forms of populism; however, it is not otherwise particularly robust. A minimal definition is required to encompass all the necessary territory (Norris & Inglehart, 2019, p. 24).

A less pejorative approach has been offered by Ostiguy (2017), who defined populism as 'style'. Following Ostiguy, Moffitt (2017) has argued that, in Australia and New Zealand, populism as style focuses on both discursive and performative elements of political actors and is characterised by appeals to 'the People' versus 'the Elite' and by 'bad manners' and 'low' behaviours (e.g. coarse and colourful, rather than technocratic, language). The essence of populism is a relationship between populist leaders and the 'authentic' people—who are not necessarily 'pure' or 'virtuous'—who wish their neglected interests to be fully represented in government (Ostiguy, 2017, p. 91). This approach has some merit but may also be too narrow.

Weyland's political-strategic approach emphasises 'personalistic leadership that rests on direct, unmediated, un-institutionalised support from large masses of mostly unorganised followers' (2017, p. 48). Populism is distinguished from fascism by the opportunism displayed by its leaders, who place vote maximisation ahead of ideological purity. Further, populists retain some commitment to democracy, whereas fascists do not, creating an even clearer divide. Again, this approach may fail to capture all necessary facets of the phenomenon. Meanwhile, some economists have identified populism with economic irresponsibility, where politicians maximise their popularity while in government via unsustainable expenditure (Dornbusch & Edwards, 1991; Sachs, 1989). However, over the last two decades, the use of populist appeals by subsequent fiscally responsible governments in various countries (most notably in Latin America) presents a counterexample.

Laclau has proposed a more promising concept of populism, which conceives of 'the people' in terms of the construction of a popular hegemonic bloc. In this vision, populism forms an essential component of democracy. Populists seek to promote universal ideas of justice by creating 'empty signifiers' (Laclau, 2005, p. 131). The 'people' and 'the elite' are symbolic containers for content that is specific to political context and culture, thereby maximising the concept's travel potential. Laclau was one of the first scholars of populism to focus on its discursive elements, a direction followed in much subsequent research. Aslanidis (2016) abandoned Laclau's post-structuralist, interpretative and very broad definition of discourse, while still drawing on his central insights. He proposed the idea of a 'populist frame' that discursively mobilises the sovereign people against the elite. This frame can be captured empirically through textual analysis of populist discourse—an approach that is now followed by most researchers in the field.

While paying due respect to Mudde's contribution, Aslanidis rejects the idea of populism as ideology of any kind, thick or thin. Populism, as used in the language of political parties and movements, is a discursive mode of operation or strategy. The 'sovereignty of the people' is a key component of the populist frame, in addition to being central to democratic discourse in general. Some, including left-wing cultural theorist Stuart Hall (Williams, 2012), have questioned the existence of such a thing as 'the people'; a statement oddly reminiscent of Margaret Thatcher's denial of 'society' (as quoted in Thatcher, 2013). Of course, such concepts as 'the people' and 'populism' are discursive constructions in themselves, as Laclau and Aslanidis have pointed out. Such constructions become 'real' when they resonate with attitudes and behaviour and are given status in normative debate and, often, in constitutional laws or norms. The idea of 'the people' can hardly be rejected out of hand without removing one of the foundations of democracy itself. For example, consider the normative force of the first words of the United States Constitution: 'We the People'.

In constructing the concept of the 'people' as a symbolic signifier, in Laclau's terms, the key distinction exists between inclusionary and exclusionary populism (Mudde & Kaltwasser, 2013). When employed as a vehicle by the authoritarian right, populism becomes exclusionary. The people are unified according to their purity; a division is created between them and the corrupt elite and, crucially, other excluded groups who become, by definition, outsiders. Müller (2016) has contended that, by delineating insider and outsider groups in this way, this form of populism becomes a form of identity politics. The substantive identity of the 'pure' people can vary—the people could be, for example, white, working-class, Christian, 'hard working folk' or a designated nation. The 'ordinary people' are typically defined in nationalistic or ethnocentric terms (Donovan & Redlawsk, 2018; Mudde, 2013, 2014). Therefore, those who oppose them are part of the corrupt elite (and, thus, not part of 'the people') and cannot be legitimate (Müller, 2016). The denial of the possibility of legitimate opposition is the last step in the transformation of this form of populism from its origins as a democratic movement into one that more loosely resembles authoritarianism, as seen in contemporary examples such as Viktor Orbàn's Hungary.

Left-wing populists define the people more broadly. As a democratic movement of the left, populism defines the people as a super-majority—or, as famously popularised by Occupy Wall Street, 'the 99 per cent'. Historically, populism emerged from the democratic left—other contemporary examples of populism have continued this tradition (Katsambakis, 2016; March, 2007; Mouffe, 2018; Ramiro & Gomez, 2017). Populism arose during the so-called 'gilded age', a late 19th-century period in the United States that was characterised by economic growth, but also punctuated by recessions and further characterised by extreme poverty and economic inequality. Business elites encouraged political corruption and successfully influenced politicians not to regulate or legislate in the public interest. Populists mobilised 'the people' against elites in a movement that included both blacks and whites and was eventually incorporated into the Democratic Party (Goodwyn, 1976).

When mapped globally, varieties of populism can also be found across the range of the widely identified second dimension of party competition: from conservative, traditionalist, authoritarian or parochial values, at one end, to cosmopolitan, liberal and multicultural values, at the other (Norris & Inglehart, 2019). 'The people' are defined narrowly or broadly, across different dimensions (Abts & Rummens, 2007; Font, Graziano &

Tsakatika, 2019; Stanley, 2008, p. 107). In contrast to standard accounts of populist movements and leaders delineating a homogenous 'people', inclusionary populism (e.g. Syriza in Greece and Podemos in Spain) may involve a highly heterogeneous and pluralist vision of 'the people' (Font et al., 2019, p. 6). Anti-pluralism does not appear to be a necessary condition of populism across all its discourses, unless one wishes to narrow its definition.

A concept of populism that focuses on the language of popular sovereignty against undemocratic elites makes sense as a minimal definition that can operationalise classification of parties and movements. Quantitative textual analysis also encourages estimates of degrees of populism, rather than a strict dichotomy. However, populism works not only due to the grievances on which it may feed, but also because, discursively, it taps into democratic norms and values. Indeed, as discussed in Chapter 3 (Comparative Study of Electoral Systems, 2016; Norris & Inglehart, 2019), one can identify populist norms in public attitudes and opinions. In a world of norms, we return to ideology, even in inchoate form. To identify the intellectual origins of popular norms, we must address democratic theory.

Surprisingly, most work on populism has hitherto ignored democratic theory as a source of norms. However, continuing a long tradition of debate, some social choice theorists have identified populism as one of two alternative traditions of democracy. Institutionally, populism is based on the principle of responsible party government, in contrast with an opposing 'liberal' theory (Riker, 1982). Riker identified this form of populism as the model of responsible party government advocated in the United States in the 1950s (American Political Science Association, 1950). Based on an idealisation of Westminster democracy, as practised in the United Kingdom, responsible party government requires internally democratic political parties, the construction of party programs (presented to voters in advance of elections) and the granting of a mandate to implement those policies if a party gains office.

Riker (1982) himself became a critic of populist democracy as he defined it. Using social choice theory, derived from Arrow (1951), he argued that true democratic majority cannot be guaranteed on any political decision, that the inevitable fate of democratic politics is chaos and disequilibrium and that only a thin or minimalist liberal democracy is feasible, based on retrospective accountability of governments to voters and with constitutional limits on majority rule. This line of thinking followed influential ideas promoted by Schumpeter, which have since become known as the theory of democratic elitism (Bachrach, 1967; Riker, 1982; Schumpeter, 1942).

From the 1950s onwards, this populist model of democratic responsiveness to mass opinion has attracted sustained criticism from social choice theorists, liberals, neoliberals and some empirical political scientists. Meanwhile, political theorists who have defended populism in these terms have contested these social choice arguments (e.g. McLean, 2002; Radcliffe, 1993; Weale, 1984). Ultimately, the choice between elitist/liberal and populist forms of democracy relates to values (Dowding, 2006; Mackie, 2003). The normative ideal and practice of responsible party government remains central to much research into electoral politics (Adams, 2001). However, inspection of critiques of populism in mainstream political science demonstrates that, when many political scientists and politicians talk of 'liberal democracy', they often mean its elitist version.

Populists are critical of liberal democracy when it merges with elitism, pointing out its limitations in addressing economic and political problems: a shrinking of the 'space reserved to politics and to the people' (Pinelli, 2011, p. 15). Populists continue to use traditional institutional forms to gain election; however, many also advocate for more direct forms of expressing the will of 'the people', such as referendums. From the populist perspective, the shifting of some decision-making to unelected or technocratic elites distances government from the people, diminishes citizens' capacity to express their will and supports a (likely nefarious) elite consensus. In response, their critics disdainfully describe populism as a 'degraded form of democracy' (Müller, 2016, p. 10).

Liberal/elitist forms of democracy seek to limit the power of the majority by means of two mechanisms: constitutional limits to government authority (Urbinati, 2017) and the separation of powers, thereby giving often privileged minorities rights of both veto and influence. Populists oppose such limits to democratic majoritarianism. If liberal democracy is defined in terms of its constitutionalism, this forms the most important difference between liberal and populist democracy. This distinction is crucial for understanding populism in New Zealand. Even more so than the United Kingdom, New Zealand almost wholly lacks constitutional limits on government authority, other than by way of democratic election—an almost perfect case of institutional populism. As Palmer and Butler put it, New Zealand's constitution is 'dangerously incomplete, obscure, fragmentary and far too flexible' (2016, p. 13). Subject only to a majority in its single-chamber parliament, virtually every constitutional rule can be altered easily, without judicial review.

In normative terms, then, there exist two dominant ways of framing populism: one negative, which portrays it as a disorder or affliction, presenting a threat to liberal democracy, and another (now somewhat less emphasised) neutral or even positive, which conceives of populism as a social movement that aims to promote and expand democracy and remove control from economic and political elites with excessive power.

Norris and Inglehart (2019) have recently clarified the debate by distinguishing between populist and authoritarian attitudes. They identify a first-order principle regarding 'who should rule' common to all forms of populism: the claim that the people, rather than the 'establishment', elected representatives or, worse, technocrats and experts, are the true and legitimate sources of political and moral authority. The second-order principles that emerge from these principles and the concrete policies that flow from them can, however, take a variety of forms: for instance, in either authoritarian or liberal directions. Populism that seeks to implement authoritarian values emphasises security and order, conformity to a certain way of life, tradition or group, and obedience to strong leadership. By contrast, libertarian populism may prioritise participatory styles of politics and include rhetoric against financial elites, neoliberalism and mainstream political parties, while also supporting or at least tolerating more progressive social attitudes (Norris & Inglehart, 2019, p. 11). Therefore, whereas populist rhetoric pushes grievances upwards towards elites, authoritarian rhetoric directs grievances outwards towards scapegoat groups perceived as threatening the values and norms of the in-group (Norris & Inglehart, 2019, p. 7).

Norris and Inglehart have continued to accept the idea that populism sits in opposition to pluralism, a core tenet of both democracy and liberalism (Abts & Rummens, 2007; Mudde, 2017; Müller, 2016; Norris & Inglehart, 2019). Populism is posited to be the opposite of pluralism, due to claims that it seeks to attack the role of representation in representative democracy (Taggart, 2000), prioritising unity (not pluralism) and the unmediated relationship between (strong) leaders and the people

(Urbinati, 2017, p. 575). We argue that this is a narrow identification of populism. Logically, accusations of anti-pluralism apply only to exclusionary and authoritarian forms.

An inclusionary form of populism, by definition, will acknowledge difference while also building majority coalitions across society around concerns that all can share, by means of strategic or 'heresthetic' leadership: a strategy by which a person or group affects the context of a decision-making process to ensure that they prevail (Nagel, 1993). In broad terms, this social choice concept has much in common with Laclau's constructivist theory of establishing a popular hegemony. It also counters the criticism of the 'general will' as a naïve concept. Majorities are constructed via mobilisation, discourse and coalition building; few, if any, practical political actors can deny this point, populists and non-populists alike. Of those who accuse populism of being necessarily anti-pluralist we might ask: is this opposition to populism anti-majoritarian? Do they agree with Riker's (1982) claim that there can be no substantive content or moral force to the notions of majority rule and popular will? If so, can someone who claims the mantle of a democrat deny the principle of majority rule? Further, if majority rule, imperfect though it may be, is denied as a principle, what are the normative and behavioural bonds of cohesion that maintain a polity and make it possible for those who lose a debate to accept the result? Schumpeter's position provides the clearest answer to this question—trust in established elites and a constitutional order that suppresses majority rule, reinforced, if necessary, by the coercive power of the state. In situations where these values come into conflict, people face stark and uncomfortable choices.

If we set aside a view of populism as inherently exclusionary and authoritarian and acknowledge its nuanced and complex relationship with democracy, both historically and in contemporary normative theory, we may approach a more firmly grounded concept of populism that defines its opposite as elitism rather than pluralism. We make one key concession: as noted, populism has a dark side—even an initially democratic and inclusionary movement may be perverted if authoritarians assume leadership and themselves become an elite. Indeed, authoritarian populist movements are often led by persons with elite backgrounds and may make exclusionary appeals to the people on cultural issues to draw attention away from continued elite power and privilege. In so doing, they render populism a caricature of its own original aims, identifying it with politicians and movements whose actions and rhetoric increasingly smack of neo-fascism, if not fascism itself.

In this book, we define populism in two senses. First, in terms of normative political theory, populism is founded on the people's belief in government as its source of ultimate sovereignty and has both moral and pragmatic foundations. Foundations are moral in that the source of collective decisions should be collective deliberation among the people, all with equal claims to speak, and pragmatic in terms of scepticism regarding the claims of elites to superior wisdom and judgement over 'the mass'. Populism can be channelled indirectly through the institutions of representative democracy, or by other more direct means, but preferably where constitutional barriers to executive authority and legislative power do not strongly inhibit majority rule, thereby avoiding a wide separation of powers and the existence of multiple veto points. In our second sense of populism, we define it as a discursive or rhetorical strategy, in those terms discussed earlier in this chapter (Aslanidis, 2016). In passing, we also note that a populist frame may be used by those whose norms are not populist. Much of the confusion regarding populism is due to the use of populist discourse to promote parties or movements whose objectives are not populist in relation to normative democratic theory. For example, the style and rhetoric of current British Conservative Party leader Boris Johnson could be described as populist; however, his party's objectives are not.

To operationalise the concept of populism, we apply it at two levels: the discourse of political parties and its resonance(s) in mass opinion. For party discourse, the idea of a discursive frame is attractive because it may cut across both inclusionary/democratic and exclusionary/ authoritarian boundaries. Regarding mass opinion, we first turn to the work of those who have pioneered a series of survey instruments to capture the phenomenon in public attitudes, including those who designed the Comparative Study of Electoral Systems module from which we draw. In both empirical applications of the concept, we also reject a binary populist/non-populist distinction; there exist continuums of discourse, attitudes and behaviour that run between populism and elitism. As outlined in Chapters 3 and 4, we refined our selection of instruments, using additional items from the New Zealand Election Study, to better separate out populist and authoritarian values and preferences.

Populism in New Zealand: Historical Patterns and Contemporary Context

In the terms we have clarified above, New Zealand has, in many respects, a populist political culture and populist political institutions. Several accounts of New Zealand politics and political culture have pointed to traditions of populism dating back to the late 19th century, shaped partly by the wave of British settler immigrants to New Zealand who sought to apply the democratic principles of the Chartist movement (Gustafson, 2006; Moffitt, 2017; Vowles, 1987). Universal suffrage occurred in 1893—all but one of the Chartist principles were in place by the end of the 19th century; the one exception was annual parliaments. New Zealand's maximum three-year term of parliament remains much shorter than those of other democracies and has survived two elite-led attempts to extend it. Richard Seddon, who led the country's first party government from 1893 to 1906, is widely described as one of the most significant examples of local populist politics, in the vein of late 19th- and early 20th-century populism in the United States (Hamer, 1988; Nagel, 1993; Simpson, 1976). Indeed, Nagel described Seddon's substantive policies and political style as 'designed to build an overwhelming majority based on the common people of his country' (1993, p. 172). In this interpretation, the goal of populist leadership is to create lasting majorities by means of well-tuned electoral strategy. Norman Kirk, a short-lived Labour prime minister in the early 1970s, sought to shape a recasting of New Zealand national identity towards the Pacific, using rhetoric that was highly evocative of populism (Kirk, 1969).

As a small, intimate democracy whose politicians are much less isolated from citizens than in many other countries, expectations of high levels of responsiveness to public opinion were characteristic of 20th-century New Zealand politics (Vowles, 1998). The absence of both a constitution as fundamental law and judicial review of legislation, within a simple unitary state where authority is concentrated in parliament, means governments wield potentially 'unbridled power' (Palmer, 1979), even following more recent electoral and constitutional reforms. Historically, prime ministers kept copies of their manifestos close to hand in their offices (Mulgan, 1990). However, political elites began to abandon norms regarding the electoral mandate during the neoliberal policy revolution of the late 1980s and early 1990s (Chapman, 1992; Gibbons, 2000). The response to this was a crisis of political legitimacy and a successful campaign to change the electoral system from first-past-the-post to proportional representation. Arguments for reform criticised governments with strong parliamentary majorities that failed to gain majority support among voters (Katz, 1997; Royal Commission on the Electoral System, 1985). During the crucial period, strong populist sentiments existed among those seeking reform (Vowles, Miller, Lamare, Catt & Aimer, 1995; see also Chapter 7). Reassertion of norms of governments 'keeping promises' and 'doing what the people want' have been important features of what citizens have sought from government after the 1996 shift to proportional representation (Vowles, 2011).

At various periods of New Zealand's political history, episodes of populism—as discourse, style or rhetoric—have been identified across almost all major political parties and their leaders. The type of populism most commonly described is grounded in a claim to represent and give effect to the will of large majorities: a kind of moderate policy responsiveness. Former Prime Minister John Key's habit of checking public opinion in preparation for formulating and subsequently amending policy reflected the reality that, in a small, parliamentary democracy, whose citizens have easy and direct access to the political class, responsiveness to voters' concerns is valued. Further, for voters, a (relatively short) three-yearly parliamentary cycle means that a chance to sanction parties at election time is never far away.

Such a conception of policy responsiveness bears some similarities to the argument that 'ad hoc pragmatism', in the form of reactive decision-making by political leaders in real time and as political events unfold, has driven the country's trajectory of incremental and sometimes unexpected constitutional change (Palmer, 2007, p. 571). The kind of populism evident in this political culture emphasises appeals to the people and giving force to the will of majorities; however, it rarely attacks pluralist politics or suggests that political rivals are existential enemies (MacDonald, 2019). Populism, in this sense, is not perceived to be a negative feature of the political style. Neither is it restricted to marginal or ideologically exclusionary parties; rather, as Moffitt (2016) has argued, it can be thought of as a 'mainstream' feature of the political system.

Nevertheless, strands of more pathologically authoritarian populism have been identified in both New Zealand's political history and aspects of its political culture (Ausubel, 1965; Bedggood, 1975). The authoritarian populist appeals of Robert Muldoon's National

Government (1975–1984) are an obvious example, particularly in terms of anti-immigrant campaigning and a backlash against Pacific Island immigrants, in addition to attacks on the media and a bullying style of leadership that explicitly appealed to the 'ordinary people'. In a famous example, justified by an electoral mandate, Muldoon ignored constitutional and legal norms by prematurely instructing officials to ignore a law intended for repeal; however, the courts did not agree (Palmer, 1979). In more recent times, the National Party's divisive Iwi/Kiwi billboards during the 2005 election campaign, under Don Brash, demonstrated a recurrence of populist rhetoric.[1]

Muldoon's legacy continues into the 21st century, in the form of the New Zealand First Party (Joiner, 2015). Internationally, comparative studies of populism generally identify New Zealand First as the main (and usually sole) populist party active in New Zealand politics and its leader of 26 years, Winston Peters, as New Zealand's primary populist politician (Denemark & Bowler, 2002; Donovan & Redlawsk, 2018; Moffitt, 2016, 2017; Norris & Inglehart, 2017). Many scholars place New Zealand First in the company of the usual right-populist suspects in Europe.[2] Norris and Inglehart's inclusion of New Zealand First in their 2019 study of authoritarian-populist parties and Moffit's (2017) exclusive focus on Winston Peters as an exemplar of an 'Antipodean' model of populism are only two examples of the common approach taken by international scholarship.[3] New Zealand First has exhibited exclusionary populist credentials over the years, via its periodic deployment of anti-immigration rhetoric in tandem with standard populist attacks on business and bureaucratic elites. Further, it has consistently supported referendums as a means of accessing, and giving effect to, the will of the majority (the 'ordinary folk' or 'hard-working Kiwis') in the political process. These political discourses reflect the core elements of common understandings

---

1   Following in the wake of a period of significant political disagreement regarding rights of access to, and ownership over, the foreshore and seabed of the New Zealand coastline, the Iwi/Kiwi billboards implied that New Zealand beaches would fall under Māori ownership under a Labour government, whereas a National government would retain them in 'Kiwi' hands. As explained below, 'Kiwi', a colloquial label for 'New Zealander', signalled the populist idea of New Zealanders being 'one people', inclusive of Māori as citizens but failing to recognise their rights as an indigenous people and Treaty partner.

2   Some scholars have even classified New Zealand First as a 'radical right' party (Betz, 2002; Norris, 2005), which appears inconsistent with its ultimately comparatively moderate positions on both the left–right and authoritarian–libertarian dimensions.

3   See also Moffitt's (2016) list that identifies key populist actors globally.

of populism (as identified earlier)—creating moral divides between 'the people' and elites, on one hand, and stressing the desirability of direct expression of the *vox populi*, on the other.

However, New Zealand First also presents a contrast to many authoritarian–populist parties. While advocating for referendums and opposing some aspects of minority rights (e.g. designated Māori seats in parliament), New Zealand First has seldom, if ever, sought to subvert the democratic process or to undermine constitutional limitations in the way described by Urbinati (2017); nor has it questioned the role of representation in democracy (Taggart, 2000). Indeed, its multiple periods of government participation reflect that, while its leader's rhetorical flourishes may be frequently anti-establishment, they are not anti-system.[4]

It is, moreover, precisely New Zealand First's movement in and out of government that demonstrates another feature of its discourse and style. As MacDonald noted, New Zealand First cannot be simply categorised as a 'populist party'; rather, it moves between populism and pluralism, 'selectively and strategically deploying and pulling back populism when required' (2019, p. 228). In opposition and during election campaigns, it has deployed a liberal degree of populist rhetoric; however, it has also engaged in regular pluralist politics during those periods in which it has held responsibilities in government.[5] Thus, while New Zealand First can, to some extent, fit the right-leaning or authoritarian–populist mould that forms the focus of most international studies, its populism in these terms is periodic, inconsistent and is as much rhetorical style—or performance, as described by Moffitt (2016)—as it is ideology.

Meanwhile, changes in society from the late 20th into the early 21st centuries increasingly complicate the analysis of populism in New Zealand. First, the Māori population has increased and Māori have become more active in national political institutions. Māori elites based in *iwi* (tribal) organisations and educational organisations have advanced strong claims for greater recognition of Māori status as an indigenous people with Treaty rights, as agreed between the British Crown and Māori chiefs at Waitangi in 1840. An alleged remark by Treaty negotiator

---

4   New Zealand First has participated in three governments: in full coalition with the centre-right National Party (1996–1998), as a support party for the 2005–2008 Labour-led government and from 2017 onwards in formal coalition with the Labour Party.

5   MacDonald (2019) also contested the tendency of scholars, as outlined and criticised in the first section of this chapter, to identify populism and pluralism as polar opposites.

William Hobson that European settlers and Māori had become 'one people' (Colenso, 1890) is used by conservative Pākehā, such as former National and ACT party leader Don Brash, to promote a single national identity and deny Māori 'special treatment'. However, Māori are a distinct people with their own language and culture. Meanwhile, after increased immigration, New Zealand has become one of the most ethnically and culturally diverse countries in the world, raising further questions regarding a definition of 'the people'.

In all accounts of populism, the identity of 'the people' is crucial, due to the structuring of a moral divide in society between authentic people and some outsider group, be it 'the establishment', business elites or, in exclusionary forms, immigrants or other social minorities. Generally, scholars assume that 'the people' is a homogenous group and, in studies that focus on right-authoritarian populism, describe an exclusionary form of boundary-drawing. On both counts, features of New Zealand's sociopolitical and historical context complicate the straightforward application of dominant accounts of populism to the country.

Moffitt has contended that a key feature of 'Antipodean' populism is that it is 'primarily "exclusive"' (2017, p. 131); it seeks to exclude identified 'others' on the material, political and symbolic dimensions identified by Mudde and Kaltwasser (2013). He further suggested that, in this model, the authentic people is 'an inherently monocultural (or sometimes in the case of New Zealand, bicultural) group' and that 'the people' face a triple enemy: the elite, immigrants and indigenous people (Moffitt, 2017, p. 133).[6] As highlighted earlier, in the example of the National Party's Iwi/Kiwi billboards, instances of right-populist discourse that deny Māori their indigenous status and Treaty rights have undoubtedly occurred over time and have not been restricted to the political fringes.

However, the delineation of insider and outsider groups in this context remains complex. In these conservative Pākehā terms, Māori are both 'inside', as equal citizens, and 'outside', in terms of their indigenous rights. Winston Peters is himself Māori. His populist rhetoric related to Māori issues does not create the 'indigenous people' as a generalised out-group. One of Peters' primary targets has been what he considers to be *iwi* elites

---

6   Moffitt (2017) also characterised the 'authentic' people in this model of populism as those in rural or agricultural regions, including small business owners or manual workers in the regions, who line up against city bureaucrats, business elites or 'welfare recipients'.

who, he argues, have benefited from a 'grievance industry' arising from the Treaty of Waitangi claims and settlement processes (Johansson, 2003, p. 66; see also Brash, 2004). These elites have benefited, he claims, at the expense of 'regular' Māori. Given that conservative Māori voters have formed a segment of New Zealand First's voter base over the years, it is certainly impossible to talk of a clear Pākehā–Māori insider/outsider dichotomy in right-populist style. Rather, the dichotomy is that of a business-elite 'outsider' that cuts across ethnic groups.

Further, ideas regarding the boundaries of the 'nation' or its dominant cultural norms are not self-evident. Historically, who or what constitutes the 'nation' or 'the people' has been an eternally challenging question, given the complex relationship among the constituent peoples of New Zealand society since the signing of the Treaty of Waitangi and the hesitant and incremental process of disentangling citizenship and national identity from their colonial origins (Barker & McMillan, 2014). Many have argued against any attempt to identify a single nation. The late historian Michael King aptly noted that New Zealand could be seen as 'representing at least two cultures and two heritages, very often looking in two different directions' (2003, p. 167). Consequently, the singularity and homogeneity of the 'nation' that is often assumed by politicians, but also by many scholars in studies of populism, are difficult to pinpoint in the New Zealand context. In such a context, it is correspondingly more difficult to sustain a political claim that a part of the people is, or embodies, the whole people (Müller, 2016; Rosenblum, 2008).

In New Zealand, the institutional and sociopolitical context further serves to weaken the incentive for, or likelihood of, strong populist rhetoric that would construct the indigenous population as one part of Moffitt's 'triple enemy' (2017). Official biculturalism (Pearson, 2001), the growing entrenchment of principles of the Treaty of Waitangi in public organisations and in policy- and law-making processes, and significant Māori representation in parliament (both via the current seven designated Māori parliamentary seats and outside of them) serve to limit the electoral cut-through of populist politics on these issues. This is not to deny periodic criticism of the 'Treaty industry', guaranteed Māori seats in parliament and 'special rights' for New Zealanders of Māori descent in election campaign rhetoric employed by politicians in New Zealand First, in centre-right National and in the neoliberal ACT Party. However, this style of populist politics is neither engaged in consistently nor tenable for most New Zealand parties that seek votes from an increasingly diverse Māori electorate with a multiplicity of actors and interests.

In addition to the complexity of identifying a singular and homogenous 'people' in a formally bicultural society, the nature of immigration and migrants' political incorporation further complicates application of the concept, in addition to the actual spread of populism. As Chapter 5 demonstrates, by international comparison, New Zealand has historically exhibited relatively high levels of support for immigration, consistent with the pattern of other settler states. Even where public support for immigration has evidenced some decline in recent years, this has occurred in the context of record levels of immigration flows and diversification of the population over the past three decades. In the 15 years preceding 2018, Asian and Pacific shares of the population had risen dramatically, reaching 15.1 per cent (compared to 9.1 per cent in 2006) and 8.1 per cent, respectively.

The consequences of immigration did become a point of debate in the 2017 election campaign; however, the significant polarisation and populist appeals seen elsewhere did not gain significant electoral traction—the basic foundations of an expansionist immigration policy remained and still benefited from cross-party consensus (Barker, 2018). A 'protective' feature in New Zealand is the size of the electorate of recent immigrant origin. Since 1975, non-citizen permanent residents have been eligible to vote in New Zealand, provided they have lived in New Zealand continuously, at some time, for a period of 12 months or more.[7] In other words, electoral law does not discriminate among nationals of different countries for the purposes of voting, even as the right to be elected to parliament remains restricted to citizens (Barker & McMillan, 2016).[8]

---

7   Aside from those people who are in New Zealand on a temporary permit (e.g. a student visa or a temporary visitor's permit), most resident visa holders are enfranchised. The criteria include those who are explicitly defined as 'permanent residents' under the 2009 *Immigration Act* and also persons on visas who are not required to 'leave New Zealand immediately or within a specific time'. Therefore, those on a long-term work visa could be eligible even though they do not hold an official 'permanent resident visa' (Barker & McMillan, 2016).

8   The 1956 *Electoral Act* had required electors to be a 'British subject ordinarily resident in New Zealand'. The 1975 *Electoral Amendment Act* dropped the requirement of being a British subject, meaning that any non-citizen who met the visa and residence test was now eligible to vote (Barker & McMillan, 2016).

On a symbolic level, the existence of the non-citizen vote constitutes an expansionist delineation of 'the people'. This does not, in and of itself, protect against the use of exclusionary populist discourse against recent immigrants; however, the non-citizen vote has the effect of generating a proportionately much larger voting population of recent immigrant origin than exists in many other countries. Although instances of exclusionary populist rhetoric in political discourse over time may be identified, the growing strength of the (recent) immigrant electorate means that political parties have an ever-stronger incentive to adopt inclusionary approaches to questions of national identity and on issues related to immigration and diversity.

Together, the bicultural context and the expansionist understanding of 'the people' in a formal electoral sense serve both to complicate the meaning of 'the people' in the New Zealand context and to mitigate any exclusionary manifestation and impact. Other structural features of New Zealand's economy and polity could also be interpreted as dampening the exclusionary populism evident in so many other countries. Recent explanations of populism emphasise the interaction of economic and cultural factors in explaining the rise in populist attitudes among voters and the timing of electoral success of populist parties and politicians (Gidron & Hall, 2017; Norris & Inglehart, 2017, 2019). White, lesser-educated/skilled men are identified as the chief supporters of populist parties and, particularly, of the authoritarian-populist right. They are argued to be motivated by declining economic and employment security following the global financial crisis combined with resistance to cultural transformations and to the 'silent revolution' that generated 'post-materialist' values, rights movements and accompanying social change. Further, citizens' perceptions of their deteriorating status—relative to other groups (Gidron & Hall, 2017), to elites (Mudde, 2016) or to the past (Gest, 2016; Hochschild, 2016)—drive a turn away from mainstream parties (who represent the 'corrupt elite') and towards populist policies and discourses. Economic and cultural insecurity is said to trigger in-group/out-group reflexes from which 'strongman' populist leaders can profit. Established, mainstream political elites are, at best, not providing solutions to the problems or, at worst, seen to have been responsible for creating or exacerbating the problems. This drives a profound distrust of the political class, which also opens the way for populist parties and politicians.

As later chapters explore in further detail, the New Zealand economy was affected less severely by the global financial crisis than many other countries. Further, a feeling of crisis in relation to immigration was palpably absent. In addition to the historically pro-immigration baseline attitudes, the absence of a land border and the country's sheer distance from conflict zones mean that immigration flows and pressure on the border have not offered a 'crisis' moment that exclusionary populist leaders could build up and exploit as they have done elsewhere in the world (Moffitt, 2016). While New Zealand's proportional electoral system does, in theory, provide a permissive opportunity structure for the electoral success and representation of a populist party, traditions in its democracy of policy responsiveness and of moderate populist rhetoric across the main political parties, anchored in the majoritarian democratic impulse, leave less scope for sustained cut-through by populist actors.

Conclusions

Bale et al. have stated that it is 'a function of the variety of usage that there is no agreement on what would constitute a canon of cases of populism' (2011, p. 114). This chapter has identified some key definitions of populism found in the international literature and outlined the approach to populism taken in this book. We argue for operationalisation of populism on two separate levels: political discourse and public attitudes. In both cases, populism and elitism form a continuum rather than a dichotomy. We argue that political history and practice in the New Zealand context does not support the dominant 'populism as authoritarianism' interpretation. Populism and authoritarianism are separate factors—one does not imply the other; however, when combined, they may form a potent mixture. New Zealand has experienced both authoritarian and non-authoritarian populism, with more experience of the latter. The argument that populism is associated with anti-pluralism will be taken up again in Chapter 8. However, New Zealand's experience of a populist campaign to establish an electoral reform that is claimed to be based on consensus necessitates careful thought.

As a value expressed in moderation across the party system, New Zealand's populism as 'moderate policy responsiveness' could, at the least, be considered normatively neutral. It might also offer some potential protection against the more destructive articulations of authoritarian and exclusionary populism found elsewhere. Considering both the historical traditions of the country's political style and the structural and institutional features of its constitution and contemporary politics, we could describe populism in New Zealand as moderate, majoritarian and mainstream, blending by turns both exclusionary and inclusionary populist discourse.

The preceding discussion of features of populism throughout New Zealand's political history, in addition to political and institutional features that affect the portability of common understandings of populism to New Zealand, has offered conceptual and empirical foundations for the subsequent chapters. These chapters, through their examination of a variety of aspects of voter attitudes in New Zealand's 2017 general election, illuminate evidence of the type(s) and degree(s) of populism that exist in New Zealand's politics.

References

Abts, K. & Rummens, S. (2007). Populism versus democracy. *Political Studies, 55,* 405–424. doi.org/10.1111/j.1467-9248.2007.00657.x

Adams, J. (2001). *Party competition and responsible party government.* Ann Arbor, MI: University of Michigan Press. doi.org/10.3998/mpub.23030

Albertazzi, D. & McDonnell D. (2008). Introduction: The sceptre and the spectre. In D. Albertazzi & D. McDonnell (Eds), *Twenty-first century populism: The spectre of Western European democracy* (pp. 1–11). Basingstoke, United Kingdom: Palgrave Macmillan. doi.org/10.1057/9780230592100

American Political Science Association. (1950). Towards a more responsible two-party system: A report of the Committee on Political Parties. *The American Political Science Review, 44*(3) (Part Two, Suppl.). doi.org/10.2307/1950997; 10.2307/1950998; 10.2307/1950999; 10.2307/1951000; 10.2307/1951001

Arrow, K. (1951). *Social choice and individual values.* New Haven, CT: Yale University Press. doi.org/10.2307/2087870

Aslanidis, P. (2016). Is populism an ideology? A refutation and a new perspective. *Political Studies, 64*(1), 88–104. doi.org/10.1111/1467-9248.12224

Ausubel, D. (1965). *The fern and the Tiki: An American view of New Zealand National Character.* New York: Holt, Reinhart and Winston.

Bachrach, P. (1967). *The theory of democratic elitism: A critique.* Boston, MA: Little Brown.

Bale, T., van Kessel, S. & Taggart, P. (2011). Thrown around with abandon? Popular understandings of populism as conveyed by the print media: A UK case study. *Acta Politica, 46*(2), 111–131. doi.org/10.1057/ap.2011.3

Barker, F. (2018). Immigration and the Key-English Government. In S. Levine (Ed.), *Stardust and substance: The New Zealand general election of 2017* (pp. 265–280). Wellington, New Zealand: Victoria University Press.

Barker, F. & McMillan, K. (2014). Constituting the democratic public: New Zealand's extension of national voting rights to non-citizens. *New Zealand Journal of Public and International Law, 12*(1), 61–80.

Barker, F. & McMillan, K. (2016). *Access to electoral rights: New Zealand* (Access to Electoral Rights Report, RSCAS/EUDO-CIT-ER 2016/5). Retrieved from cadmus.eui.eu/bitstream/handle/1814/42884/EUDO_CIT_ER_2016_05.pdf

Bedggood, D. (1975). Conflict and consensus: Political ideology in New Zealand. In S. Levine (Ed.), *New Zealand politics: A reader* (pp. 299–311). Melbourne, Australia: Cheshire.

Betz, H. G. (2002). Conditions favouring the success and failure of radical right-wing populist parties in contemporary democracies. In Y. Mény & Y. Surel (Eds), *Democracies and the populist challenge* (pp. 197–213). London, United Kingdom: Palgrave Macmillan. doi.org/10.1057/9781403920072

Brash, D. (2004, 28 January). Nationhood (Address to the Orewa Rotary Club). *New Zealand Herald.* Retrieved from www.nzherald.co.nz/treaty-of-waitangi/news/article.cfm?c_id=350&objectid=3545950

Brett, W. (2013). What's an elite to do? The threat of populism from left, right and centre. *The Political Quarterly, 8*(3), 410–413. doi.org/10.1111/j.1467-923X.2013.12030.x

Chapman, R. M. (1992). A political culture under pressure. *Political Science, 44*(1), 1–27. doi.org/10.1177/003231879204400101

Colenso, W. (1890). *The authentic and genuine history of the signing of the Treaty of Waitangi.* Wellington, New Zealand: New Zealand Government Printer.

Comparative Study of Electoral Systems. (2016). *CSES Module 5: Democracy divided? People, politicians and the politics of populism.* Retrieved from cses.org/wp-content/uploads/2019/03/CSES5_ContentSubcommittee_Final Report.pdf

Denemark, D. & Bowler, S. (2002). Minor parties and protest votes in Australia and New Zealand: Locating populist politics. *Electoral Studies, 21*, 47–67. doi.org/10.1016/S0261-3794(00)00034-2

Donovan, T. & Redlawsk, D. (2018). Donald Trump and right-wing populists in comparative perspective. *Journal of Elections, Public Opinion and Parties, 28*(2), 190–207. doi.org/10.1080/17457289.2018.1441844

Dornbusch, R & Edwards, S. (Eds). (1991). *The macroeconomics of populism in Latin America.* Chicago, IL: University of Chicago Press.

Dowding, K. (2006). Can populism be defended? William Riker, Gerry Mackie and the interpretation of democracy. *Government and Opposition, 41*(3), 327–346. doi.org/10.1111/j.1477-7053.2006.00182.x

Font, N., Graziano, P. & Tsakatika, M. (2019). Varieties of inclusionary populism? SYRIZA, Podemos and the five star movement. *Government and Opposition.* [Advance online publication]. doi.org/10.1017/gov.2019.17

Galston, W. (2018). *Anti-pluralism: The populist threat to liberal democracy.* New Haven, CT: Yale University Press. doi.org/10.2307/j.ctt21668rd.8

Galton, G. J. (2016). *The new minority: White working class politics, immigration and inequality.* New York: Oxford University Press.

Gibbons, M. (2000). *Election programmes in New Zealand politics* (Unpublished doctoral thesis). University of Waikato, New Zealand.

Gidron, N. & Hall, P. A. (2017). The politics of social status: Economic and cultural roots of the populist right. *British Journal of Sociology, 68*(S1), S57–S84. doi.org/10.1111/1468-4446.12319

Goodwyn, L. (1976). *Democratic promise: The populist moment in America.* New York: Oxford University Press.

Gustafson, B. (2006). Populist roots of political leadership in New Zealand. In R. Miller & M. Mintrom (Eds), *Political leadership in New Zealand* (pp. 51–69). Auckland, New Zealand: Auckland University Press.

Hamer, D. (1988). *The New Zealand liberals: The years of power, 1891–1912.* Auckland, New Zealand: Auckland University Press.

Hochschild, A. (2016). *Strangers in their own land.* New York: New Press.

Johansson, J. (2003). Leadership and the campaign. In J. Boston, S. Church, S. Levine & N. Roberts (Eds), *New Zealand voters: The general election of 2002* (pp. 59–74). Wellington, New Zealand: Victoria University Press.

Joiner, M. (2015). New Zealand First. In J. Hayward (Ed.), *New Zealand Government and Politics* (6th ed.) (pp. 251–260). Melbourne, Australia: Oxford University Press.

Kaltwasser, C. R., Taggart, P., Espejo, P. O. & Ostiguy, P. (2017). Populism: An overview of the concept and the state of the art. In C. R. Kaltwasser, P. Taggart, P. O. Espejo & P. Ostiguy (Eds), *The Oxford handbook of populism* (pp. 1–25). Oxford, United Kingdom: Oxford University Press.

Katsambakis, G. (2016). Radical left populism in contemporary Greece: Syriza's trajectory from minoritarian opposition to power. *Constellations, 23*(3), 391–403. doi.org/10.1111/1467-8675.12234

Katz, R. (1997). *Democracy and elections.* New York: Oxford University Press.

King, M. (2003). *The Penguin history of New Zealand.* Auckland, New Zealand: Penguin Books.

Kirk, N. (1969). *Towards nationhood: Selected extracts from the speeches of Norman Kirk.* Palmerston North, New Zealand: New Zealand Books.

Laclau, E. (2005). *On populist reason.* London, United Kingdom: Verso.

MacDonald, D. (2019). Between populism and pluralism: Winston Peters and the international relations of New Zealand First. In F. Stangel, D. MacDonald & D. Nabers (Eds), *Populism and world politics* (pp. 227–249). Basingstoke, United Kingdom: Palgrave Macmillan.

Mackie, G. (2003). *Democracy defended.* Cambridge, United Kingdom: Cambridge University Press. doi.org/10.1017/CBO9780511490293

March, L. (2007). From vanguard of the proletariat to vox populi: Left-populism as a 'shadow' of contemporary socialism. *SAIS Review of International Affairs, 27*(1), 63–77. doi.org/10.1353/sais.2007.0013

Marx, K. (1998). The Communist manifesto. In M. Cowling (Ed.), *The Communist manifesto: New interpretations* (pp. 14–39). New York: New York University Press. (Original work published 1848)

McLean, I. (2002). William H. Riker and the invention of heresthetic(s). *British Journal of Political Science, 32*, 535–558. doi.org/10.1017/S0007 123402000224

Moffitt, B. (2016). *The global rise of populism.* Stanford, CA: Stanford University Press.

Moffitt, B. (2017). Populism in Australia and New Zealand. In C. R. Kaltwasser, P. Taggart, P. O. Espejo & P. Ostiguy (Eds), *The Oxford handbook of populism* (pp. 121–139). Oxford, United Kingdom: Oxford University Press. doi.org/ 10.1093/oxfordhb/9780198803560.013.5

Mouffe, C. (2018). *For a left populism.* London, United Kingdom: Verso.

Mudde, C. (2004). The populist zeitgeist. *Government and Opposition, 39*(4), 541–563. doi.org/10.1111/j.1477-7053.2004.00135.x

Mudde, C. (2007). *Populist radical right parties in Europe.* Cambridge, United Kingdom: Cambridge University Press.

Mudde, C. (2013). Three decades of populist radical right parties in Western Europe: So what? *European Journal of Political Research, 52*(1), 1–19. doi.org/10.1111/j.1475-6765.2012.02065.x

Mudde, C. (2014). Fighting the system? Populist radical right parties and party system change. *Party Politics, 20*(2), 217–226. doi.org/10.1177/1354068813519968

Mudde, C. (2015). The problem with populism. *The Guardian.* Retrieved from www.theguardian.com/commentisfree/2015/feb/17/problem-populism-syriza-podemos-dark-side-europe

Mudde, C. (2016). *The populist radical right: A reader.* London, United Kingdom: Routledge.

Mudde, C. (2017). Populism: An ideational approach. In C. R. Kaltwasser, P. Taggart, P. O. Espejo & P. Ostiguy (Eds), *The Oxford handbook of populism* (pp. 27–47). Oxford, United Kingdom: Oxford University Press. doi.org/10.1093/oxfordhb/9780198803560.013.1

Mudde, C. & Kaltwasser, C. R. (2013). Exclusionary vs. inclusionary populism: Comparing contemporary Europe and Latin America. *Government and Opposition, 48*(2), 147–174. doi.org/10.1017/gov.2012.11

Mulgan, R. (1990). The changing electoral mandate. In M. Holland & J. Boston (Eds), *The fourth Labour government: Politics and policy in New Zealand* (pp. 11–21). Auckland, New Zealand: Oxford University Press.

Müller, J. W. (2016). *What is populism?* University Park, PA: University of Pennsylvania Press.

Nagel, J. (1993). Populism, heresthetics and political stability: Richard Seddon and the art of majority rule. *British Journal of Political Science, 23*, 139–174. doi.org/10.1017/S0007123400009716

Norris, P. (2005). *Radical right: Voters and parties in the electoral market.* Cambridge, United Kingdom: Cambridge University Press.

Norris, P. (2020). *Measuring populism worldwide* (HKS Working Paper No. RWP20-002). Retrieved from www.hks.harvard.edu/publications/measuring-populism-worldwide

Norris, P. & Inglehart, R. (2017). Trump and the populist authoritarian parties: The *Silent Revolution* in reverse. *Perspectives on Politics, 15*(2), 443–454. doi.org/10.1017/S1537592717000111

Norris, P. & Inglehart, R. (2019). *Cultural backlash. Trump, Brexit and the rise of authoritarian-populism.* New York: Cambridge University Press. doi.org/10.1017/9781108595841

Ostiguy, P. (2017). Populism: A socio-cultural approach. In C. R. Kaltwasser, P. Taggart, P. O. Espejo & P. Ostiguy (Eds), *The Oxford handbook of populism* (pp. 73–99). Oxford, United Kingdom: Oxford University Press. doi.org/10.1093/oxfordhb/9780198803560.013.3

Palmer, G. (1979). *Unbridled power.* Auckland, New Zealand: Oxford University Press.

Palmer, G. & Butler, A. (2016). *A constitution for Aotearoa-New Zealand.* Wellington, New Zealand: Victoria University Press.

Palmer, M. (2007). New Zealand constitutional culture. *New Zealand Universities Law Review, 22,* 565–597.

Pearson, D. (2001). *The politics of ethnicity in settler societies: States of unease.* Basingstoke, United Kingdom: Palgrave.

Pinelli, C. (2011). The populist challenge to constitutional democracy. *European Constitutional Law Review, 7,* 5–16. doi.org/10.1017/S1574019611100024

Radcliffe, B. (1993). Liberalism, populism and collective choice. *Political Research Quarterly, 46*(1), 127–142. doi.org/10.1177/106591299304600109

Ramiro L. & Gomez, R. (2017). Radical-left populism during the Great Recession: *Podemos* and its competition with the established radical left. *Political Studies, 65*(1), 108–126. doi.org/10.1177/0032321716647400

Riker, W. (1982). *Liberalism against populism: A confrontation between the theory of democracy and the theory of social choice.* San Francisco, CA: W.H. Freeman.

Rosenblum, N. (2008). *On the side of the angels: An appreciation of parties and partisanship.* Princeton, NJ: Princeton University Press.

Royal Commission on the Electoral System. (1985). *Toward a better democracy.* Wellington, New Zealand: Government Printing Office.

Sachs, J. (1989). *Social conflict and populist policies in Latin America.* (Working Paper 2897). Retrieved from www.nber.org/papers/w2897

Schumpeter, J. (1942). *Capitalism, socialism and democracy.* New York: Harper.

Simpson, T. (1976). Huey Long's other island: Style in New Zealand politics. In S. Levine (Ed.), *New Zealand politics: A reader* (pp. 149–162). Melbourne, Australia: Cheshire.

Stanley, B. (2008). The thin ideology of populism. *Journal of Political Ideologies, 13*(1), 95–110. doi.org/10.1080/13569310701822289

Taggart, P. (2000). *Populism*. Buckingham, United Kingdom: Open University Press.

Thatcher, M. (2013, 8 April). Margaret Thatcher: A life in quotes. *The Guardian*. Retrieved from www.theguardian.com/politics/2013/apr/08/margaret-thatcher-quotes

Urbinati, N. (2017). Populism and the principle of majority. In C. R. Kaltwasser, P. Taggart, P. O. Espejo & P. Ostiguy (Eds), *The Oxford handbook of populism* (pp. 571–589). Oxford, United Kingdom: Oxford University Press. doi.org/10.1093/oxfordhb/9780198803560.013.31

Vowles, J. (1987). Liberal democracy: Pākehā political ideology. *New Zealand Journal of History, 21*, 215–227.

Vowles, J. (1998). Aspects of electoral studies, present and past: New Zealand voters and 'The System', 1949–1996. *Political Science, 50*, 90–110. doi.org/10.1177/003231879805000105

Vowles, J. (2011). Why voters prefer coalitions: Rationality or norms? *Political Science, 63*, 126–145. doi.org/10.1177/0032318711403917

Vowles, J., Aimer, P., Catt, H., Lamare, J. & Miller, R. (1995). *Towards consensus? The 1993 general election and referendum in New Zealand and the transition to proportional representation*. Auckland, New Zealand: Auckland University Press.

Weale, A. (1984). Social choice versus populism? An interpretation of Riker's political theory. *British Journal of Political Science, 14*(3), 369–385. doi.org/10.1017/S0007123400003653

Weyland, K. (2017). Populism: A political-strategic approach. In C. R. Kaltwasser, P. Taggart, P. O. Espejo & P. Ostiguy (Eds.), *The Oxford handbook of populism* (pp. 48–72). Oxford, United Kingdom: Oxford University Press. doi.org/10.1093/oxfordhb/9780198803560.013.2

Williams, Z. (2012). The Saturday interview: Stuart Hall. *The Guardian*. Retrieved from www.theguardian.com/theguardian/2012/feb/11/saturday-interview-stuart-hall

2

POPULISM AND THE 2017 ELECTION— THE BACKGROUND

Jack Vowles

Introduction

As the 23 September 2017 general election approached, there was little reason to expect a significant advance of the populist right in New Zealand. New Zealand's two mainstream parties, National and Labour, maintained their dominant roles in the party system, despite New Zealand's mixed member proportional (MMP) system having been in place since 1996. The National Party, in power since 2008, retained a high level of political support, despite the retirement of popular prime minister John Key late in 2016. Consequently, neither party seemed in danger of capture by authoritarian populism.

Until the 2017 election, the party most identified with populism in New Zealand, New Zealand First, continued to languish in party preference polling, very rarely registering more than 10 per cent, significantly less than the numbers it had secured in its 1996 heyday, when it had briefly entered government in coalition with National. Admittedly, some political commentators were anticipating a revival of New Zealand First, given low polling for the main opposition (Labour) between the 2014 election and mid-2017. However, Labour recovered much of its lost ground a few weeks before the campaign began. Whatever momentum there might have been for New Zealand First during the campaign was abruptly halted. Following the publication of leaked information that New Zealand First party leader Winston Peters had been overpaid in his state pension payments for several years, the party's polling numbers halved.

The election results gave New Zealand First 7.2 per cent of the votes (down from 8.7 per cent in 2014) and nine seats in the 120-member parliament. Nonetheless, New Zealand First was in a pivotal position and, following lengthy negotiations, elected to form a government with the Labour and Green parties. An election that was expected to be 'more of the same' had resulted in a party widely identified as 'populist' gaining a considerable measure of power. Opinion was divided regarding the consequences: on the one hand, New Zealand First had entered government before, with few adverse effects; on the other, examples of radical right populism elsewhere gave reasons for concern, particularly among observers outside New Zealand.

This book takes these differences of perspective as its starting point. Does it make more sense to interpret the 2017 election, and the public mood that shaped it, as an exception to the international authoritarian populist wave? Or, alternatively, can one identify in the 2017 New Zealand election a somewhat distinctive, but nonetheless recognisable, form of the phenomenon?

The data used here were mostly gathered from the 2017 New Zealand Election Study (NZES), comprising a random sample of 3,455 persons from the electoral rolls. In the weeks following the election, respondents answered questions that gathered information regarding their political behaviour and political attitudes at the time of the election. The dataset also contains a module of questions specifically designed to inquire into populism, crafted by the planning committee of an international collaborative research programme: the Comparative Study of Electoral Systems. This chapter provides a background analysis of the 2017 election and addresses some key implications, in the context of the evolution of the party system and the potential for populist politics in New Zealand.

As explained in Chapter 1, populism is far from a new phenomenon in New Zealand. New Zealand First is not the only New Zealand party running for office at recent elections with policies and leadership compatible with some aspects of populism. The Conservative Party, led by property manager Colin Craig, gained 4 per cent of the vote in 2014. In left–right terms, the Conservative Party is significantly right; however, New Zealand First may be classified as slightly left of centre (Vowles, 2014).

Unpacking the 2017 Election

As New Zealanders began to anticipate the 2017 election, a year or so before the likely date most commentators were expecting that the National-led government, who had been in power since 2008, would secure a fourth parliamentary term. It was thought that the 2017 election would have a similar result to the previous election in 2014.

National continued to dominate the political polls, while Labour, the key opposition party, continued to poll between 25 and 30 per cent, which was insufficient to present itself as the potential core of an alternative government. Its main ally, the Green Party, was tracking at approximately 10 per cent. The two parties combined very rarely managed to close the gap between themselves and National, whose numbers often approached 50 per cent. The only prospect of a change of government lay with New Zealand First and its pivotal position in the left–right dimension of the party system—one expectation of the eventual outcome that was borne out.

These expectations were shaken by an unexpected event. On 16 July, to draw attention to the inadequacy of welfare benefits to provide sufficient income, Green Party co-leader Metiria Turei admitted to historic benefit fraud. This caused a temporary poll shift—the Greens moved up to almost 14 per cent, gaining left-leaning support at the expense of Labour. In the face of this Labour poll decline, from an already low level, Labour leader Andrew Little resigned, paving the way for Ardern to replace him on 1 August. Meanwhile, further scrutiny of Turei's claims, which made the news on 3 August, raised doubts regarding her integrity and threw the Green Party into disarray: the party's poll surge evaporated, dropping back to 8 per cent. Turei resigned on 9 August, followed by polling that put the party at less than 5 per cent, below the threshold for representation. Thereafter, Labour began its poll recovery. On 27 August, information was leaked that stated Winston Peters had been overpaid by his pension for some years. Figure 2.1 displays the polling data and the shifts in vote intentions that followed these events.

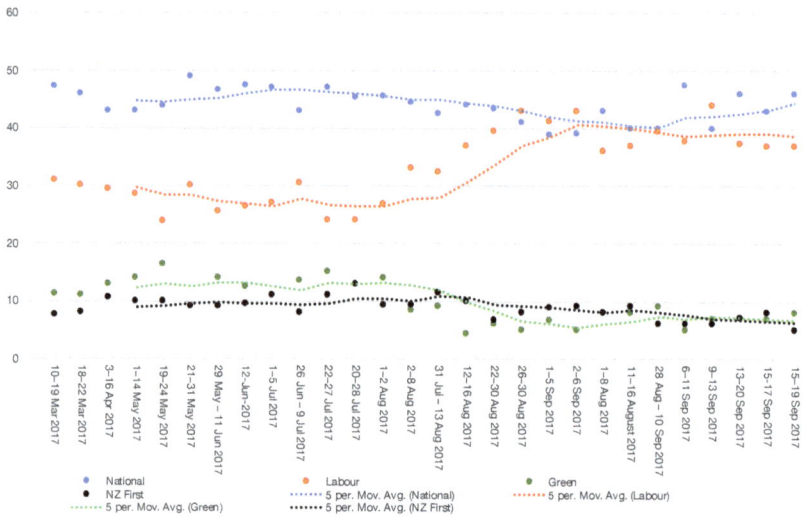

Figure 2.1: Political polls (March–September 2017).

Source: Clifton (2017a, 2017b); Curia (2019a–c); *New Zealand Listener* (2017a–c); Mills (2018). Includes Colmar Brunton, Reid Research, Roy Morgan and Bauer polls throughout and the last UMR-Insight polls during the campaign.

Table 2.1 displays the results of the election, compared with those of 2014. The balance of votes shifted approximately 5 percentage points leftward; however, the combined centre-left grouping of Labour-plus-Green still lagged behind the centre-right. Opposition votes consolidated behind Labour, primarily at the expense of the New Zealand First and Green parties. Therefore, the 'populist vote' shrank in 2017, particularly if one includes the Conservative Party in that grouping. The Conservative collapse from 4 per cent to only 0.2 per cent of the party vote is also one of the key elements of the leftward aggregate shift in the votes.

This reading of the aggregated results is confirmed in Table 2.2, which displays an estimation of the flows of votes between the 2017 and 2014 elections, including those flows in and out of non-voting and the votes of those ineligible in 2014. Each cell represents a percentage of those eligible to vote in 2017. The 'total 2017 row' represents the percentages of the votes cast or not cast in 2017. Reading across the rows for each party indicates the sources of each party's 2017 votes. The 'total 2014' row represents the percentages of the votes cast or not cast in 2014, including those ineligible to vote then. Reading up and down the columns indicates where the 2014 votes went in 2017. Several small parties drop out of the picture, including neoliberal ACT and United Future—their party votes were too few for even marginally credible estimation of flows. The exception is The Opportunities Party (TOP), a new liberal-centre party founded by wealthy philanthropist Gareth Morgan. It appears that TOP took votes equally from the right and the left.

Table 2.1: The 2017 and 2014 elections—party votes and seats

	2014		2017	
	% votes	seats	% votes	seats
National Party	47.0	*60	44.4	56
Labour Party	25.1	32	36.9	46
New Zealand First (NZF) Party	8.7	11	7.2	9
Green Party	10.7	14	6.3	8
ACT	0.7	1	0.5	1
The Opportunities Party (TOP)	-	-	2.4	0
Māori Party	1.3	2	1.2	0
Aotearoa Legalise Cannabis Party	0.5	0	0.3	0
Conservative (CONS)	4.0	0	0.2	0
MANA	1.4	0	0.1	0
Ban1080	0.2	0	0.1	0
New Zealand People's Party	-	-	0.1	0
United Future (UF)	0.2	1	0.1	0
New Zealand Outdoors Party	-	-	0.1	0
Democrats for Social Credit	0.1	0	0.0	0
Internet Party**	-	-	0.0	0
Total		121		120
Left (Labour, Green, MANA)	37.2	46	43.3	54
Right (National, ACT, CONS)	51.7	61	45.1	57
Centre (NZF, Maori, TOP, UF)	10.2	14	10.9	9
Others	0.8	0	0.6	0

Note: * National lost the Northland electorate seat to New Zealand First at a by-election early in 2015, bringing its seats down to 59.

** With MANA in 2014.

Source: Electoral Commission (2014, 2017).

Table 2.2: Estimated flows of votes (2014–2017)

2017 Votes	2014 Votes									2017 (%)	N
	Non-vote	National	Labour	Green	NZF	Conservative	Mana	Māori	In-eligible		
Non-vote	13.73	3.21	1.91	0.36	0.61	0.24	0.16	0.12	2.35	21.3	279
National	2.7	26.25	0.71	0.41	1	1.51	0	0.14	0.55	34.7	8,906
Labour	3.59	3.29	13.89	4.06	2.12	0.38	0.36	0.25	0.68	28.8	8,027
Green	0.76	0.35	0.81	2.31	0.09	0.03	0.24	0.05	0.21	4.9	2,932
New Zealand First (NZF)	0.64	1.15	0.55	0.19	2.35	0.56	0.04	0.03	0.07	5.6	1,770
Conservative	0.0	0.01	0.0	0.0	0.01	0.12	0.0	0.03	0.0	0.1	59
Mana	0.01	0.0	0.01	0.0	0.0	0.0	0.05	0.01	0.0	0.8	22
Māori	0.03	0.17	0.1	0.06	0.06	0.04	0.11	0.32	0.02	0.9	269
The Opportunities Party	0.36	0.53	0.25	0.36	0.12	0.07	0.05	0.04	0.04	1.9	1,049
2014 (%)	22.1	35.2	18.3	7.8	6.4	3.0	1.01	0.96	3.96	100	
N	654	1,0202.0	4,634	3,889	1,761	537	115	97	1,111		2,3698

Note: These data are sourced from the Vote Compass dataset. Thanks are due to Clifton van der Linden and Vox Pops Labs for agreement regarding its use. While not selected randomly, the large sample increases confidence in estimating between-party shifts. The data are weighted by a series of iterations on the two marginal percentage (Total %) frequencies, to represent as closely as possible the actual distributions of votes/non-votes in each election. The unweighted sample sizes summed up by row and column appear in the bottom and right margins of the table as an indication of the caution to be followed with small cell sizes. As with the NZES Panel, non-voters, particularly those in 2017, are significantly under-represented; therefore, the non-vote cells and flows must be treated much more cautiously. From these estimates, approximately 46 per cent of those eligible to vote voted for the same party in 2017 as in 2014 (comprising 62 per cent of voters). Therefore, approximately 38 per cent changed party or moved in or out of voting. To test this data against the NZES, a weighted turnover table derived from the NZES 2017–2014 Panel (N = 1,361), augmented by voters ineligible in 2014, is very close to the same distribution across the diagonal (stable voting) cells (see Table A2.1).

Source: Vote Compass post-election sample.

A significant shift also occurred in Māori politics. In 2017, the tide had run out for the Māori Party. Its objective had been to defend Māori rights under the Treaty of Waitangi, bringing Māori culture and values into the heart of government. By accepting a ministerial position in the National Government from 2008 onwards, although not within Cabinet, the party received its opportunity. Some progress was made—the right of Māori to claim customary rights over foreshore and seabed areas was restored and the government founded *whanau ora*, an innovative health initiative based on Māori values. However, the government was failing to address increasing social problems that most affected those on low incomes, among whom Māori remain concentrated.

Among Māori, class politics began to reassert its salience at the expense of indigenous rights. Following Māori Party member of parliament (MP) Hone Harawera's departure from the party, and his establishment of left-wing MANA, Harawera sought and gained support from the radical Pākehā left. However, he also procured an alliance with the Internet Party—a party formed by Kim Dotcom, a German internet entrepreneur accused of intellectual property theft, who was in New Zealand resisting extradition to the United States. This proved to be a misstep—Harawera lost his seat in 2014. He ran again in 2017, having made an agreement with the Māori Party that it would not contest his seat, in return for no MANA candidates in the remaining Māori electorates. The strategy failed—as Lara Greaves and Janine Hayward argue in Chapter 7, the MANA/Māori Party deal was probably irrelevant. MANA had lost its *mana* (prestige or status). Several key advisors no longer backed the party and had shifted to Labour (Burr & Templeton, 2017; Small, 2014). The votes of the discontented flowed back to Labour, both from former MANA and former Māori Party voters.

Of more significance for our discussion, the collapse of the Conservative Party mostly benefited National—half of the Conservative vote swung to them. Only one in six and one in seven of the Conservative Party votes in 2014 went to New Zealand First and Labour, respectively. Consistent votes for each party between the two elections can be read diagonally in the shaded cells in Figure 2.2. The core populist vote for New Zealand First and the remaining Conservatives was less than 3 per cent. The greatest shift of New Zealand First votes was to Labour. Approximately half of the new voters who were ineligible to vote in 2014 failed to vote in 2017. Of those who did vote, very few opted for New Zealand First.

Figure 2.2: Content analysis (most important issue).

Note: The word cloud is based on a word-count content analysis and illustrates the 70 most popular words. Words with no political content were dropped and some were consolidated: for example, 'taxation' into 'tax', healthcare into 'health'. The data were sourced from those freshly sampled in 2017, with oversamples resampled to bring them into the same proportions as the electoral rolls.

Source: New Zealand Election Study (2017).

Two possible interpretations follow—either populist voters for New Zealand First and the Conservatives in 2014 had their populism overshadowed by an increased salience of left–right issues or populists shifted to Labour because the party had taken on board some key populist concerns, particularly the restriction of immigration. The salience of policy issues in 2017 is the next port of call for analysis, taking advantage of the following open-ended NZES question: 'what was the single most important issue for you in the 2017 election?' The electronically captured text of the responses was analysed and used to generate the word cloud illustrated in Figure 2.2.

Figure 2.2 provides a visual impression of the content of the open-ended responses. However, it is not entirely accurate as an estimate of individual responses; despite the question wording, many respondents mentioned multiple issues. Further, the number of words captured for each respondent varied considerably; therefore, the cloud reflects how many words people wrote—some many more than others and some none at all. Table 2.3 more accurately compares the number of words counted to the codes assigned on inspection of the data, one code entry per respondent, and makes comparison with similar codes used for the comparable question in the 2014 NZES (Vowles, Coffé & Curtin, 2017, p. 13).

The 2017 coding column provides a more accurate representation of issue salience. The figure and table provide much the same narrative; however, the economy pushes ahead more significantly in the table. Comparison with issue salience in 2014 puts the economy in the same leading position; however, the salience of health and housing doubled in 2017 and immigration appeared as a primary concern for 6 per cent of those answering the question. In 2014, immigration scored less than 1 per cent. Environment was up, inequality stable and poverty down; however, this is in the context of increased concern regarding other social issues. The key insight is that the 2017 election pushed social issues (e.g. health and housing) significantly closer to the fore than in 2014.

Table 2.3: Issue salience (by word count and codes)

	Word count (N) 2017	Coding 2014 (%)	Coding 2017 (%)
Economy	211	19	14
Housing	207	5	11
Health	188	3	8
Poverty	112	7	4
Tax	110	4	6
Inequality	104	7	7
Education	92	3	4
Immigration	92	1	5
Environment	84	2	5
Welfare	18	1	3
N		2,835	3,455

Note: The issue coding frames in 2014 were slightly different—there was no top-level code for poverty in 2014; rather, it was included under inequality.

Source: New Zealand Election Study (2017).

Social issues and concerns regarding public services have traditionally been thought to benefit the centre-left; however, populists may also capture votes from people with such concerns. As explained in Chapter 1, two main explanations for the rise of populism have been posited. One identifies populism as a response to economic malaise, stagnation or economic crisis among those most affected. When current elites fail to address the problem, particularly if they belong to the centre-left, populists may begin to attract the votes of those who feel most vulnerable. Using strong emotional appeals, populists promise strong leadership, playing into the anti-establishment elements of populist ideology.

In 2011 and 2012, net immigration into New Zealand was effectively zero. By 2013, the New Zealand economy was exhibiting strong growth, compared to other comparator countries, and received 'rockstar' status from commentators (Vowles, Coffé & Curtin, 2017, p. 96). Immigration rose quickly. In 2017, New Zealand had a net gain of 70,000 immigrants, contributing approximately 1.5 per cent to population growth that year (Statistics New Zealand, 2018b). Such a high level of immigration puts pressure on infrastructure, services and housing, particularly where new arrivals are concentrated in New Zealand's largest city—Auckland. Rising house prices have made life difficult for low- and middle-income home buyers. A shortage of housing has led to increasing homelessness and even affected the employed. Competition in the labour market from new immigrants may be responsible for little or no recent wage growth in New Zealand. Easy access to cheap labour may reduce incentives for business to increase productivity. The growth benefits of current levels of immigration tend to be unevenly distributed. The shift in issue salience between 2014 and 2017 is a consequence of the unease and outright concern of many New Zealanders regarding the direction that has been taken by their country, in the context of increasing evidence of the failure of recent economic growth to benefit most low- and middle-income earners.

On the surface, the condition of the New Zealand economy in 2017 did not provide much economic ammunition for populism. As shown in Figure 2.3, the official estimate of economic growth in New Zealand rose to a high point of 4 per cent in 2016, before dropping back to a (still apparently healthy) 3 per cent in 2017. These recent rates outstrip growth in comparator countries such as Australia, the United States, Japan and the United Kingdom. This is the 'headline' narrative that shaped most political and economic commentary regarding the National-led government and underpinned perceptions of the government's competence within New Zealand and favourable impressions of the state of New Zealand's economy internationally. However, the underlying picture is less rosy; due to high levels of net immigration, in terms of growth per person, the trend flattened at approximately 2 per cent per year in 2013 and more than halved in 2017 to only 0.7 per cent.

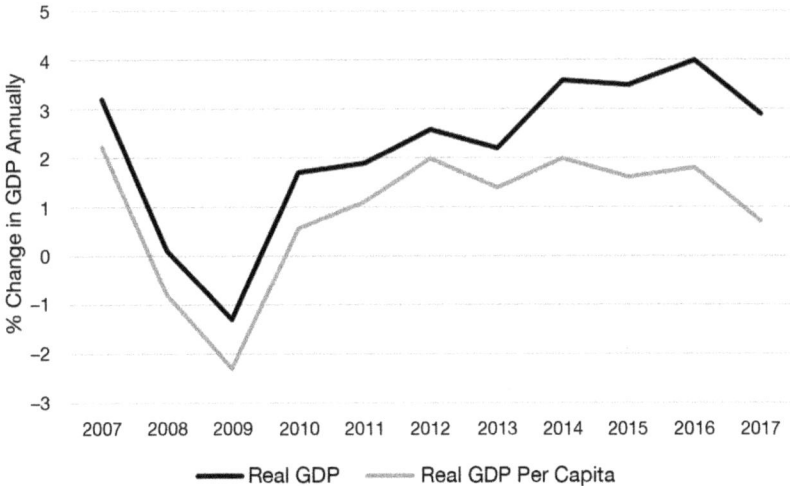

Figure 2.3: Real GDP and real GDP per capita in New Zealand (2007–2017).
Source: Reserve Bank of New Zealand (2018); Statistics New Zealand (2018a).

Discussion of immigration into contemporary New Zealand leads to an exploration of the second alternative explanation of the development of populism: the cultural dimension. In Europe and the United States, populism often represents white nationalism that is triggered by rising rates of immigration and, most of all, rising numbers of refugees from other cultures that threaten the dominance of established ethnic groups. People with lower levels of education are particularly likely to embrace populism on these grounds. In Australia, populism in the form of the One Nation Party also represents resistance to the recognition of Indigenous Aboriginal peoples and to efforts to improve their status. In New Zealand, by contrast, as explained in Chapter 1, populism in the form of New Zealand First is inclusive of indigenous Māori. Several New Zealand First MPs, including Winston Peters himself, are of Māori descent and identify as Māori. Despite this, New Zealand First takes a conservative position on New Zealand's founding document, the Treaty of Waitangi between the Crown and Māori, opposing granting it any form of constitutional status.

Like the lobby group, Hobson's Pledge, led by former National Party and ACT leader Don Brash, New Zealand First stands for 'One Nation' and is opposed to what it interprets to be 'separatism' among Māori. Under Brash's leadership between 2003 and 2006, the National Party adopted a strong 'One Nation' platform with strong populist undertones and was rewarded by a dramatic boost in polling preferences. However, following 2008, National governed with the support of the Māori Party and set aside populist appeals to 'One Nation'. It presided over several significant Treaty settlements and, while continuing to oppose the existence of the Māori parliamentary seats in principle, refrained from implementing their abolition in practice.

Immigration into New Zealand over the previous 30 years has made it one of the most culturally diverse countries in the world. Despite occasional outbursts of racism in individual behaviour and in public discourse, new immigrants are, for the most part, accepted. New Zealand is the most recently peopled landmass of a significant size. The first Māori settlers arrived less than 1,000 years ago and other peoples arrived only in the last two centuries. Many New Zealanders are descended from relatively recent immigrants or are immigrants themselves. The Māori word for New Zealand Europeans is 'Pākehā'.[1] The population remains majority Pākehā at just over 70 per cent; however, incoming migrants have increasingly mixed origins. The recently released 2018 census puts the foreign-born population at 27 per cent. Over the period 2015–2017, the main source countries were Australia, predominantly comprising New Zealanders returning home, followed by the United Kingdom, China and India. More broadly, of those permanently entering the country, approximately a third have come from Asian countries, a quarter from Europe and a fifth from Australia (Statistics New Zealand, 2018c). Increasing diversity can produce a cultural backlash, to which the Asian population has been most vulnerable. Since inception, the New Zealand First Party has been a focus for criticism of Asian immigration (see e.g. Peters, 2005). Meanwhile, the National Party welcomes immigrants from everywhere,

---

1   According to the Māori dictionary (n.d.), 'Pākehā' means 'New Zealander of European descent'—probably originally applied to English-speaking Europeans living in Aotearoa/New Zealand. According to Mohi Tūrei, an acknowledged expert in Ngāti Porou tribal lore, the term is a shortened form of *pakepakehā*, which was a Māori rendition of a word or words remembered from a chant used in a very early visit by foreign sailors for raising their anchor (*TP* 1/1911: 5). Others claim that *pakepakehā* was another name for *tūrehu* or *patupairehe* (mythical human-like beings with fair skin and hair). Despite claims made by some non-Māori speakers, the term does not normally have negative connotations.

particularly valuing those who bring investment into New Zealand, many of whom come from mainland China. Labour has also tended to welcome immigration, particularly from the Pacific Islands, and Pacific Island communities continue to provide Labour with strong electoral support.

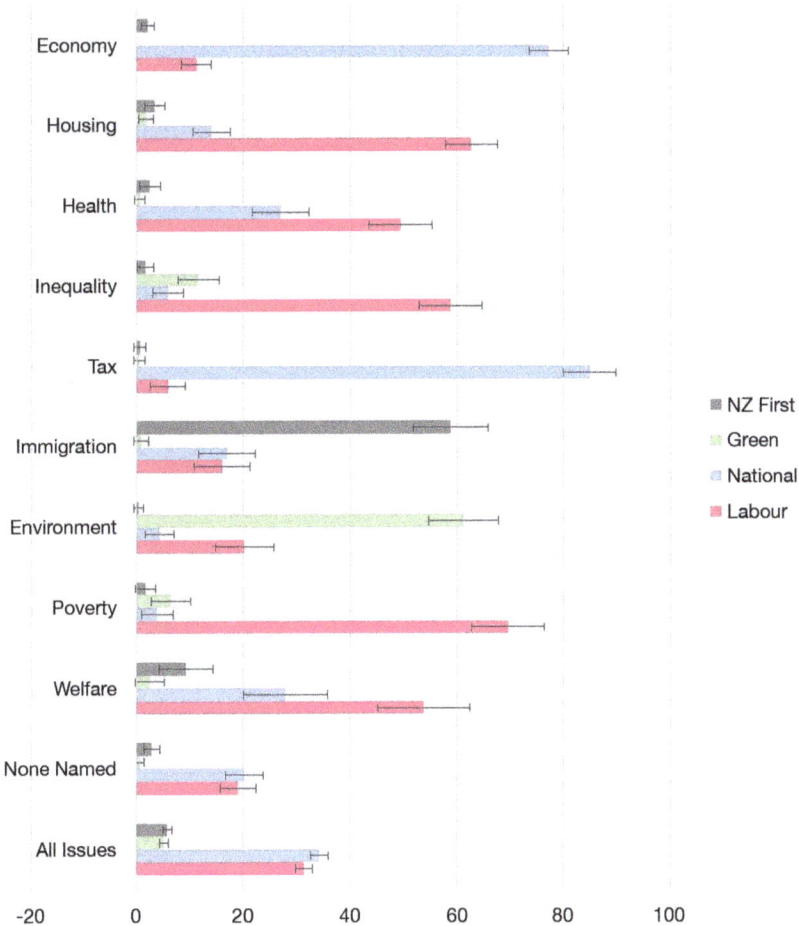

Figure 2.4: Parties closest to voters' positions on different issues.
Source: New Zealand Election Study (2017).

NZES respondents were asked which party was the closest to their position on the issue they identified as most important. Only 16 per cent did not, or could not, name a party that championed their issue. As expected, those who named immigration were most likely to choose New Zealand First. Figure 2.4 demonstrates that New Zealand First has a distinctive command of immigration, but no other issue, much as the Green Party has a commanding position on the environment. Similarly, National is dominant in approval of its conservative positions on the economy and taxes and Labour is dominant on approval of its positions on social issues—housing, health and inequality. There is no evidence of a New Zealand First breakthrough on any issue other than immigration. Instead, the strongest impression is one of Labour successfully mobilising opinion on its issues of traditional strength: support for public services, more active housing policies and the reduction of poverty. Nonetheless, Labour also identified high levels of immigration as a contributing factor to pressures on infrastructure, social services and housing, and entered the 2017 election with promises to reduce immigration by 20,000–30,000 annually (New Zealand Labour Party, 2017). New Zealand First promised even greater restrictions: to a net 10,000, annually.

Alignment and Stability of the Party System

Another correlate of the development of populism elsewhere has been the dealignment or realignment of party systems. Party systems have fragmented, allowing new parties to emerge. Voting choices have become more volatile from one election to the next, making governments more likely to change more frequently than in the past and potentially affecting governability. Figures 2.5 and 2.6 situate New Zealand in the international context of other members of the Organisation for Economic Development and Cooperation (OECD), comparing changes in the number of effective elective political parties and in net vote volatility between 1991 and 2007, and 2008 and 2016. Compared with most other OECD countries, relative to their number weighted by shares of votes cast, New Zealand's party system is smaller post 2008 than it was before and vote choices between elections have become less, rather than more, volatile. The contexts of different countries matter, of course. The first period marks New Zealand's transition to an MMP system and the second the stabilisation of vote choices that followed this (Vowles, 2014). Post-communist countries were also in transition during the 1990s and have somewhat stabilised since.

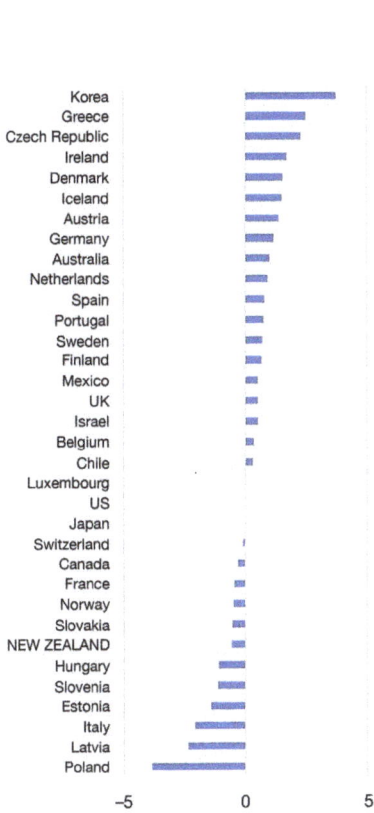

Figure 2.5: Change in number of effective parties in OECD countries (2016–2007/2007–1990).

Note: The effective number of electoral parties is weighted by the proportional shares of votes cast, estimated as 1 divided by the squares of the fractional vote shares of all parties scoring 1 per cent or more (i.e. as fractions of 1).

Source: Gallagher (2019).

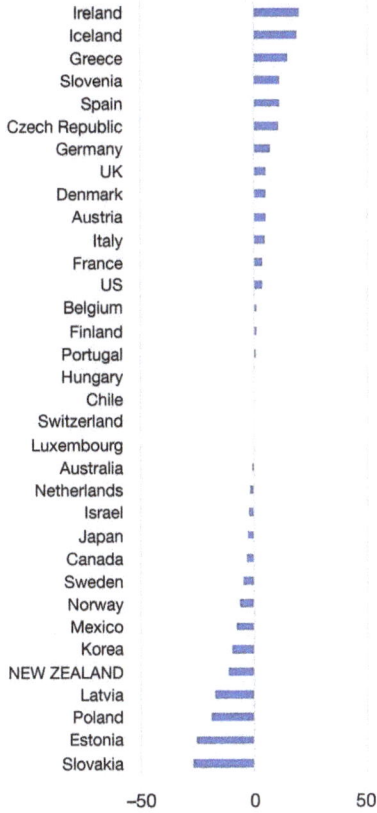

Figure 2.6: Change in electoral volatility in OECD countries (2016–2007/2007–1990).

Note: Net electoral vote volatility is estimated by adding the absolute differences between party vote shares between the election in question and the previous one and dividing the resulting sum by 2. This figure is also based on unpublished data generously provided by Scott Mainwaring (for which thanks are due).

Source: Alcántara (2012); Emmanuele (2015); Mainwaring, Gervasoni and Espana-Najera (2017).

If we refocus analysis away from change and examine the absolute levels of recent and current estimates of effective party system size and vote volatility, New Zealand has scored comparatively low on both counts since 2008. The average number of effective elective parties across the OECD countries between 2008 and 2016 was five and the average vote volatility between elections was 18. In New Zealand, over the three elections between 2008 and 2014, the comparable figures were 3.1 and 8.8. In 2017, the effective number of elective parties slightly shrank to 2.9; net volatility had risen to 13.5, which was still well below the OECD average. In comparative contexts, electoral politics in New Zealand is stable, particularly when compared to many of the long-established democracies in western Europe.

Acknowledging this, like citizens in other OECD countries, New Zealanders are in two minds regarding political parties and the governments formed by them. As later chapters will discuss in greater depth, public trust in parties and politicians has not fully recovered from a crisis of legitimacy in the late 1980s and early 1990s, which followed rapid neoliberal economic and social reforms that led to electoral system change in 1996. Consistent cognitive or affective ties to political parties have not recovered either—levels of party identification are considerably lower than those estimated before the mid-1980s.

Nonetheless, approximately 60 per cent of the NZES sample chose a party when asked if they thought themselves 'generally speaking' close to a particular party; 38 per cent chose the 'no party' option. The phrase 'generally speaking' is included to elicit ties to parties that persist beyond a single election. However, in practice, this estimate still demonstrates much between-election volatility (Aimer, 1989). Those nominated as 'very close' comprised only 7 per cent of the whole sample; most who nominated parties as 'close' chose the 'fairly close' option (37 per cent of all respondents). National had the most who were particularly close: 28 per cent of respondents compared to Labour's 20 per cent. The Green Party scored just over 5 per cent and New Zealand First only 3.5 per cent. The low level of core partisan commitment to New Zealand First is notable.

The ideological and structural alignment of the New Zealand party system up to the mid-20th century was classically defined by Chapman (1962), who characterised it as predominantly urban versus rural but also crosscut by differences between higher or lower socio-economic groups. In terms of ideology, the cleavage was both one-dimensional (between the interests of owners and wage workers) and two-dimensional (in terms of social structure). Chapman identified signs of this pattern changing in the early 1980s; others similarly identified de-alignment (Aimer, 1989; Bean, 1984; see also Vowles 1998). The process that occurred from 1984 to 1990 may be interpreted as a realignment that failed, requiring a change of electoral system to recognise that New Zealand had become a moderate multi-party system—moderate, but still 'multi'.

The nature of the post-MMP realignment, if it can be identified as such, continues to unfold as successive elections produce various iterations of outcomes within their apparent parameters. Since 2005, the number of parties has stabilised and vote choice volatility has decreased, giving some grounds to assume that a new pattern is emerging. However, on face value, the urban–rural divide seems alive and well, particularly since 2008. Figure 2.7 plots the effects of the urban–rural characteristics of general electorates on Labour and National voting across the electorates since 1972, using census data broken down by electorate, and the percentage employed in agriculture as a proxy for the urban–rural divide.[2] The Māori electorates are left out of this picture, because their numbers are few and they overlie the general electorates, which makes combined analysis problematic. The percentage of the labour force in agriculture is simply regressed against the vote percentages for the two parties, the unstandardised parameter estimates or coefficients providing the data plotted in Figure 2.7. Averaged over time, there appears to be a consistent pattern—for each 1 percentage difference across the urban–rural divide, the National Party vote is approximately half a percentage point up towards the rural electorates and Labour is approximately half a percentage point down (that is, towards the urban electorates).

---

2   It must be acknowledged that this proxy variable is approximate and does not fully account for both urban growth and changes in agricultural production and employment over the period. However, any error associated with these measurement issues is likely to be very minor and, therefore, unlikely to affect the broad patterns uncovered.

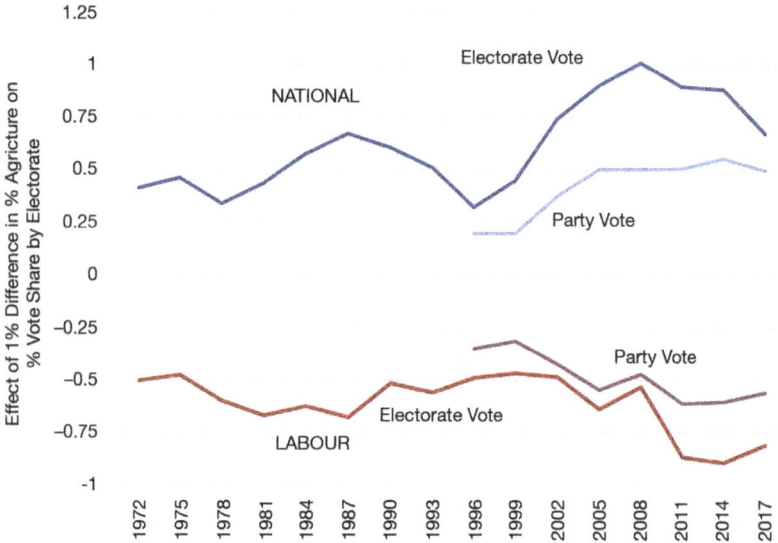

Figure 2.7: The urban–rural divide and major party voting (1972–2017).
Source: Author's research based on data from Statistics New Zealand and the Electoral Commission.

Figure 2.7 indicates fluctuations in this general pattern. Interpretation is complicated by electoral system change and the crisis in legitimacy that preceded this. The single electorate vote prior to MMP continues after the change in the form of the electorate or candidate vote: the new party vote is an addition. However, MMP introduced a new logic—the party vote determining the overall seat count—with electorate outcomes simply incorporated within the totals. Casting an electorate vote under MMP is not the same as it was under the old system, where one could cast a personal vote without worrying regarding its consequences for the overall outcome. MMP changes the data in a further way. The number of general electorates decreased from 95 to 60 in 1996 and, since this time, has crept upward only marginally. This affects the urban–rural boundary, with more mixing between provincial urban and rural communities within electorates. In 1993, across the 95 general electorates, the average percentage in agriculture was 9.9 per cent and the standard deviation as 11.2. In 1996, with 60 general electorates, the average was 9.5 per cent and the standard deviation was 9.9. While the narrowing of the standard deviation is lower than might have been expected, caution is still required.

The most significant point is a reduction in the number of solidly rural electorates, making a lower proportion of cases responsible for plotting the rural end of the slopes estimated.

While one can read consistency into these data over the long term, significant variations are also apparent. From the mid-1970s until 1987, as the blue and red lines in Figure 2.7 move further apart, the urban–rural dimension became more significant in shaping vote choices for both major parties: an intensification of that alignment, rather than a weakening of it. From 1987 to 1996, the alignment weakened, and then began to strengthen again as the party system stabilised from 1999 and 2002 onwards. The urban–rural effect on National's electorate vote in 2008 was particularly significant. Meanwhile, the other two parties' party votes were much less affected. However, comparing the electorate votes of 1972 and 1975 with the party votes of 2017 reveals little difference. Chapman's primary social structure dimension remains alive and continues to underpin the New Zealand party system.

Further scrutiny suggests that the story is not quite so simple. Figure 2.8 illustrates the R-squared statistic that estimates the variance explained by each model, from which estimates were derived for Figure 2.7. These drop precipitously following the transition to MMP; however, they rise again for National between 2002 and 2008. The lower R-squared value tells us that, if we plotted the regressions for each party and election (drawing the slope estimates or trend lines), more of the data points representing electorates would be further from those lines, indicating further variation that is not explained post-MMP—more electorates that are 'out-of-line' relative to their position, when plotted against the overall pattern. The lower number of purely rural electorates provides one explanation; however, further investigation indicates non-linearity elsewhere, when the R-squared value is low.[3] A pattern consistent with the urban–rural divide remains, but intermediate electorates diverge from this. Although fewer mixed electorates fit the pattern as closely as in the past, the urban–rural divide continues as strongly as before when one compares communities that are most strongly urban or rural.

---

3   Thanks are due to Alistair Gray for his help in uncovering these subtleties.

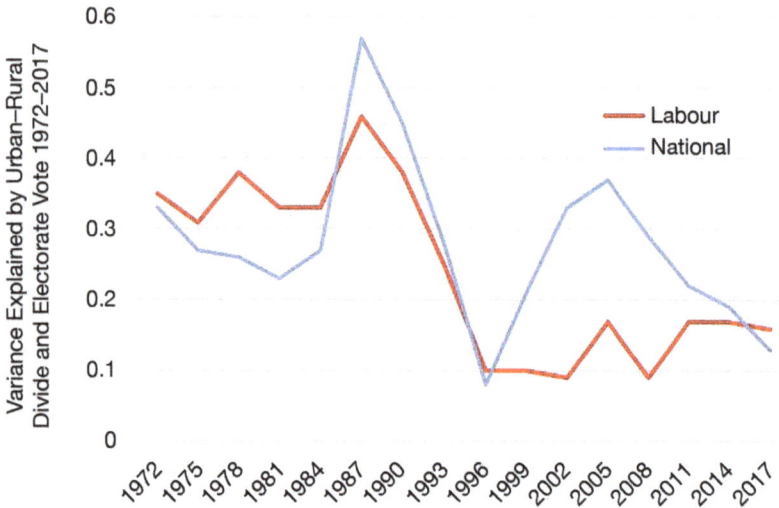

Figure 2.8: Variance explained by the urban–rural divide on the electorate vote (1972–2017).

Source: Author's research based on data from Statistics New Zealand and the Electoral Commission.

Regarding the second dimension of the social structure, the de-alignment process is more clearly apparent, as Figure 2.9 shows. Here, we define class voting as the difference in the Labour party vote between those households dependent primarily on manual and service occupations and those dependent primarily on wage and salary earners in non-manual occupations: managers, professionals, semi-professionals, clerical and sales workers (excluding non-voters).[4] The progressive decline of this form of class voting in the old established democracies is so widely known as to become a cliché of electoral politics: the new element is its close-to-complete collapse at the 2017 election, for which there occurred a 2002 precedent. This very closely replicates findings from recent elections in the United Kingdom, Germany, France and the United States: an apparent death of class voting (Dalton, 2020, p. 163).

---

4   This follows Alford (1962). In multiple working-adult households, we classify occupational class of the household by the occupation of the male in the household (the respondent himself or the respondent's partner). This reflects the reality of gender pay inequity, meaning that, in most cases, the occupation of the male is a better guide to the economic position of the household. The NZES does not ask for the gender of respondents' partners; however, because the majority of couples comprise a male and a female, this classification is the best reflection of the economic position of a male–female household that can be estimated from our data.

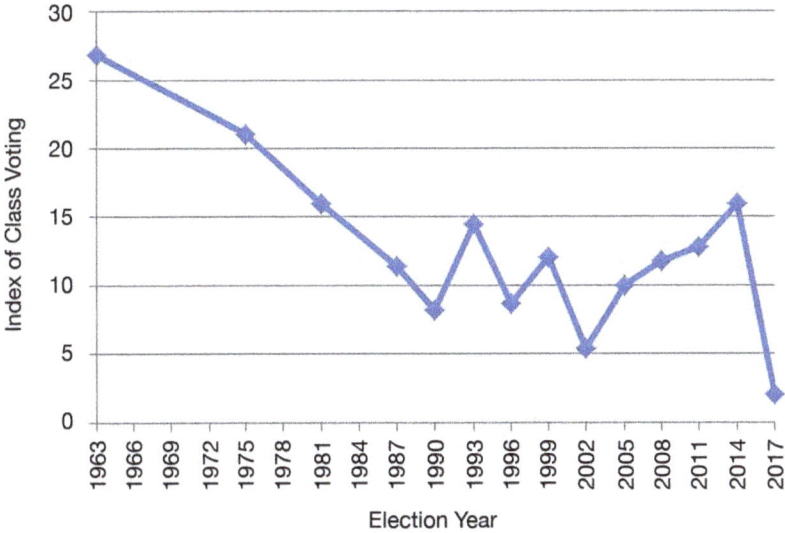

Figure 2.9: The Alford Index of class voting in New Zealand (1963–2017).
Source: Levine & Robinson (1975); Bean (1984); New Zealand Election Studies (1987–2017).

While the decline has been progressive since 1963 (the first data available), the 1990 height of the legitimacy crisis highlights the New Zealand story; in 1987, approximately 45 per cent of people in manual or service households voted Labour and, in 1990, only 32 per cent did so. Labour has never recovered this earlier share of the votes of its traditional supporters (Vowles, 2014, p. 40). In 2017, 30 per cent in this group continued to vote Labour. Meanwhile, in NZES samples, households mostly dependent on people in manual or service occupations have declined from approximately 40 per cent to 30 per cent of the total. To compensate for this compounded loss of votes, Labour has survived as a major party by collecting more votes from people in non-manual households.

In the 21st century, analysis of party system alignment comprises more than occupational categories, which have become more complex and less strongly associated with overall social positions and other definitions of class. More encompassing models of social structure are required to allow identification of relationships with vote choice after controlling for how each aspect of social position is mutually affected by all other relevant factors. Table 2.4 lists the variables from our baseline multinomial, multivariate model of the social and demographic correlates of voting choice—this is the appropriate approach, because the various party choices and non-vote are unordered categories. Vote National is the base category in the model (details of which are found in Table A2.2); the other categories are non-vote, Labour, Green, New Zealand First, Conservative and 'Other'. We include non-vote in the model but do not report it here because it is a significant element in overall voting choice, which affects the distribution of party choices. The baseline model accounts for approximately 10 per cent of the variation in voting choices in 2017.

Table 2.4: The social and demographic structural correlates of voting choice

Baseline model	
Occupation household	No occupation reported
	Farming household
	Manual/service household
	(Ref.: non-manual household)
Sector of employment	Public sector
	Self-employed
	(Ref.: private sector wage salary)
Assets	High-risk assets
	Low-risk assets only
	(Ref.: no. assets)
Income quintiles (1–5)	
On benefit	Yes
	(Ref. No)
Education	School qualification
	Post-school qualification (excluding university)
	University
	(No qualification)
Gender	Female
	(Ref.: male)
Age (18+)	
Ethnicity	Māori
	Asian
	Pasifika
	(Ref. Pākehā)

Baseline model	
Living in urban area	Major urban (100,000+ inhabitants)
	(Ref. not major urban)
Membership union	Yes
	(Ref.: No)
Church attendance	Never–at least once a week (0–1, five-point scale)

Note: Bracketed categories are reference categories in the analyses: the category to which an effect is estimated. For example, 'female' is estimated against the reference category 'male'. Low-risk assets are defined by answering yes to one of three questions: do respondents own a home, house or apartment; any savings or a contributory pension plan? High-risk assets are defined by answering yes to owning one of a business; a property, farm or livestock or stocks, shares or bonds? Ethnic identity is defined as strongest where multiple identifications were reported. Income is based on breaking household income into quintiles, augmented by a five-category question on relative income. Union household is defined by anyone in the household indicating that they were a member.

Source: New Zealand Election Study (2017).

Table 2.4 outlines the key variables. Occupational differences are crosscut by location in the public or private sectors; public sector employees are more dependent on a strong public sector for their security and incomes. Low-risk assets, such as owning a home, having savings or a contributory pension scheme, offer people security without much risk. High-risk assets, such as owning a rental property, a business or stocks and shares, may provide higher reward but also greater risk. This assets variable is categorised into those with no assets, those with low-risk assets only and those with high-risk assets. This group contains a few who possess high-risk assets but no low-risk assets; however, this is a very small group. Household income also shapes opportunities and security, as does receiving some kind of benefit (excluding New Zealand Superannuation, the universal pension available to all at age 65). Education shapes opportunities, income and social attitudes; people who are more educated tend to adopt more liberal positions.

Compared to occupation, other categories—assets, income, age, gender and ethnicity—are even more fundamental attributes affecting opportunities and life choices. Age is relevant for generational differences between older people, who have been able to benefit from rising house prices, and younger people, for whom acquisition of such assets has become more difficult. Gender and ethnicity also have well-known implications for social position. Finally, union membership tends to mobilise people towards the left and forms a residual element of Labour tradition. Church attendance is expected to mobilise people towards more socially conservative positions. We report the findings from this model in Figures 2.10–2.13, plotting predicted probabilities for all significant variables, plus 95 per cent confidence intervals. The full model is given in Table A2.2.

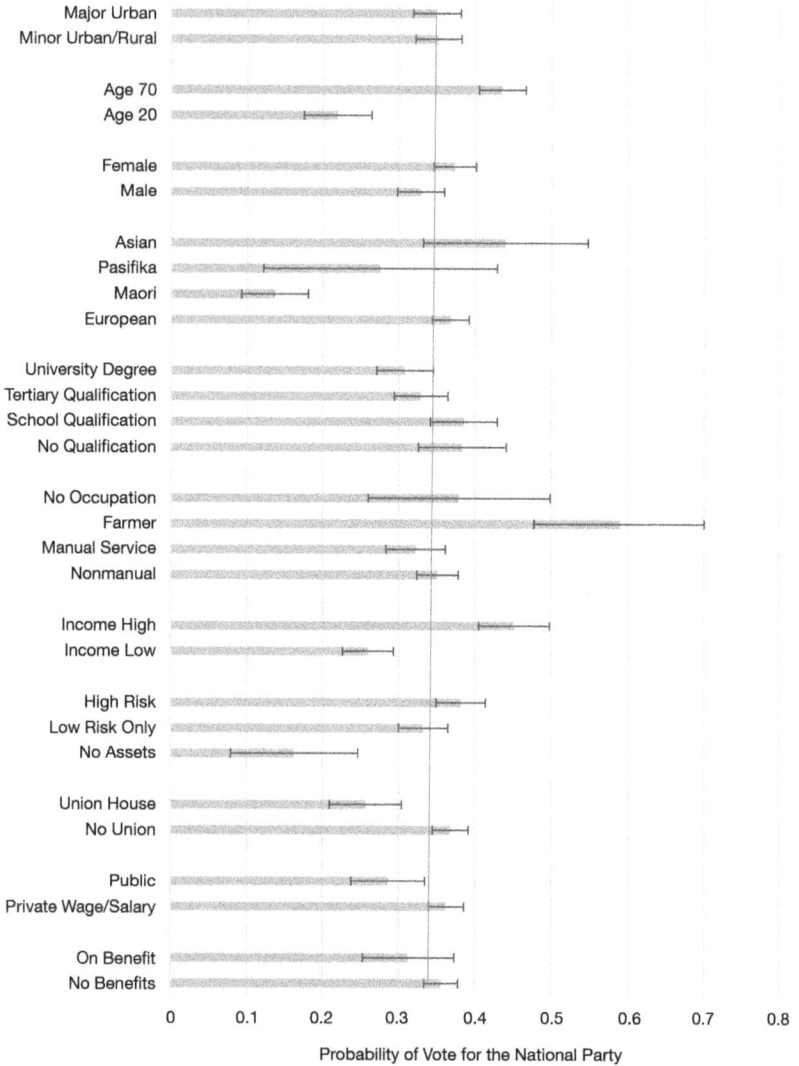

Figure 2.10: Probabilities of party vote for the National Party.
Source: New Zealand Election Study (2017).

The vertical line in Figure 2.10 represents National's party vote as a percentage of the entire electorate, including non-voters, making it possible to benchmark the probability estimates to the entire enrolled electorate. As expected, the National Party was more likely to receive the votes of older people and Pākehā and less likely to appeal to Māori. Despite the gender contrast between the Labour and National leaders, women were slightly more likely to vote National than men. National took votes relatively evenly across all educational categories but was more likely than average to receive the votes of those with only a high school qualification. It should be no surprise that farmers strongly support National; however, National's appeal to manual/service voters matched its overall level of electoral support. High incomes and both kinds of assets attract people to National. As expected, people in those households dependent on public sector employment and union members are less likely to support National. This picture of the National Party vote is exactly what one would expect, indicating that the New Zealand party system is still strongly aligned in reference to differences in social locations and opportunities. NZES data appear to indicate that National did marginally better in major urban electorates than elsewhere; however, comparison with official data indicates that this is probably an artefact of a slighter lower response rate among National rural voters.

Figure 2.11 confirms that, all else equal, Labour's new female leadership is associated with a gender gap—women are more likely to vote Labour than men. Labour's strong support among Māori is also apparent (see Chapter 6 for more details). This confirms the absence of a manual–non-manual divide among those who vote Labour. However, income, high-risk assets and support among beneficiaries and those in union households confirm the persistence of a significant residue of Labour's traditional support. Sector of employment has little apparent effect on voting. Regarding education, with all else being equal, it seems that Labour appeals more to those with higher rather than lower education; however, the confidence intervals overlap. Youth enthusiasm for Labour, evident during the election campaign, is not reflected in these data. Labour performed best in major urban areas, net of all other factors in the model. Further analysis indicates a linear relationship across the urban–rural divide; Labour fared worse in rural areas, better in country towns, better again in provincial towns or cities and best in urban areas, which is consistent with official data.

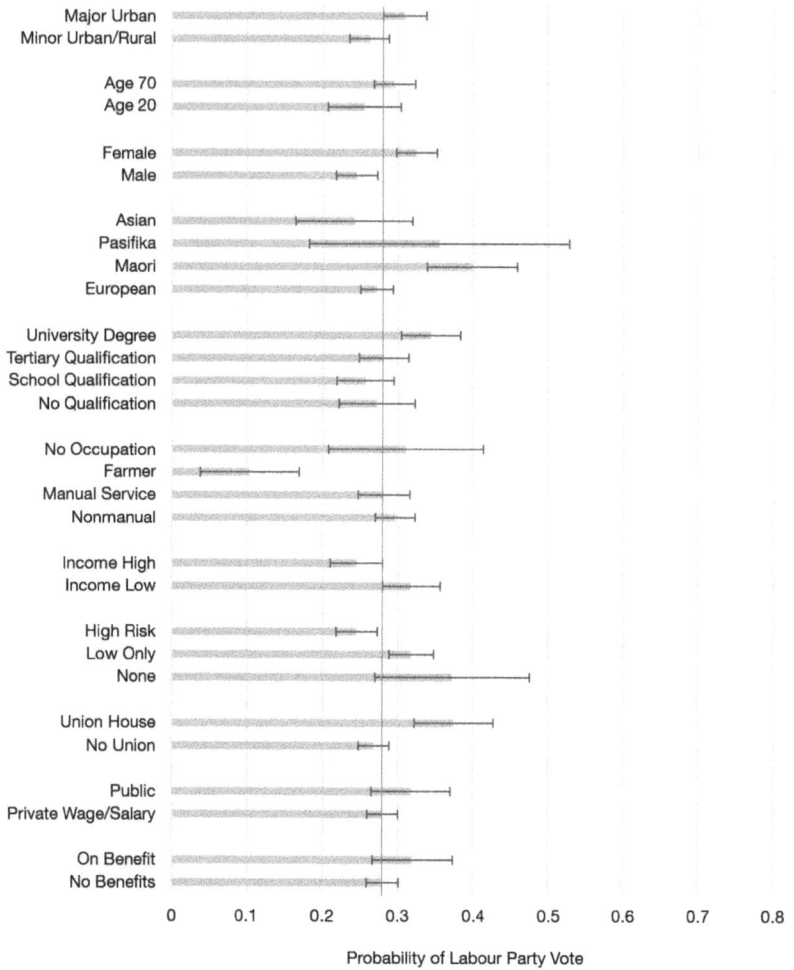

Figure 2.11: Probability of Labour Party vote.
Source: New Zealand Election Study (2017).

Age and education are the two strongest associations with party vote for the Green Party, as shown in Figure 2.12. The Green Party does not fare so well among ethnic minorities, aside from Māori, among whom it receives votes equivalent to its overall share of the vote. Lower income and dependence on non-manual and public sector jobs also shape the Green Party vote. The Green Party is confirmed as a party of predominantly middle-class, young and relatively well-educated radicals, which is quite different to the support profile of the Labour Party, excepting a slight tendency to appeal more to members of union households and to major urban residents.

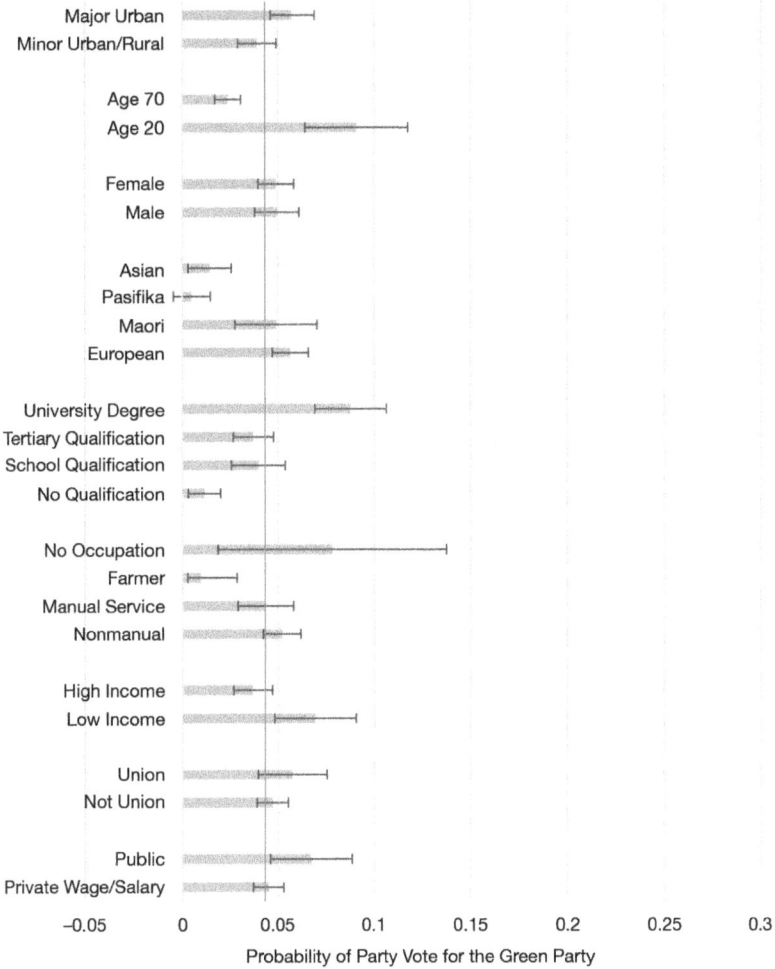

Figure 2.12: Probability of vote for the Green Party.
Source: New Zealand Election Study (2017).

As shown in Figure 2.13, New Zealand First, in some respects, represents the other side of the coin to the Green Party. It appeals more to the older population and to men and has effectively zero support among ethnic minorities, other than Māori, who are slightly more likely to vote for the party than average. The lower the education level, the more likely a vote for New Zealand First. This is one of the indicators of a populist party; however, confidence intervals do overlap. In other respects, New Zealand First shares with Labour and the Green Party an appeal to those on low incomes and to union members. New Zealand First's possible appeal to

Pasifika people merits further investigation. However, caution is advised, because the confidence intervals are very wide and Pasifika responses rates to the NZES are very low. New Zealand First's left–right orientation on these factors is consistent with its membership of a centre-left-led coalition. In terms of its profile on age and education, and in its slightly greater appeal to those outside major cities, New Zealand First has more in common with the National Party.

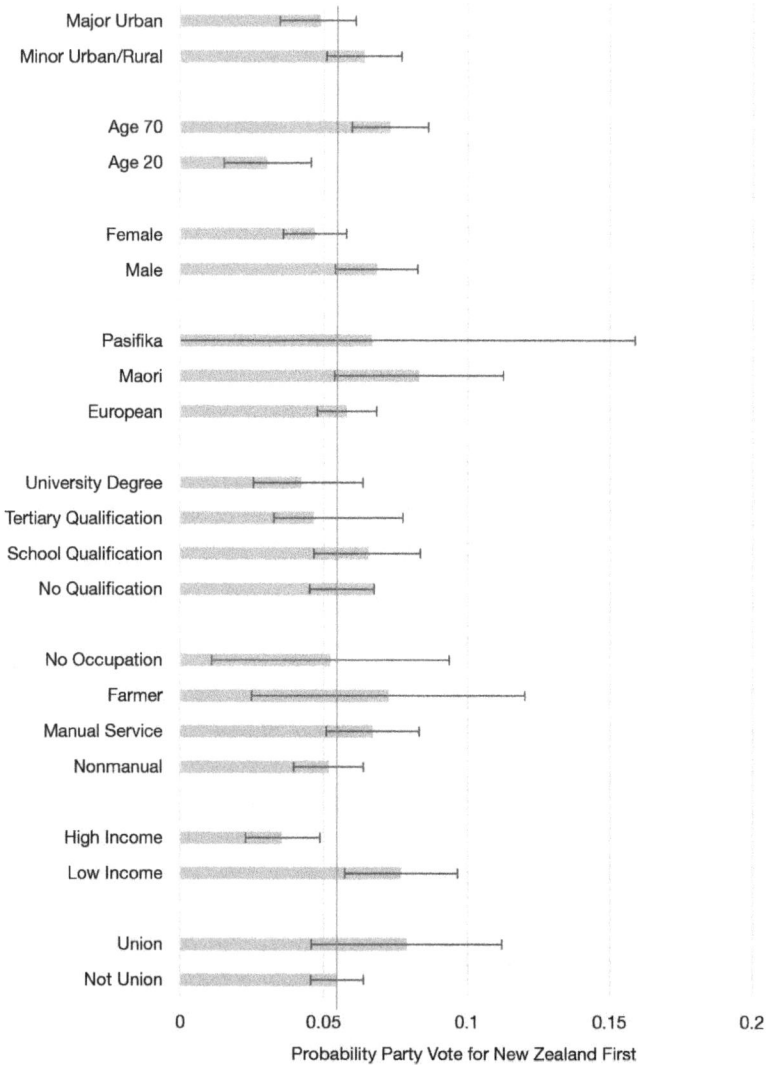

Figure 2.13: Probabilities of party vote for New Zealand First.
Source: New Zealand Election Study (2017).

Conclusions

Comparatively speaking, New Zealand's electoral politics are stable. Two centre-focused major political parties remain dominant; however, when in government, they are required to share power with much smaller parties that may exert some leverage over their major party coalition parties. One of these, New Zealand First, owes much of its appeal to populism, despite being a party of the centre on the left–right dimension. However, its foundation of electoral support is small and the party lost ground at the 2017 election.

To the extent that any election can signal a national shift of priorities, 2017 saw New Zealand take a step to the left—embodied by concern regarding healthcare, housing and other social issues. Increased concern for the environment helped to keep the Green Party in parliament and increased concern regarding high rates of immigration provided a foundation for New Zealand First. However, greater control of immigration was also a Labour issue, framed in terms of economic and social consequences rather than in relation to nationalism or ethnocentrism. Therefore, the coalition government announced in October had an underlying logic and coherence.

In the United States and Europe, immigration is a matter of concern because many newcomers are refugees or enter illegally—borders have proven difficult to control. Due to New Zealand's geographical distance and separation from other landmasses, almost all illegal immigration is limited to those who overstay previously granted rights of entry. Refugees are admitted through official channels; however, the quota is low relative to those of other countries. Those refugees that are admitted are provided with significant support to adjust to New Zealand and do not present a matter of wide concern; indeed, the New Zealand First Party is on record for advocating a modest increase of the quota and agreeing to this in government. The numbers of immigrants received by New Zealand are among the highest in the world (by head of population), yet concern regarding immigration is relatively low. Opinions consistent with ethnocentric and nationalist populism can be found in New Zealand but there is little or no foundation for mobilising these widely. Although a cultural dimension that spans the differences between social conservatives and social liberals can be identified in public opinion and party policies, it remains secondary rather than dominant.

The economic and social pressures created by high levels of legally sanctioned immigration have been more effectively mobilised across the traditional left–right dimension. Representing this ideological cleavage, despite the neoliberal revolution of the late 1980s and early 1990s, electoral system change and the global financial crisis, the party system remains relatively well-aligned across the urban–rural dimension, crosscut by differences between social groups in terms of incomes, assets and opportunities. While this socio-economic dimension is no longer based on occupational status, its foundations in differences between those who own more and those who own less, little or nothing remain strongly apparent. The focus of class politics has shifted away from status-based occupational differences towards those rooted in production, assets and property. With a government of the centre-left in office, authoritarian populists are likely to advance only if that government is perceived to fail and disappoint; however, New Zealand's apparently populist party is part of that same government. Winston Peters (aged 74 in early 2020) is unlikely to maintain his political career for much longer. There may be a more successful future for authoritarian populism in New Zealand than in 2017, or even 2020; however, it is as yet impossible to predict what this might be.

References

Aimer, P. (1989). Travelling together: Party identification and voting in the New Zealand General Election of 1987. *Electoral Studies, 8*(2), 131–142. doi.org/10.1016/0261-3794(89)90030-9

Alcántara, M. (2012). *Elections in Latin America 2009–2011: A comparative analysis* (Working Paper No. 386). Retrieved from kellogg.nd.edu/publications/workingpapers/WPS/386.pdf

Alford, R. R. (1962). A suggested index of the association of social class and voting. *The Public Opinion Quarterly, 26*(3), 417–425.

Bean, C. (1984). *A comparative study of electoral behaviour in Australia and New Zealand* (Unpublished doctoral thesis). Australian National University, Canberra, ACT.

Burr, L. & Templeton, S. (2017). Willie Jackson confirms Labour Party candidacy. *Newshub*. Retrieved from www.newshub.co.nz/home/politics/2017/02/willie-jackson-confirms-labour-party-candidacy.html

Chapman, R. M. (1962). The general result. In R. M. Chapman, W. K. Jackson & A. Mitchell (Eds), *New Zealand politics in action: The 1960 general election* (pp. 235–298). London, United Kingdom: Oxford University Press.

Clifton, J. (2017a). New Zealand Election 2017: Undercurrents of change in new poll. *Noted.* Retrieved from www.noted.co.nz/currently/currently-politics/new-zealand-election-2017-undercurrents-of-change-in-new-poll

Clifton, J. (2017b). Why Labour's last-minute leadership change may be its salvation. *Noted.* Retrieved from www.noted.co.nz/currently/currently-politics/why-labours-last-minute-leadership-change-may-be-its-salvation

Curia. (2019a). *Archives Colmar Brunton.* Retrieved from www.curia.co.nz/company/colmar-brunton/page/1/

Curia. (2019b). *Archives Reid Research.* Retrieved from www.curia.co.nz/company/reid-research/page/1/

Curia. (2019c). *Archives Roy Morgan.* Retrieved from www.curia.co.nz/company/roy-morgan/

Dalton, R. J. (2020). *Citizen politics: Public opinion and political parties in advanced industrial democracies* (7th ed.). Thousand Oaks, CA: CQ Press.

Electoral Commission. (2014). *Summary of overall results.* Retrieved from archive.electionresults.govt.nz/electionresults_2014/e9/html/e9_part1.html

Electoral Commission. (2017). *2017 general election—official result..* Retrieved from www.electionresults.org.nz/electionresults_2017/

Emanuele, V. (2015). *Dataset of electoral volatility and its internal components in Western Europe (1945–2015).* Rome, Italy: Italian Center for Electoral Studies. doi.org/10.7802/1112

Gallagher, Michael. (2019). *Election indices dataset.* Retrieved from www.tcd.ie/Political_Science/staff/michael_gallagher/ElSystems/index.php

Levine, S. & Robinson, A. (1975). New Zealand post-election survey, 1975. ADA Dataverse, V2. doi.org/10.26193/UM8HWF

Mainwaring, S., Gervasoni, C. & Espana-Najera, A. (2017). Extra- and within-system electoral volatility. *Party Politics, 23*(6), 623–635. doi.org/10.1177/1354068815625229

Mills, S. (2018). Survey findings and the 2017 election. In S. Levine (Ed.), *Stardust and substance: The New Zealand general election of 2017* (pp. 365–378). Wellington, New Zealand: Victoria University Press.

New Zealand Election Study. (2017). *New Zealand Election Study* [dataset]. Retrieved from www.nzes.org/exec/show/data

New Zealand Labour Party. (2017). *Making immigration work for New Zealand.* Retrieved from www.labour.org.nz/immigration

New Zealand Listener. (2017a). New Zealand Election 2017: Undercurrents of change in new poll. *New Zealand Listener*, 8 June.

New Zealand Listener. (2017b). Why Labour's last-minute leadership change may be its salvation. *New Zealand Listener*, 4 August.

New Zealand Listener. (2017c). Poll: Labour, National, and the crucial 8%. *New Zealand Listener*. 8 September.

Pākehā. (n.d.). In *Māori Dictionary*. Retrieved from maoridictionary.co.nz/search?idiom=&phrase=&proverb=&loan=&keywords=pakeha

Peters, W. (2005). Securing our borders and protecting our identity. *Scoop*. Retrieved from www.scoop.co.nz/stories/PA0505/S00702.htm

Reserve Bank of New Zealand. (2018). *Real GDP*. Retrieved from www.rbnz.govt.nz/statistics/key-graphs/key-graph-real-gdp

Small, V. (2014). Matt McCarten new Labour Chief of Staff. *New Zealand Herald*. Retrieved from www.stuff.co.nz/national/politics/9763705/Matt-McCarten-new-Labour-chief-of-staff

Statistics New Zealand. (2018a). *Gross Domestic Product: December 2017 quarter* (Series SNEA.SG09RAC00B01NZD). Retrieved from www.stats.govt.nz/information-releases/gross-domestic-product-december-2017-quarter

Statistics New Zealand. (2018b). *International travel and migration: March 2018*. Retrieved from www.stats.govt.nz/information-releases/international-travel-and-migration-march-2018

Statistics New Zealand. (2018c). *International visitor arrivals to New Zealand: December 2017*. Retrieved from www.stats.govt.nz/reports/international-visitor-arrivals-to-new-zealand-december-2017

Vowles, J. (1998). Waiting for the realignment: The New Zealand party system 1972–1993. *Political Science 48*(2), 184–209. doi.org/10.1177/003231879704800203

Vowles, J. (2014). Putting the 2011 election in its place. In J. Vowles (Ed.), *The new electoral politics in New Zealand: The significance of the 2011 election* (pp. 27–52). Wellington, New Zealand: Institute for Governance and Policy Studies.

Vowles, J., Coffé, H. & Curtin, J. (2017). *A bark but no bite: Inequality and the 2014 New Zealand general election*. Canberra, Australia: ANU Press. doi.org/10.22459/BBNB.08.2017

Appendices

Table A2.1: Estimated flows of the votes (2014–2017) (New Zealand Election Survey Panel)

2017 Vote	Non-vote	National	Labour	Green	NZ First	Conservative	Ineligible	N
Non-vote	12.2	2.8	2.9	0.8	0.9	0.7	1.3	289.0
National	4.5	25.8	0.5	0.2	0.8	1.0	1.0	466.0
Labour	4.1	3.6	13.6	2.7	2.8	0.2	1.1	387.0
Green	0.4	0.6	0.6	2.2	0.4	0.1	0.6	66.0
New Zealand First	0.7	0.9	0.3	0.1	2.8	0.6	0.0	76.0
Conservative	0.0	0.0	0.0	0.0	0.0	0.1	0.0	2.0
The Opportunities Party	0.5	0.4	0.3	0.3	0.1	0.1	0.1	25.0
Total	22.5	34.6	18.5	6.4	7.9	2.9	4.1	1,344.0

Note: This table presents equivalent data to Table 2.2, estimated from the 2017–2014 Panel, following iterative weighting on the marginal frequencies. Comparison with Vote Compass data indicates close correspondence between the matching consistent non-voter and party cells. For the 2017 and 2014 Panels, as for the NZES in general, reported vote is validated from official records. Given wide confidence intervals for other cells, assessment of differences between this and the Vote Compass data is a matter of judgement; however, evidence of significant cell consistency between the two data sources and larger Ns in the Vote Compass data give some grounds for confidence in the Vote Compass small cell estimates.

Source: New Zealand Election Study (2017).

Table A2.2: Party voting groups and social structure—multinomial logit model

Reference National	Non-vote	rse	Labour	rse	Green	rse	NZF	rse	Other	rse
Age in years	-0.038 **	0.007	-0.012 **	0.003	-0.040 **	0.005	0.001	0.006	-0.022 **	0.005
Female	-0.457 *	0.220	0.168	0.104	-0.158	0.168	-0.630 **	0.174	-0.684 **	0.166
(Male)										
ethnic										
Māori	1.454 **	0.280	1.347 **	0.202	1.046 **	0.289	1.221 **	0.267	2.269 **	0.236
Pasifika	-0.741	0.923	0.246	0.403	-1.889	1.020	0.902	0.570	-1.153	0.825
Asian	0.421	0.388	-0.312	0.232	-1.387 **	0.414	-15.714 **	0.225	-0.581	0.445
Other	-15.229 **	1.046	1.509	1.035	0.130	1.430	-14.877 **	1.026	0.994	1.352
(Pākehā)										
School qualification	-0.229	0.338	-0.113	0.170	1.468 **	0.450	-0.185	0.239	0.421	0.317
Tertiary qualifications	-0.254	0.328	0.122	0.168	1.650 **	0.446	-0.180	0.247	0.651 *	0.304
University degree	-0.490	0.392	0.430 *	0.185	2.640 **	0.446	-0.318	0.305	1.075 **	0.316
(No qualification)										
Manual service	0.452	0.232	0.099	0.123	-0.015	0.212	0.265	0.187	0.007	0.191
Farmer	-0.405	0.547	-1.585 **	0.371	-2.746 **	1.040	-0.266	0.395	-0.624	0.470
No occupation	1.001	0.677	0.005	0.297	0.717	0.490	0.394	0.428	-0.585	0.601
(Occupation)										
Household income	-0.213 *	0.094	-0.244 **	0.041	-0.310 **	0.067	-0.335 **	0.066	-0.177 **	0.063

Reference National	Non-vote	rse	Labour	rse	Green	rse	NZF	rse	Other	rse
Low-risk assets	-1.051 *	0.461	-0.741 *	0.297	0.307	0.519	-0.392	0.430	-0.969 *	0.444
High-risk assets	-0.128	0.229	-0.390 **	0.110	-0.239	0.180	-0.068	0.191	-0.086	0.180
Union household	-0.357	0.348	0.824 **	0.142	0.616 **	0.210	0.743 **	0.252	0.599 **	0.205
Major urban	-0.466	0.240	0.163	0.105	0.307	0.174	-0.253	0.184	0.068	0.167
Public sector	0.639 *	0.296	0.443 **	0.142	0.676 **	0.211	0.168	0.244	0.521 *	0.210
Self-employed	0.457	0.272	-0.003	0.137	0.354	0.237	0.151	0.213	0.155	0.211
On benefit	0.044	0.294	0.388 *	0.155	0.223	0.242	-0.065	0.254	-0.008	0.244
Church Attendance	-0.531	1.014	-0.192	0.465	-0.832	0.862	0.313	0.752	0.837	0.642
Constant	3.081 **	0.734	1.436 **	0.404	-1.521 *	0.761	-0.124	0.684	-0.066	0.628
R2	0.102									
N	3,295									

Source: New Zealand Election Study (2017).

3

MEASURING POPULISM IN NEW ZEALAND

Lara Greaves and Jack Vowles

If populism is a coherent, underlying set of attitudes that is present in the minds and emotions of voters, it should be measurable by asking people questions in surveys (Geurkink, Zaslove, Sluiter & Jacobs, 2019).[1] Indeed, using somewhat different approaches, various efforts have been made to measure populist public attitudes within and across nations (Gidron & Bonikowski, 2013; Norris & Inglehart, 2019; Roodujin, 2018; see also Castanho Silva, Jungkunz, Helbling & Littvay, 2019). In this chapter, we consider two alternative ways of measuring populism using questions from the 2017 New Zealand Election Study (NZES), some of which form part of the Comparative Study of Electoral Systems (CSES) (Module 5) (CSES, 2019) designed to measure populism, and others that are specific to the NZES.[2] Following Mudde (2004), the CSES questions were principally designed to estimate exclusionary populism and comprise three core domains: antipathy towards elites, representative democracy and outgroups (Hobolt, Anduiza, Carkoglu, Lutz & Sauger, 2016). As explained in Chapter 1, we argue that an exclusionary form of

---

1   It is necessary to provide a brief note on some terminology used in this chapter (see De Vaus [2014] for further information). We aim to measure populism and authoritarianism through survey questions. In survey research and scale development, researchers aim to measure an underlying latent construct through survey questions (sometimes called 'items'). Multiple questions comprise a scale, which can be defined as a set of questions that work together to measure an underlying construct.
2   Charles Crothers contributed to an earlier version of this chapter—we acknowledge and thank him for his work and comments on the final draft.

populism provides too narrow a definition, regardless of context; defining populism in such terms is even more problematic in (post)colonial societies such as New Zealand.[3] Drawing on some CSES questions and other questions specific to the NZES, we instead develop two scales, following Norris and Inglehart (2019), which split populism away from authoritarianism. We then analyse scores on this measure of populism and authoritarianism across a range of demographics, to investigate who is more likely to endorse populism and authoritarianism.

Populism in the Comparative Study of Electoral Systems and the New Zealand Election Study

The CSES is a collaborative project that includes more than 60 election studies worldwide. Participating nations run the same module of questions, alongside some other core questions and demographics, to allow for the creation of a cross-national, open-access dataset. The latest module, included in the 2017 NZES, examines populism. For the purposes of the CSES module, populism was defined as 'citizens' attitudes towards political elites, majority rule and outgroups in representative democracy' (Hobolt et al., 2016, p. 3) (see Figure 3.1).

The set of 17 questions was conceptualised as a triangle. The corners represent three key aspects of populism: attitudes towards political elites, attitudes towards majority rule and representative democracy and attitudes towards the out-group (assumed to be immigrants). In the following sections, we present the questions and the percentages of participants who agreed with them, alongside a discussion of how these relate to the measurement of populism in New Zealand.

---

3   Some would label New Zealand as a postcolonial nation; that is, we *experienced* colonisation. However, many Māori academics argue that the nation is not postcolonial because Māori are *still experiencing* colonisation and its effects (Smith, 2012).

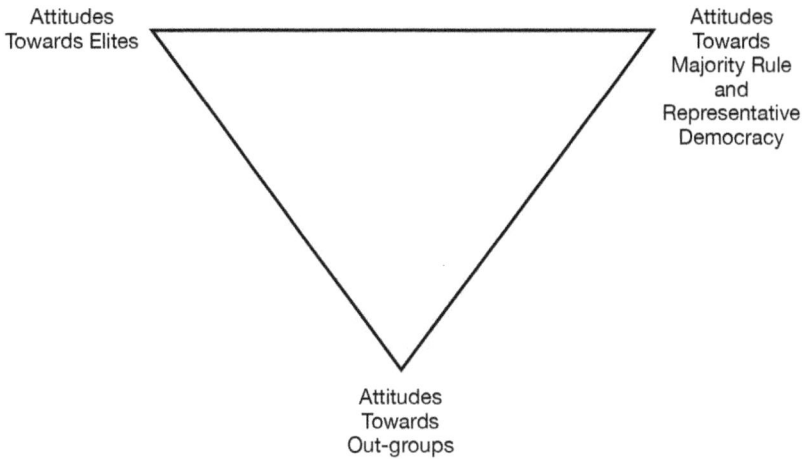

Figure 3.1: The components of populist attitudes.
Source: Reproduced from Hobolt et al. (2016).

The Components of Populism in New Zealand?: Attitudes towards Political Elites

A core element of exclusionary or authoritarian populism is the creation of contrast between 'us' (the pure, regular, ordinary people) and 'them' (the corrupt, untrustworthy, polluted elites) (Mudde, 2007; Mudde & Kaltwasser, 2012). This contrast positions elites as uncaring and untrustworthy: a 'problem' for ordinary New Zealanders. To assess attitudes towards elites, participants were asked to rate the following questions on a scale from 1 ('strongly agree') to 5 ('strongly disagree'):

- 'Most politicians do not care about the people' (31 per cent agreed or strongly agreed)
- 'Most politicians are trustworthy' (in this case, 36 per cent disagreed or strongly disagreed)[4]
- 'Politicians are the main problem in New Zealand' (20 per cent agreed or strongly agreed).

---

4   In scale development, it is best practice to include a balanced number of negatively and positively worded items, to avoid agreement bias—the tendency to agree with survey items and statements in general (De Vaus, 2014).

One aspect of this anti-elite component of populism is the idea that, if one perceives elites as untrustworthy, it follows that they also engage in corruption. An additional question, rated on a scale of 1 ('very widespread') to 4 ('very unusual'), asked participants about the extent to which they perceive that corruption is a regular part of politics:

- 'How widespread or unusual do you think corruption such as bribe-taking is among politicians and public servants in New Zealand?' (22 per cent felt it was 'very' or 'quite' widespread).

This question refers to the level of *perceived* corruption—here, there exists an inherent assumption that very little *actual* corruption occurs in many established democracies (Kaufmann, Kraay & Mastruzzi, 2007; Zirker & Barrett, 2017). Therefore, the question is intended to measure the perception that elites are corrupt, rather than experiences of actual corruption. Indeed, New Zealand ranks highly in the 2018 Transparency International anti-corruption index, ranking second of 180 nations (Transparency International, 2018). Despite this relatively high ranking, the level of agreement to the corruption question demonstrates that approximately one in every five participants feels that corruption is 'very' or 'quite' widespread.

Finally, a question was designed to specifically index left-wing populism (Hobolt et al., 2016), tapping into the idea that large corporations wield some control over politicians, because political elites ally with the interests of such groups rather than everyday people:

- 'Most politicians care only about the interests of the rich and powerful' (35 per cent agreed or strongly agreed).

Together, this group of questions creates an index of views regarding political elites and their role: as caring and trustworthy or uncaring 'sell-outs', only interested in helping the rich and powerful. However, herein lies a problem that has been highlighted by various critics (see, e.g. Geurkink et al., 2019). Some of these questions are very close, in conceptual terms, to questions used to estimate external political efficacy. External political efficacy is defined as the sense that politicians are responsive to the demands of public opinion or, more specifically, the wishes of the person being surveyed or interviewed (Craig & Maggiotto, 1982; Easton, 1965, 1975; Norris, 2011). If elites are indeed unresponsive, and voters perceive them to be so, does this make the people, by definition, populist? Further, if a specific group of voters feels particularly ignored, does this make them more populist?

Two key efforts have been made to address this potential problem: using exploratory and confirmatory factor analysis,[5] researchers have found sufficient separation between sets of questions relating to external efficacy and to populism (Geurkink et al., 2019). However, this is not the case for the CSES instruments. Indeed, the efficacy question defined by Geurkink et al. is very close to the first CSES populism question listed above as part of 'attitudes to elites'[6] and another addresses trust in politicians. In the article in question, this forms another measurable dimension that is distinct from populism. Indeed, almost all the CSES 'attitudes to elites' questions can be criticised as relating to external political efficacy. A better approach is to identify more deep-seated populist attitudes and distinguish these from short-term responses to 'representation gaps' that affect political efficacy (Kaltwasser, Vehrkamp & Wratil, 2019). Fortunately, the CSES contains two other questions that may be used together as an alternative estimate of external efficacy (Ikeda, Kobayashi & Hoshimoto, 2008). These ask participants to rate: (a) 'who is in power' and (b) 'voting' on a 1–5 scale, where 1 is that it will not make any difference and 5 is that it makes a 'big' difference (see Vowles, 2016).

Challenges to Representative Democracy

Another component of the CSES version of populism concerns majoritarian political values, coupled with dislike of the current system of representative democracy (Hobolt et al., 2016; Kriesi, 2014). This scale positions the 'regular people' (as opposed to the elites) as the majority, who are viewed as those who should be making the decisions in a democracy. Higher endorsement of this dimension could lead to support for changes to the system, to include a more direct link between political decisions and the people, in part by removing the power of politicians. The first

5   These are statistical techniques that allow researchers to determine which survey questions tap into the same underlying latent construct as other questions. They allow researchers to see which questions 'hang together', or have similar 'factor loadings', to create a scale (De Vaus, 2014).
6   'Politicians are not interested in what people like me think' and 'Political parties are only interested in my vote, not my opinions'.

question can be interpreted as favouring greater use of direct democracy, rather than representative democracy (rated on a scale from 1 ['strongly agree'] to 5 ['strongly disagree']):

- 'The people, and not politicians, should make our most important policy decisions' (51 per cent agreed or agreed strongly).

This suggests that New Zealanders tend to support the use of direct rather than representative democracy and decision-making through referenda or other methods by which regular, everyday people may have their voices heard on policy matters. Work with survey data in New Zealand has shown that support for referenda has increased over time and may now be as high as 70 per cent (Bowler, Donovan & Karp, 2007; Greaves & Milne, 2019).[7]

The next question investigates the notion of compromise. In politics, particularly in a mixed member proportional (MMP) system, compromise is part of the decision-making process, whether it be with coalition partners or other groups (Church & McLeay, 2003; McLeay & Vowles, 2007). This question indicates the extent to which participants disagree with compromise, which inevitably moderates any ideologically motivated policy that they might support, and also tests 'anti-pluralism':

- 'What people call compromise in politics is really just selling out on one's principles' (38 per cent strongly agreed or agreed).

There also exists a question regarding protecting the rights of minorities, which is worded using very broad language that could include a range of groups. Attitudes towards minority rights have been linked to exclusionary populism; diverse groups, based on gender, sexuality, ethnicity, religion or culture, have been framed as receiving a disproportionate amount of power. In the case of New Zealand, this manifests in relation to a cisgender,[8] straight, Pākehā, 'Kiwi' and secular (or Christian) majority (Plattner, 2010). However, this statement received a relatively low level of support:

- 'The will of the majority should always prevail, even over the rights of minorities' (28 per cent strongly agreed or agreed).

---

7   This high level of support includes favouring referendums in general, so including advisory referendums, not necessarily binding ones, both of which are features of New Zealand politics.
8   People whose gender identity matches what their culture expects their gender to be, based on their biological sex at birth.

Populists may also wish to bypass traditional representative democracy via a strong leader who can act as a conduit between the will of the people and political decisions (Canovan, 1999; Gidron & Bonikowski, 2013; Ionescu & Gellner, 1969). This hypothetical strong leader would possess the power to override typical policy processes and ignore other politicians and the media (Hobolt et al., 2016; Kriesi, 2014). A notable recent example of this is Donald Trump's announcements of policy, and various other communications, via Twitter (Norris & Inglehart, 2019). The survey asked a question regarding support for the idea of such a strong leader, rated on the same 1 ('strongly agree') to 5 ('strongly disagree') scale:

- 'Having a strong leader in government is good for New Zealand, even if the leader bends the rules to get things done' (43 per cent agreed or strongly agreed).

These results are striking; however, they should be interpreted with some caution. This question is double-barrelled: it indicates support for both a strong leader in government and a leader who bends rules. Therefore, some people may have disagreed regarding rule-bending but nevertheless selected 'agree' due to their strong desire for a strong leader. Regardless of how people read this question, the results indicate that nearly half the participants feel that such a leader would be a good thing for New Zealand.

Attitudes towards Outgroups

Finally, to create the 'pure' authentic, real people under the CSES working definition of populism, there exists a dimension of opposition towards 'the other', the out-group (Hobolt et al., 2016). However, besides excluding those 'elites' (investigated in the first dimension), the out-group must be defined. This is where the CSES approach to populism encounters the greatest difficulty in the New Zealand context. The classic outgroup targets of populism are generally immigrants, particularly those from ethnic minority groups, religions or cultures that are viewed as distant from, or threatening towards, the majority (Mudde & Kaltwasser, 2012; Norris & Inglehart, 2019; Zaslove, 2008). However, how does this component of the scale, or working definition, fit in the context of a vocal, indigenous minority? In the New Zealand context, many of these questions lack applicability because they mix concepts.

To use a cliché, New Zealand is a land of immigrants, at least relative to most European nations. The majority group in New Zealand (European, also called Pākehā) only became the majority approximately six to seven generations ago (in about 1860). Indeed, many Pākehā are more recent immigrants than this (Phillips, 2015). As of the 2018 New Zealand Census, people of European descent comprise the majority of the population (70.2 per cent), followed by indigenous Māori peoples (16.5 per cent), those of Asian descent (15.1 per cent; largely those of Chinese, Filipino and Indian ethnicities), Pacific peoples (8.1 per cent; more than two-thirds of whom are New Zealand–born) and other ethnicities such as Middle Eastern, African and Latin American peoples (2.7 per cent). The 2018 Census also showed that 27 per cent of the population were born outside New Zealand (Statistics New Zealand, 2019).

There is still considerable debate regarding New Zealand national identity and the extent to which it includes elements of Māori versus European cultures (biculturalism) and/or multiculturalism (see, e.g. Bell, 2009, 2014; McIntosh, Liu, McCreanor & Teaiwa, 2005). For the CSES definition of populism to gain leverage, national identity must be defined in such a way that distinguishes between insiders and outsiders (Hobolt et al., 2016). In the broader literature, this component of populism has been called 'nativism'; this is yet another concept that is difficult to define. In one line of thinking, nativism has been defined as opposition to minority groups within one's country due to their foreign connections (Higham, 2002). However, Mudde has described nativism as 'an ideology which holds that states should be inhabited exclusively by members of the native group' (2007, p. 19). There are clear problems with applying the concept of nativism to New Zealand, where the majority group have colonised an indigenous group that still comprise a large, vocal and politically conscious minority. Therefore, a problem is posed regarding defining 'the other'.

Many of the questions in this scale domain could be understood by respondents as a reference to outsiders or ethnic minority groups. However, others more specifically mention 'immigrants' (again, rated on a five-point agreement scale):

- 'New Zealand culture is generally harmed by immigrants' (22 per cent strongly agree or agree)
- 'Immigrants increase crime rates in New Zealand' (16 per cent strongly agree or agree)
- 'Immigrants are generally good for New Zealand's economy' (reverse-worded; 15 per cent disagreed/strongly disagreed).

The results demonstrate that a minority, albeit a substantial minority, of participants (15–22 per cent) are comfortable expressing explicit prejudice towards immigrants to New Zealand. It should be noted that this attitudinal dimension is usually difficult to measure. Asking people to indicate agreement with such explicit statements underestimates the prevalence of these views due to social desirability bias.[9] People struggle to accurately estimate their own prejudice; a degree of implicit or unconscious bias is evident in the majority of people (for a summary that is relevant to New Zealand, see Blank & Houkamau, 2017). Therefore, this set of questions likely underestimates anti-immigrant prejudice.

In developing the populism scale, Hobolt et al. (2016) note that, across nations, the most visible and controversial out-group is immigrants (Zaslove, 2008). The questions allow the participants to transpose their own ideas of who the 'immigrants' are onto the question. Most immigrants to New Zealand comprise those from the 'Anglosphere' (Australia, the United Kingdom and the United States) and Europe (Ministry of Business, Innovation and Employment, 2016). While some negativity exists regarding English 'Pommie' immigrants,[10] it is usually comparatively inoffensive (NZPA, 2010). Scores on this dimension are more likely to indicate prejudice towards immigrants from regions viewed as having cultures dissimilar to New Zealand (e.g. Asia, India and the Middle East). International testing of these questions has suggested that endorsement of these statements is related to prejudice towards Muslim immigrants, in particular (Hobolt et al., 2016). Further, in support of these international findings, past national survey research has shown that New Zealanders hold more anger and less warmth towards Arabs and Muslims, as compared to other groups (Shaver, Sibley, Osborne & Bulbulia, 2017; Shaver, Troughton, Sibley & Bulbulia, 2016).

While these first questions aim to detect direct, explicit prejudice towards immigrants, other components (of the attitudes towards out-groups questions) involve positioning national identity and what immigrants (or others) *must do* to be a 'New Zealander'. Exclusionary populists wish to create a solid, national in-group identity, one that cannot be penetrated by outsiders/immigrants. However, the existence of a relatively large and

---

9   'Social desirability bias' is the idea that people want to present themselves in a positive light, even in an anonymous questionnaire (De Vaus, 2014).

10   The term 'Pommie' is also found in South Africa and Australia—its origins are a contraction of 'pomegranate', referring to the tendency of light-skinned people to suffer from acute sunburn.

vocal indigenous group problematises the position of nativists. The New Zealand national identity—the 'we' that populists attempt to define—is altered by the (post)colonial context and the existence of a clear indigenous minority group, members of which can assert a more authentic claim to the national identity than those descended from later colonists. Indeed, work on implicit association tests has shown that Pākehā New Zealanders equally associate Pākehā and Māori symbols and faces to New Zealand, whereas this was not the case in Australia with Indigenous Australians (Sibley & Barlow 2009; Sibley, Liu & Khan, 2008).

Past research has documented several strategies that New Zealand nativists have used to claim the 'New Zealand' identity. For example, some adopt a superordinate 'New Zealander' category that includes certain tokenistic aspects of Te Ao Māori (the Māori world) but not those more confronting or demanding aspects such as reparations for past injustices (Sibley, 2010). Symbolically, many embrace Māori culture as part of the national identity with the use of the haka (ceremonial dance) in sports games or a pōwhiri (welcome) to greet international guests. However, support for Māori reparations by way of claims to redress past injustices is much weaker; for example, in the 2017 NZES, 33 per cent of eligible voters were opposed to legal recognition of the Treaty of Waitangi. Some opponents of recognition of Māori rights seek to fast track the claims settlement process while framing it as the 'Treaty-grievance industry' (Barnes et al., 2012; Sibley 2010; Smith & Abel, 2015; see also Chapter 7). Such opponents argue against claims to Māori sovereignty and self-determination and continue to repeat calls to abolish the Māori electorates. The conservative Pākehā approach, as explained in Chapter 1, is to postulate the existence of only 'one nation' or 'one people', folding Māori into a superordinate, inclusive New Zealander or 'Kiwi' category. Examples of people classifying themselves into the superordinate 'New Zealander' category may be observed in the inaugural parliamentary speeches of Māori members of parliament (MPs) Winston Peters and Simon Bridges (Bridges, 2010). Another example is the 2006 national census controversy, in which 430,000 people (11.1 per cent of the population) identified with the 'New Zealander' label regarding their ethnicity; later analyses showed that almost all of these were of Pākehā descent (Kukutai & Didham, 2009). A universal scale of populism is unlikely to draw out this complexity.

These issues surrounding national identity mean that it is difficult to conceptualise a national identity with standardised comparative questions. In the NZES, we used modified versions of the CSES questions.

We measured the extent to which people believe that 'to be a true New Zealander it is important' to abide by the following four statements (rated on a 1 ['very important'] to 4 ['not important at all'] scale):

- 'To have been born in New Zealand' (47 per cent rated this as 'fairly' or 'very' important)
- 'To have Māori ancestry' (13 per cent rated this as 'fairly' or 'very' important)
- 'To be able to speak English OR Māori' (75 per cent rated this as 'fairly' or 'very' important)
- 'To follow New Zealand customs and traditions' (80 per cent rated this as 'fairly' or 'very' important).

The results suggest that those who rated New Zealand birth and/or Māori ancestry as important view immigrants as not fully meeting the criteria of a 'true New Zealander', thereby rendering them less strongly identified with the 'New Zealander' in-group. Endorsement of these ideas constitutes what has been called nativism, or a preference for people born/from here. However, translation of these concepts into the New Zealand context is problematic. Both Māori, as tangata whenua (people of the land), and tauiwi (those without iwi—non-Māori) may feel as though they are from New Zealand; most New Zealand–born Pākehā have no citizenship rights other than in New Zealand and some can claim New Zealand descent over several generations. It would have been difficult to word the third question in such a way as to make sense to participants regarding the nature of 'New Zealand ancestry'. Thus, we aimed to investigate the Pākehā heritage side of 'New Zealand ancestry' with an additional question. Averaged together with the Māori ancestry question, this possibly gives the most accurate representation of this aspect of nativism:

- 'For one's grandparents to have been born in New Zealand' (26 per cent rated this as 'very' or 'fairly' important).

Leaving aside debates regarding what exactly constitutes New Zealand customs (Bell, 2009, 2014; McIntosh et al., 2005), the final question of this component asks whether minorities *should* assimilate. Unlike questions relating to in-group exclusivity, these are both components of national identity that may be attained, albeit with some effort, by immigrants (Humpage & Greaves, 2017):

- 'Minorities should adapt to the customs and traditions of the majority' (38 per cent 'strongly agreed' or 'agreed').

Again, in the New Zealand context, it is unclear how this question would be read by participants. The Pākehā majority could read 'minorities' as relating to both Māori and immigrants. Populist rhetoric in New Zealand has often targeted Māori. This question was placed in the questionnaire before questions on immigrants, which may have helped to mitigate the conflation; however, it is still unclear whether this means one group (Māori), the other (immigrants) or both.

To test how this scale 'fits' the New Zealand context (statistically), we conducted an exploratory factor analysis on the CSES populism questions. On CSES-based assumptions, there would be three underlying factors; however, using the NZES data, we found five—the attitudes towards out-groups questions split into three (see Table A3.1). We present a visual representation of this in Figure 3.2. One of these factors contained the immigration-related questions; another included the questions relating to certain aspects of being a 'true New Zealander' that were unobtainable to immigrants, such as being born in New Zealand, having grandparents born here and having Māori ancestry (we can call this 'in-group exclusivity' or simply nativism). A final factor—cultural adaptation or conformity—related to those aspects of being a 'true New Zealander' that were obtainable for more recent migrants: following 'New Zealand customs and traditions' (whatever they are) and being able to speak English or te reo Māori (the Māori language). In summary, New Zealand presents an intriguing case in relation to out-group attitudes; we await further analysis of how these questions fit other colonised countries when CSES data are collected and become available. Some preliminary evidence is already available: compared to six alternative scales, the CSES populism scale rates high on internal coherence and external validity but low on conceptual breadth and cross-national validity—the latter is a concern, given the comparative purpose of the CSES (Castanho Silva et al., 2019). Meanwhile, the CSES anti-elitist populism scale correlates (weakly) at $r = -0.21$, with a scale comprising the two external efficacy questions discussed earlier.

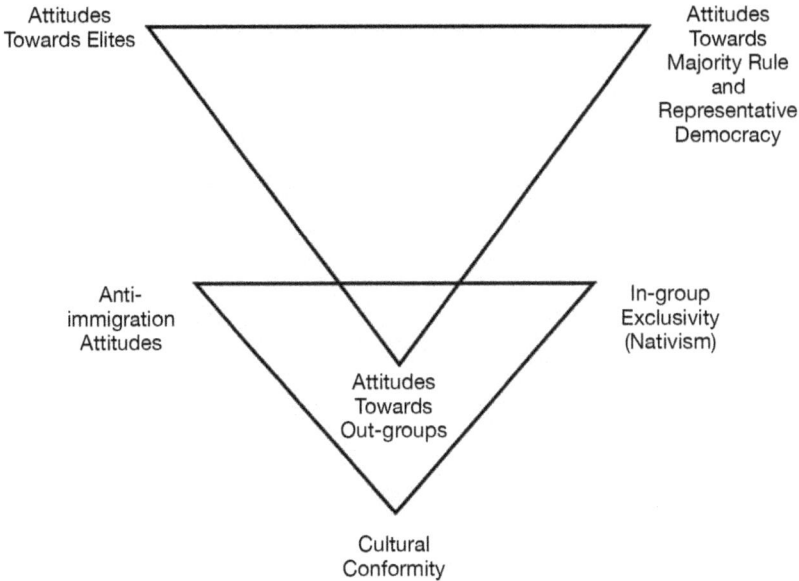

Figure 3.2: Five-factor structure underlying the CSES questions in the NZES.
Source: Adapted and modified from Hobolt et al. (2016).

Given this, our ability to compare across countries is questionable. From the first release of the CSES Module 5, available at the time of writing, there were 13 other countries for comparison: eight European (Austria, Germany, Greece, Hungary, Ireland, Italy, Lithuania and Montenegro), three Asian (Hong Kong, South Korea and Taiwan), one North American (the United States) and one South American (Chile) nation (CSES, 2019).

In our analysis of these data, based on the scales discussed above, New Zealand scored lowest (was the least apparently populist) on two of the three dimensions: anti-elite attitudes and attitudes to 'out-groups'. The 'out-group' finding is as expected; defining who is 'out' or 'in' is more difficult in New Zealand than elsewhere. The anti-elite finding is reinforced by longitudinal analysis of external political efficacy in New Zealand, which has continued to improve following a trough in the early 1990s (Vowles, 2018); however, this simply underpins our earlier scepticism regarding at least one instrument included in the scale. New Zealand also scored second lowest on negative attitudes to representative democracy. This is despite high levels of support for direct democracy in New Zealand and a relatively high desire for strong leadership. In summary, there are many weaknesses associated with using the CSES populism scale in the New

Zealand context and, indeed, elsewhere. There are more appropriate ways to conceptualise populism in New Zealand. We now move on to attempts to generate scales more consistent with our own theory, following the approach of Norris and Inglehart (2019), which separates populism and authoritarianism.

Populism and Authoritarianism

Critical examination of populist theory in Chapter 1 and the empirical analysis presented above both confirm that an alternative operationalisation of the concept is required. As noted previously, it is necessary to isolate exclusionary (anti-immigrant) components, particularly in the New Zealand context. Norris and Inglehart develop separate estimates of authoritarianism and populism, defining populism as 'a style of rhetoric reflecting first-order principles about who should rule, claiming that legitimate power rests with "the people" not the elites' (2019, p. 4). They define authoritarianism as 'a cluster of values prioritising collective security for the group at the expense of liberal autonomy for the individual' (p. 7). We now present questions that could be used as proxy measures for these concepts, drawing on those included in the 2017 NZES. We present the source (either CSES or NZES) and the percentage of participants who agreed or strongly agreed with the question in parentheses.

Populism

We estimated populist attitudes from six questions that position 'the people' as the legitimate source of power, versus 'the elites'. These were drawn from three CSES questions and three questions specific to the NZES ($\alpha = 0.74$):[11]

- 'The people, and not politicians, should make our most important policy decisions' (CSES; 51 per cent strongly agreed or agreed)
- 'Most politicians care only about the interests of the rich and powerful' (CSES; 35 per cent strongly agreed or agreed)
- 'How widespread or unusual do you think corruption such as bribe-taking is among politicians and public servants in New Zealand? (CSES; 22 per cent selected 'very' or 'quite' widespread)

---

11   This estimate is derived from a Cronbach's Alpha test. Generally, a score of 0.7 or above is considered to indicate that an index reliably captures an underlying dimension.

- 'What people call compromise in politics is really just selling out on one's principles' (CSES; 38 per cent strongly agreed or agreed)
- 'The New Zealand Government is largely run by a few big interests' (NZES; 40 per cent strongly agreed or agreed)
- 'Where 1 means government should listen more to experts and 5 means government should listen more to the public, where would you put your view?' (NZES; 43 per cent selected 4 or 5, indicating that they believe that government should listen to the public more).

As previously examined during exploration of the CSES dimensions, we note that several of these questions still overlap with external efficacy; therefore, they could be estimating either short-term perceptions generated by a highly unpopular government or other group-defined perceptions of elite unresponsiveness. Indeed, our scale based on these populism questions correlates at r = –0.15 (weakly) with a scale based on the two efficacy questions, a better separation than that of the equivalent CSES instrument. That scale also clearly appears as a separate factor when added to our analysis—that is, as based on the two 'who is in power/ voting makes a difference' questions discussed earlier.

Authoritarianism

Next, we estimated authoritarianism from six questions ($\alpha = 0.72$) that prioritise group cohesion and conformity and seek collective security over individual (and minority) rights and freedoms.

This scale related, in part, to the desire for a strong leader:

- 'Having a strong leader in government is good for New Zealand, even if the leader bends the rules to get things done' (CSES; 43 per cent strongly agreed or agreed)
- 'A few strong leaders could make this country better than all the laws and talk' (NZES; 51 per cent strongly agreed or agreed).

Another two questions investigated attitudes towards majority rule:

- 'The will of the majority should always prevail, even over the rights of minorities' (CSES; 28 per cent strongly agreed or agreed)
- 'Minorities should adapt to the customs and traditions of the majority' (CSES; 38 per cent strongly agreed or agreed).

Last, we included questions regarding harsh punishment for breaking rules:

- 'The death penalty should be brought back for some murders' (NZES; 40 per cent strongly agreed or agreed)
- 'What young people need most of all is strict discipline by their parents' (NZES; 54 per cent strongly agreed or agreed).

Since their development nearly 70 years ago, definitions and operationalisations of authoritarianism have been the subject of much debate (Adorno, Frenkel-Brunswik, Levinson & Sanford, 1950; MacWilliams & Tillman, 2016). There exists general agreement that authoritarianism is characterised by a strong desire to maintain social order and conformity, at the expense of individual autonomy. One consistent way that this has been investigated is by the centring of measurement on attitudes to child-rearing practices (Feldman, 2003; Feldman & Stenner, 1997; Stenner, 2005). Disagreement emerges regarding measurements that include attitudes that may be endogenous to what authoritarianism is supposed to explain, such as support for the death penalty (as included in the scale being used here). However, our selection of questions compares favourably to those recently used by the British Election Study (BES) and justified as useful, if not ideal (MacWilliams & Tillman, 2016). It may be noted that, like ours, the BES questions also encounter the issue of agreement bias (De Vaus, 2014).

Generally, political psychology research in New Zealand has measured authoritarianism with the right-wing authoritarianism (RWA) scale (Altemeyer, 1981, 1988, 2007), as part of a body of work driven by social psychologists working on the dual process model of ideology and prejudice (Duckitt, 2001; Duckitt & Sibley, 2010). The model analyses the personal and contextual factors that predict prejudice, including RWA. A body of work using a short-form version of the scale has emerged from the New Zealand Attitudes and Values Study, including exploring the predictors of RWA and demonstrating how authoritarianism relates to out-group prejudice in the New Zealand context (see e.g. Brune, Asbrock & Sibley, 2016; Duckitt & Sibley, 2016; Satherley & Sibley, 2018; Sibley et al., 2019).

Although we operationalise authoritarianism in a slightly different way, the scales broadly tap the same underlying construct—being motivated by a desire to maximise social conformity. Since the 1990s, the NZES has included three questions that measure authoritarian attitudes, included in the scale explained earlier. Authoritarian attitudes have been particularly useful in explaining opposition to the MMP electoral system (Lamare & Vowles, 1996). Therefore, past work from other New Zealand studies in the area of authoritarianism may inform our analysis. However, we are aware of no past work that has assessed populism in New Zealand voters as an attitudinal construct. Related work has investigated demographic and political differences between supporters of New Zealand First or related constructs such as nationalism, patriotism or different aspects of the New Zealand identity (e.g. Greaves et al., 2015; Humpage & Greaves, 2017; Osborne, Satherley, Yogeeswaran, Hawi & Sibley, 2019; Satherley, Yogeeswaran, Osborne & Sibley, 2019).

Our factor analysis supports the theoretical expectation that populism and authoritarianism are distinct dimensions. The three-factor out-groups dimensions also remain distinct in our alternative NZES approach (see Table A3.2). We expected them to be significant, particularly for opinion on immigration (see Chapter 5). However, populism and authoritarianism do correlate moderately (r = 0.28). In other words, a simple linear regression indicates that an extreme authoritarian is likely to be 0.25 higher on the 0–1 populism scale than an extreme liberal, with a constant term of 0.38, which indicates the extent to which the most liberal person is closer to the elitist than the populist end of the dimension. However, the variance explained is only approximately 8 per cent. Therefore, we argue that, while these two scales of populism and authoritarianism could be improved, they represent a better conceptualisation of these constructs than the CSES model and, therefore, the best possible version, given that we are limited by those questions present in the 2017 NZES. Nonetheless, these weaknesses present opportunities to continue developing questions for later iterations of the study.

Social and Demographic Correlates of Populism and Authoritarianism

Finally, we turn to the socio-demographic correlates of populism and authoritarianism in New Zealand.[12] The multivariate analyses below use ordinary least squares regression to control for the independent effects of the different variables on populism and authoritarianism. To use an example, we may find that residents of major urban centres are less populist than those outside them; however, the effects may simply be driven by a third variable, such as higher average level of education. Therefore, we analysed each of the following while also controlling for each of the variables in each analysis: generation (war and interwar, baby boomer, generation X, millennial or generation Z), gender (binary: women or men), LGBT+ (identifying as gender- or sexuality-diverse), ethnicity (Māori, Asian or Pasifika, allowing for multiple identities), occupational type (non-manual, manual labour or farmer), assets owned (no assets, low-risk assets or high-risk assets), household income in quintiles, whether someone reported a religious denomination, whether they lived in a major urban area (an area with population over 100,000) and education (whether they held a university degree). We only briefly discuss gender and Māori ethnicity because they are addressed in greater detail in Chapters 6 and 7, respectively. Table A3.3 displays the coefficients and other details of the model.

We report the data here in Figure 3.3. Each bar represents the probabilities that the average person in the group in question will be populist (in the first panel) and authoritarian (in the second), where the least populist/authoritarian person scores 0 and the most scores 1. It also displays 95 per cent confidence intervals.

---

12   Throughout this work, we have replaced missing data (when people did not answer the question or selected the 'don't know' option) with the neutral/scale mid-point response to the question (where such mid-points exist). While we cannot know how these participants truly scored on the measures (although a 'don't know' response can be argued to imply neutrality or at least indifference), we have taken this standard approach for missing data throughout this chapter and the book as a whole. Including 'don't know' responses, the questions had rates of missing data between 6 per cent (n = 214; for the question regarding government listening to experts versus the public) and 16 per cent (n = 556; for the question regarding whether government is run by big interests); however, the rate of missing data was at the lower end of this range for most questions. We re-ran the model reported below, dropping all cases with missing values on the populist and authoritarian questions—results were almost identical.

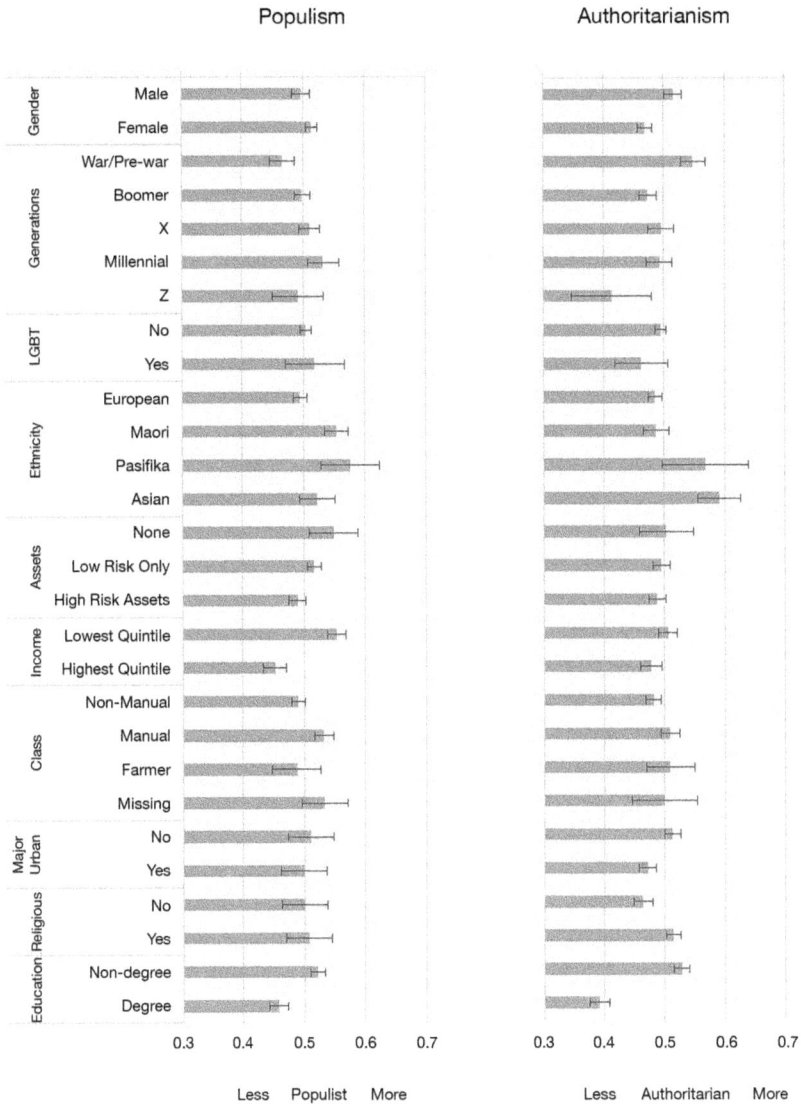

Figure 3.3: Relative probabilities of being populist and authoritarian by social groups.

Source: New Zealand Election Study (2017) (from Table A3.3).

Generational Differences

Following the example of Norris and Inglehart (2019), participants were split into different generations: the war and interwar generation (born before 1945), baby boomers (born 1946–1964), generation X (born 1965–1979) and millennials (born 1980–1996). We also added a low number of generation Z participants (born after 1997, aged 20 and under at the time of the 2017 election). In theory, older generations should be more authoritarian, whereas younger generations (generation X onwards), who came of age during times of increased protest and counterculture, should be less so (Norris & Inglehart, 2019). However, recall that our populism questions still contain attitudes to elites often used to estimate external political efficacy. The 2017 election marked the election of the first millennial prime minister: Ardern was born in 1980. Indeed, it produced a younger cohort of MPs overall; approximately 37 per cent were under 45 years of age. This may represent a generational shift, as political elites tend to be of the older generations (James, 2018), resulting in a better relationship between elites and younger generations.

Figure 3.3 shows that the average person in the earliest generational group is expected to score 0.46 on the populist scale, compared to a millennial, who scores 0.53. The confidence intervals for these two groups do not overlap; therefore, we can be reasonably sure that this constitutes a real difference. Indeed, this pre-1945 generation exhibits both the lowest populism and the highest authoritarianism. The generational pattern for the populism measure shows increasing propensity towards populism in recent generations, except generation Z. However, generation Z had the lowest average score for authoritarianism, followed by baby boomers. The timeline for generational change in authoritarianism and populism may be different in New Zealand, as compared to other nations. Baby boomers grew up in a time of increased unrest in New Zealand, in the face of Robert Muldoon's authoritarian style of leadership (see Chapter 1). Many were coming of age in the 1970s, a period of political activism and mobilisation, in tandem with a Māori cultural renaissance (Walker, 2004): the issues spanned Māori rights, second-wave feminism, environmentalism, anti-nuclear campaigning and actions to support the anti-apartheid movement in South Africa. For instance, in 1981, over 150,000 people took part in protests against apartheid during the South African rugby team tour of New Zealand (Chapple, 2014). The pattern of results for populism could relate to the closeness of the measure to external efficacy; however, adding a control for this in an alternative version of our populist model makes almost no difference to the results.

Gender and LGBT+

In this study, gender was coded as a woman/man binary, although 12 participants (0.4 per cent of the sample) identified as gender diverse. Analysis of this group as a single category was undesirable due to the small sample size and the likely diversity within, so we instead folded these participants into the LGBT+ group (Lesbian, Gay, Bisexual, Transgender and further rainbow community identities). The 2017 NZES included sexual orientation for the first time. Participants could select from heterosexual or 'straight', gay or lesbian, bisexual or bi-curious, pansexual or open and asexual: for analysis, we included these categories together. It is crucial to investigate LGBT+ scores on the authoritarian dimension, as the community is often a target of conservative rhetoric regarding changing values (Pappas, Mendez & Herrick, 2009; Spierings, Lubbers & Zaslove, 2017). As far as we are aware, no prior research has analysed populism in the LGBT+ community and very little has examined authoritarian-type measures within this population (Pacilli, Taurino, Jost & van der Toorn, 2011; Warriner, Nagoshi & Nagoshi, 2013). We would broadly expect LGBT+ people to score lower in terms of authoritarianism, as they are less likely to endorse traditional roles and people that score higher in authoritarian measures have been shown to be more homophobic/heterosexist (Cowie, Greaves & Sibley, 2019; Pacilli et al., 2011).

Regarding gender, we found that women scored slightly higher in terms of populism than men, albeit well within confidence intervals. Women scored significantly lower on authoritarianism than men. Again, it may be that women are (slightly) more populist than men or, more likely, that they are lower in external efficacy. The result for authoritarianism is to be expected, given that authoritarianism is generally associated with more rigid and traditional gender roles, which may restrict women's rights (Duckitt & Sibley, 2010). LGBT+ participants were not statistically distinguishable from heterosexual and cisgender participants regarding populism; however, as expected, they tended to be less authoritarian, although this difference was within confidence intervals.

Ethnicity

In the American and British contexts, authoritarian populism has been identified as an 'angry white man' phenomenon (Ford & Goodwin, 2010; Kimmel, 2017). One explanation for the rise of authoritarian populism posits such factors as decline in trust and economic power, the rise of liberal values and increased immigration. These tendencies have caused a 'cultural backlash', wherein those of European descent, especially men, become angry (Ford & Goodwin, 2010; Kimmel, 2017; Norris & Inglehart, 2019). According to this logic, we could expect Pākehā to exhibit higher scores on populism and authoritarianism. However, we found that those only identifying as Pākehā had the lowest average score for populism, with the average score for Asian participants being similar and Pasifika and Māori scoring highest. We also found ethnic group differences in relation to authoritarianism; Māori had a lower score, although not significantly different to that of Pākehā, whereas Asian and Pasifika populations had higher average scores. In summary, there existed minor ethnic group differences, perhaps relating to different perceptions of the responsiveness of elites in the past and differences in authoritarianism across ethnicity, which may relate to cultural differences in the construct.

Socio-Economic Status

We also investigated two variables relating to socio-economic status. In theory, those who are more vulnerable to shifts in the economic system (e.g. the automation of jobs) or those associated with globalisation (e.g. work shifting overseas) are expected to be more populist and authoritarian (Mudde & Kaltwasser, 2012; Norris & Inglehart, 2019). Such shifts represent a threat to their economic livelihoods. However, we tested the 'offshorability' of jobs (Blinder & Krueger, 2013) and the relative skill specificity of occupations (Iversen & Soskice, 2001) and found no significant results when education was taken into account. Traditional occupational classifications work more effectively for this analysis; indeed, those in manual service professions have the highest average scores for both populism and authoritarianism. Assets matter little to authoritarianism; however, those with low-risk and, most of all, high-risk assets were less prone to populism. Those with high household incomes—estimated as the difference between the lowest and the highest quintiles—were both less populist and less authoritarian. Therefore, in New Zealand, working in a manual service profession predicts higher degrees of populism and authoritarianism, independent of education level, the offshorability of one's job or relative skill level.

Religiosity and Rurality

We expected that rural people and religious people would score higher on authoritarianism and, possibly, populism than other groups (Kimmel, 2017; Lockhart, Sibley & Osborne, 2019; Norris & Inglehart, 2019; Scoones et al., 2018). Further, we theorised that the higher populism of rural and religious people, as demonstrated by prior research, could have been driven by socio-economic indicators; therefore, we controlled for this in our analyses. Religious people are more likely to hold conservative values and may subscribe to authoritarianism as a 'cultural backlash' to a society that is becoming more socially liberal (Norris & Inglehart, 2019). Those outside major urban centres may be more authoritarian due to selective migration. Prior research in New Zealand has shown that those who live in cities are more open to experience, a personality trait closely associated with liberal values (Greaves et al., 2015). Reflecting our expectations, we found that those residing outside major urban centres were likely to be more authoritarian but were not significantly more populist than their major urban counterparts. Similarly, those with a religion were no less or more populist than non-religious people but were significantly more authoritarian.

Education

Lower education levels have been a consistent predictor of populism in the international context; however, some authors have suggested that this may be due to the radical-right, exclusionary, authoritarian and nativist components of populism, rather than populism in and of itself (Rooduijn, 2018). The results of our study reflected this—those with a university degree scored lower on populism than those without one. Further, a similar pattern was found for authoritarianism. These results reflect the existing research, both nationally and internationally, showing that those with lower education tend to adopt populist or conservative, authoritarian values at higher rates than those with more education (Duckitt & Sibley, 2016; Kimmel, 2017; Norris & Inglehart, 2019; Satherley et al., 2019; Sibley et al., 2019).

In summary, our investigation of populism in New Zealand reveals that baby boomers, millennials, Māori, Pasifika, manual service workers, those with no assets and people without degrees score higher on authoritarianism and populism. This is perhaps unsurprising—some of these groups may be more likely to hold a negative view of the state and elites, because they feel that the state has been insufficiently responsive to their interests; such experiences may shape feelings of low political efficacy. For some of these groups (e.g. manual service workers), this may represent a more recent shift or a type of 'cultural backlash' scenario, whereas for others, these higher scores likely represent a long history of the state being unresponsive to the group's needs (e.g. Māori) or generational differences in political socialisation (e.g. baby boomers, millennials). In relation to authoritarianism, we found that older people tended to have higher scores, as did Pasifika and Asian participants, men, manual service workers, rural-dwellers, the religious and those without university degrees. While these scales may still be subject to limitations, the results for authoritarianism largely reflect past work using RWA scales and the results for populism represent an initial exploration of a construct not previously measured in a national study in New Zealand.

Conclusion

In this chapter, we examined the CSES model of (exclusionary) populism in New Zealand and the level of support for the various questions among NZES participants. In comparing the CSES three-dimensional model of populist attitudes across countries, New Zealand scored lowest on two of three indicators (attitudes towards elites and attitudes towards outgroups) and second lowest on the negative attitudes towards representative democracy measures. These findings suggest that, among a limited group of nations, New Zealand is relatively low in terms of populism, as defined in these terms. However, this group of nations includes the United States, Germany and Austria, where populism is recognised to be a major phenomenon. This gives support to an interpretation of the New Zealand case as one of 'exceptionalism'. However, given reservations regarding the utility of CSES instruments as a cross-national operationalisation of populism, a claim that New Zealand is exceptional would be a risky interpretation. There is more of a case for exceptionalism in terms of indigenous visibility and ethnic diversity; however, these characteristics are shared with some other countries.

We presented an alternative approach, comprising two scales that separated populism and authoritarianism. The key disadvantage of this alternative is the loss of a comparative dimension; however, it addresses the flaw identified in CSES operationalisation. That is, collinearity between populism and external political efficacy makes it difficult to separate out short-term responses to peoples' sense of exclusion from more deep-seated populist attitudes. The NZES enables us to include an independent control variable for external efficacy; however, it may be that some of the instruments in our own populist scale are too closely associated with efficacy. The absence of a clear authoritarian–liberal dimension, except as in part summed up as 'attitudes to representation', represents another flaw in the CSES model.

In terms of age and generational experiences, some groups (but not all) demonstrated the expected differences in their levels of populism and authoritarianism. Māori and Pasifika were more populist than other ethnic groups. Baby boomers, generation X and millennials were more populist than the war and pre-war generation or generation Z. All other generational groups were less authoritarian than the war and pre-war generations, with generation Z being the least authoritarian. However, when it came to socio-economic position and education, those in manual labour professions with no assets and lower levels of education all scored relatively high on the populism scale. Depending on social identity, some of these results are likely related to different phenomena; that is, some groups may always have had negative views towards elites, whereas for others, the results may relate to a rising discontent or 'cultural backlash'.

Broadly speaking, there appears to be no evidence for a significant populist or authoritarian mood of discontent, although New Zealanders are relatively evenly distributed across the two dimensions, with most falling in the middle. However, as illustrated by the experience of New Zealand in the 1970s and early 1980s under the Muldoon government, there exists potential for greater mobilisation of authoritarian attitudes, particularly when opinion, activism and policy turn in the other direction. Support for strong political leadership is relatively high, as is a belief in the need for strong discipline of children (both receiving approximately 50 per cent support). Authoritarian responses have remained stubbornly high since these questions were first asked in 1996. Consequently, future research must generate better estimates of populist attitudes and values, not only in New Zealand but also elsewhere.

References

Adorno, T. W., Frenkel-Brunswik, E., Levinson, D. & Sanford, N. (1950). *The authoritarian personality*. New York City, NY: Harper.

Altemeyer, B. (1981). *Right-wing authoritarianism*. Winnipeg, Canada: University of Manitoba Press.

Altemeyer, B. (1988). *Enemies of freedom: Understanding right-wing authoritarianism*. San Francisco, CA: Jossey-Bass.

Altemeyer, B. (2007). *The authoritarians*. Winnipeg, Canada: University of Manitoba Press.

Barnes, A. M., Borell, B., McCreanor, T., Nairn, R., Rankine, J. & Taiapa, K. (2012). Anti-Māori themes in New Zealand journalism—Toward alternative practice. *Pacific Journalism Review: Te Koakoa, 18*(1), 195–216. doi.org/10.24135/pjr.v18i1.296

Bell, A. (2009). Dilemmas of settler belonging: Roots, routes and redemption in New Zealand national identity claims. *The Sociological Review, 57*(1), 145–162. doi.org/10.1111/j.1467-954X.2008.01808.x

Bell, A. (2014). *Relating indigenous and settler identities: Beyond domination*. London, United Kingdom: Palgrave MacMillan. doi.org/10.1057/9781137313560

Blank, A. & Houkamau, C. (2017). *REWIRE: The little book about bias*. Auckland, New Zealand: Oranui Press.

Blinder A. S. & Krueger, A. B. (2013). Alternative measures of offshorability: A survey approach. *Journal of Labor Economics, 31*(2), S97–S128. doi.org/10.1086/669061

Bowler, S., Donovan, T. & Karp, J. (2007). Enraged or engaged? Preferences for direct citizen participation in affluent democracies. *Political Research Quarterly, 60*(3), 351–362. doi.org/10.1177/1065912907304108

Bridges, S. (2010). Diversity enriches the view. In M. Bargh (Ed.), *Māori and Parliament: Diverse strategies and compromises* (pp. 138–141). Wellington, New Zealand: Huia.

Brune, A., Asbrock, F. & Sibley, C. G. (2016). Meet your neighbours: Authoritarians engage in intergroup contact when they have the opportunity. *Journal of Community and Applied Social Psychology, 26*, 576–580. doi.org/10.1002/casp.2289

Canovan, M. (1999). Trust the people! Populism and the Two Faces of Democracy. *Political Studies, 47*(1), 2–16. doi.org/10.1111/1467-9248.00184

Castanho Silva, B., Jungkunz, S., Helbling, M. & Littvay, L. (2019). An empirical comparison of seven populist attitudes scales. *Political Research Quarterly*. doi.org/10.1177/1065912919833176

Chapple, G. (2014). *When the tour came to Auckland.* Wellington, New Zealand: Bridget Williams Books. doi.org/10.7810/9781927277461

Church, S. & McLeay, E. (2003). The parliamentary review of MMP in New Zealand. *Representation, 39*(4), 245–254. doi.org/10.1080/00344890308523231

Comparative Study of Electoral Systems. (2019, 21 May). *CSES Module 5 First Advance Release* [dataset and documentation]. Ann Arbor, MI: CSES.

Cowie, L. J., Greaves, L. M. & Sibley, C. G. (2019). Sexuality and sexism: Differences in ambivalent sexism across gender and sexual identity. *Personality and Individual Differences, 148*, 85–89. doi.org/10.1016/j.paid.2019.05.023

Craig, S. C. & Maggiotto, M. A. (1982). Measuring political efficacy. *Political Methodology, 8*, 85–109.

De Vaus, D. (2014). *Surveys in social research* (6th ed.). Sydney, Australia: Allen & Unwin.

Duckitt, J. (2001). A dual-process cognitive-motivational theory of ideology and prejudice. *Advances in Experimental Social Psychology, 33*, 41–113. doi.org/10.1016/S0065-2601(01)80004-6

Duckitt, J. & Sibley, C. G. (2010). Personality, ideology, prejudice and politics: A dual-process motivational model. *Journal of Personality, 78*(6), 1861–1894. doi.org/10.1111/j.1467-6494.2010.00672.x

Duckitt, J. & Sibley, C. G. (2016). Personality, ideological attitudes, and group identity as predictors of political behaviour in majority and minority ethnic groups. *Political Psychology, 37*(1), 109–124. doi.org/10.1111/pops.12222

Easton, D. (1965). *A systems analysis of political life.* New York: Wiley.

Easton, D. (1975). A reassessment of the concept of political support. *British Journal of Political Science, 5*(4), 435–457. doi.org/10.1017/S0007123400008309

Feldman, S. (2003). Enforcing social conformity: A theory of authoritarianism. *Political Psychology, 24*(1), 41–74. doi.org/10.1111/0162-895X.00316

Feldman, S. & Stenner, K. (1997). Perceived threat and authoritarianism. *Political Psychology, 18*(4), 741–770. doi.org/10.1111/0162-895X.00077

Ford, R. & Goodwin, M. J. (2010). Angry white men: Individual and contextual predictors of support for the British National Party. *Political Studies, 58*(1), 1–25. doi.org/10.1111/j.1467-9248.2009.00829.x

Geurkink, B., Zaslove, A., Sluiter, R. & Jacobs, K. (2019). Populist attitudes, political trust and external political efficacy: Old wine in new bottles? *Political Studies* [Advance online publication]. doi.org/10.1177/0032321719842768

Gidron, N. & Bonikowski, B. (2013). *Varieties of populism: Literature review and research agenda* (Weatherhead Working Paper Series, No. 13-0004), 1–13.

Greaves, L. M., Cowie, L., Fraser, G., Muriwai, E., Huang, Y., Milojev, P. & Osborne, D. (2015). Regional differences and similarities in the personality of New Zealanders. *New Zealand Journal of Psychology, 1*, 4–16.

Greaves, L. M. & Milne, B. (2019). Referendexit: Has support for referenda decreased since the flag referendums? Findings from a New Zealand national survey (Unpublished manuscript). University of Auckland, Auckland, New Zealand.

Higham, J. (2002). *Strangers in the land: Patterns of American nativism, 1860–1925.* New Brunswick, NJ: Rutgers University Press.

Hobolt, S., Anduiza, E., Carkoglu, A. Lutz, G. & Sauger, N. (2016). *Democracy divided? People, politicians and the politics of populism* (CSES Planning Committee Final Report, CSES Module 5). Retrieved from cses.org/wp-content/uploads/2019/03/CSES5_ContentSubcommittee_FinalReport.pdf

Humpage, L. & Greaves, L. (2017). 'Truly being a New Zealander': Ascriptive versus civic views of national identity. *Political Science, 69*(3), 247–263. doi.org/10.1080/00323187.2017.1418177

Ionescu, G. & Gellner, E. (Eds). (1969). *Populism: Its meaning and national characteristics.* London, United Kingdom: Macmillan.

Ikeda, K., Kobayashi, T & Hoshimoto, M. (2008). Does political participation make a difference: The relationship between political choice, civic engagement and political efficacy. *Electoral Studies, 27*(1), 77–88. doi.org/10.1016/j.electstud.2007.11.004

Iversen, T. & Soskice, D. (2001). An asset theory of social policy preferences. *American Political Science Review, 95*(4), 875–911. doi.org/10.1017/S0003055400400079

James, C. (2018). The first post baby boomer election. In S. Levine (Ed.), *Stardust and substance: The New Zealand general election of 2017* (pp. 325–338). Wellington, New Zealand: Victoria University Press.

Kaltwasser, C. R., Vehrkamp, R. & Wratil, C. (2019). *Europe's choice populist attitudes and voting intentions in the 2019 European election.* Gütersloh, Germany: Bertelsmann Stiftung.

Kaufmann, D., Kraay, A. & Mastruzzi, M. (2007). *Measuring corruption: Myths and realities.* Retrieved from openknowledge.worldbank.org/handle/10986/9576

Kimmel, M. (2017). *Angry white men: American masculinity at the end of an era.* New York: Nation Books.

Kriesi, H. (2014). The populist challenge. *West European Politics, 37*(2), 361–378. doi.org/10.1080/01402382.2014.887879

Kukutai, T. & Didham R. (2009). In search of ethnic New Zealanders: National naming in the 2006 Census. *Social Policy Journal of New Zealand, 36,* 46–62. Retrieved from www.msd.govt.nz/about-msd-and-our-work/publications-resources/journals-and-magazines/social-policy-journal/spj36/36-in-search-of-ethnic-new-zealanders.html

Lamare, J. & Vowles, J. (1996). Party interests, public opinion and institutional preferences: Electoral system change in New Zealand. *Australian Journal of Political Science, 31*(3), 321–346. doi.org/10.1080/10361149651085

Lockhart, C., Sibley, C. & Osborne, D. (2019). Religion makes—and unmakes—the status quo: Religiosity and spirituality have opposing effects on conservatism via RWA and SDO. *Religion, Brain & Behaviour* [Advance online publication]. doi.org/10.1080/2153599X.2019.1607540

MacWilliams, M. C. & Tillman, E. (2016). *Authoritarianism and the rise of populist national parties in Europe: Preliminary findings from surveys of four European nations.* Retrieved from static1.squarespace.com/static/50bf87bfe4b090fdb6237204/t/58136bd71b631bf20f10daa4/1477667800156/EuropeanReleaseD2.pdf

McIntosh, T., Liu, J., McCreanor, T. & Teaiwa, T. (Eds). (2005). *New Zealand identities: Departures and destinations.* Wellington, New Zealand: Victoria University Press.

McLeay, E. & Vowles, J. (2007). Redefining constituency representation: The roles of New Zealand MPs under MMP. *Regional and Federal Studies, 17*(1), 71–95. doi.org/10.1080/13597560701189628

Ministry of Business, Innovation and Employment. (2016). *Migration trends 2016/2017.* Retrieved from www.mbie.govt.nz/immigration-and-tourism/immigration/migration-research-and-evaluation/migration-trends-report/

Mouffe, C. (2018). *For a left populism.* London, United Kingdom: Verso.

Mudde, C. (2004). The populist zeitgeist. *Government and opposition, 39*(4), 541–563. doi.org/10.1111/j.1477-7053.2004.00135.x

Mudde, C. (2007). *Populist radical right parties in Europe.* Cambridge, United Kingdom: Cambridge University Press.

Mudde, C. & Kaltwasser, C. R. (Eds). (2012). *Populism in Europe and the Americas.* Cambridge, United Kingdom: Cambridge University Press.

New Zealand Election Study. (2017). *New Zealand Election Study* [dataset]. Retrieved from www.nzes.org/exec/show/data

Norris, P. (2011). *Democratic deficit: Critical citizens revisited.* New York: Cambridge University Press.

Norris, P. & Inglehart, R. (2019). *Cultural backlash: Trump, Brexit and authoritarian populism.* Cambridge, United Kingdom: Cambridge University Press. doi.org/10.1017/9781108595841

NZPA. (2010, 6 April). 'Pommy git' okay, BSA rules. *New Zealand Herald.* Retrieved from www.nzherald.co.nz/nz/news/article.cfm?c_id=1&objectid=10636663

Osborne, D., Satherley, N. Yogeeswaran, K., Hawi, D. & Sibley, C. (2019). White nationalism and multiculturalism support: Investigating the interactive effects of white identity and national attachment on support for multiculturalism. *New Zealand Journal of Psychology, 48*(1), 65–74.

Pacilli, M., Taurino, A., Jost, J. & van der Toorn, J. (2011). System justification, right-wing conservatism and internalised homophobia: Gay and lesbian attitudes toward same-sex parenting in Italy. *Sex Roles, 65*(580). doi.org/10.1007/s11199-011-9969-5

Pappas, C., Mendez, J. & Herrick, R. (2009). The negative effects of populism on gay and lesbian rights. *Social Science Quarterly, 90*(1), 150–163. doi.org/10.1111/j.1540-6237.2009.00608.x

Phillips, J. (2015). History of immigration. In *Te Ara: The Encyclopedia of New Zealand.* Retrieved from www.TeAra.govt.nz/en/history-of-immigration

Plattner, M. F. (2010). Democracy's past and future: Populism, pluralism and liberal democracy. *Journal of Democracy, 21*(1), 81–92. doi.org/10.1353/jod.0.0154

Rooduijn, M. (2018). What unites the voter bases of populist parties? Comparing the electorates of 15 populist parties. *European Political Science Review, 10*(3), 351–368. doi.org/10.1017/S1755773917000145

Satherley, N. & Sibley, C. G. (2018). A dual process model of post-colonial ideology. *International Journal of Intercultural Relations, 64*, 1–11. doi.org/10.1016/j.ijintrel.2018.03.003

Satherley, N., Yogeeswaran, K., Osborne, D. & Sibley, C. G. (2019). Differentiating between pure patriots and nationalistic patriots: A model of national attachment profiles and their sociopolitical attitudes. *International Journal of Intercultural Relations, 72*, 13–24. doi.org/10.1016/j.ijintrel.2019.06.005

Scoones, I., Edelman, M., Borras Jr, S. M., Hall, R., Wolford, W. & White, B. (2018). Emancipatory rural politics: Confronting authoritarian populism. *The Journal of Peasant Studies, 45*(1), 1–20. doi.org/10.1080/03066150.2017.1339693

Shaver, J. H., Sibley, C. G., Osborne, D. & Bulbulia, J. (2017). News exposure predicts anti-Muslim prejudice. *Plos One, 12*(3), e0174606. doi.org/10.1371/journal.pone.0174606

Shaver, J. H., Troughton, G., Sibley, C. G. & Bulbulia, J. (2016). Religion and the unmaking of prejudice toward Muslims: Evidence from a large national sample. *Plos One, 11*(3), e015020. doi.org/10.1371/journal.pone.0150209

Sibley, C. G. (2010). The dark duo of post-colonial ideology: A model of symbolic exclusion and historical negation. *International Journal of Conflict and Violence, 4*(1), 106–123. doi.org/10.4119/ijcv-2818

Sibley, C. G. & Barlow, F. (2009). Ubiquity of whiteness in majority group national imagination: Australian = white, but New Zealander does not. *Australian Journal of Psychology, 61*(3), 119–127. doi.org/10.1080/00049530802239300

Sibley, C. G., Bergh, R., Satherley, N., Osborne, D., Milojev, P., Greaves, L. M., … Duckitt, J. (2019). Profiling authoritarian leaders and followers. *Testing, Psychometrics, Methodology in Applied Psychology, 26*, 1–17. doi.org/10.4473/TPM26.3.6

Sibley, C. G., Liu, J. H. & Khan, S. S. (2008). Who are 'we'? Implicit associations between ethnic and national symbols for Māori and Pākehā. *New Zealand Journal of Psychology, 37*(2), 38–49.

Smith, J. & Abel, S. (2015). Ka whaw'ai tonu matou: Indigenous television in Aotearoa/New Zealand. In W. G. Pearson & S. Knabe (Eds), *Reverse shots: Indigenous film and media in an international context: Film and media studies book 17* (pp. 175–188). Waterloo, United Kingdom: Wilfred Laurier University Press.

Smith, L. (2012). *Decolonising methodologies: Research and indigenous peoples* (2nd ed.). London, United Kingdom: Zed Books.

Spierings, N., Lubbers, M. & Zaslove, A. (2017). 'Sexually modern nativist voters: Do they exist and do they vote for the populist radical right? *Gender and Education, 29*(2), 216–237. doi.org/10.1080/09540253.2016.1274383

Statistics New Zealand. (2019). *2018 Census totals by topic – national highlights.* Retrieved from www.stats.govt.nz/information-releases/2018-census-totals-by-topic-national-highlights

Stenner, K. (2005). *The Authoritarian Dynamic.* Cambridge: Cambridge University Press.

Transparency International. (2018). *New Zealand.* Retrieved from www.trans parency.org/country/NZL

Vowles, J. (2016). Globalisation, government debt, government agency and political efficacy: A cross-national comparison. In J. Vowles & G. Xezonakis (Eds), *Globalisation and domestic politics: Parties, public opinion and elections* (pp. 155–171). Oxford, United Kingdom: Oxford University Press. doi.org/ 10.1093/acprof:oso/9780198757986.003.0008

Vowles, J. (2018). Electoral systems in context: New Zealand. In E. S. Herron, R. Pekkanen & M. S. Shugart (Eds), *The Oxford handbook of electoral systems* (pp. 805–824). Oxford, United Kingdom: Oxford University Press. doi.org/ 10.1093/oxfordhb/9780190258658.013.29

Walker, R. (2004). *Struggle without end* (2nd ed.). Auckland, New Zealand: Penguin.

Warriner, K., Nagoshi, C. T. & Nagoshi, J. L. (2013). Correlates of homophobia, transphobia and internalised homophobia in gay or lesbian and heterosexual samples. *Journal of Homosexuality, 60*(9), 1297–1314. doi.org/10.1080/009 18369.2013.806177

Zaslove, A. (2008). Here to stay? Populism as a new party type. *European Review, 16*(3), 319–336. doi.org/10.1017/S1062798708000288

Zirker, D. & Barrett, P. (2017). Corruption vs. corruption scandals in New Zealand: Bridging a wide gulf? *Political Science, 69*(1), 35–48. doi.org/ 10.1080/00323187.2017.1327798

Appendices

Table A3.1: Item content and factor loadings for the Comparative Study of Electoral Systems populism items

Item	Anti-elite	Representation	Anti-immigration	Nativism	Cultural Conformity
Compromise a sell-out	**0.453**	0.170	0.024	0.080	–0.001
Politicians don't care	**0.777**	0.124	–0.037	–0.057	–0.006
Politicians trustworthy (R)	**–0.489**	0.133	–0.011	0.129	–0.025
Politicians the main problem	**0.716**	0.106	0.013	0.016	–0.013
Politicians corrupt	**0.470**	–0.129	0.153	0.092	0.023
People decide	**0.490**	0.029	0.010	0.017	0.040
Politicians care for rich	**0.744**	–0.092	0.024	0.027	–0.025
Politicians care for rich	0.035	**0.677**	0.012	–0.040	0.068
Majority overrules minority rights	0.023	**0.752**	0.045	0.055	–0.005
Strong leader bend rules	–0.002	**0.362**	–0.028	0.125	0.027
Immigrants good for economy (R)	–0.049	0.172	**–0.593**	–0.035	0.057
Immigrants harm culture	–0.015	0.019	**0.847**	–0.034	0.052
Immigrants increase crime	0.011	0.096	**0.698**	0.023	0.017
Born in New Zealand	–0.035	0.037	0.071	**0.750**	0.045
Grandparents born in New Zealand	–0.003	0.018	0.008	**0.964**	–0.058
Have Māori ancestry	0.121	–0.222	–0.020	**0.582**	0.123
Speak English OR Māori	–0.006	–0.041	–0.018	0.013	**0.637**
Follow New Zealand customs	0.003	0.113	0.061	0.022	**0.621**

Note: Principal components, Varimax Rotation. (R) signals that an item is reverse-worded. Loadings greater than 0.30 are presented in bold.

Source: New Zealand Election Study (2017).

Table A3.2: Item content and factor loadings for the New Zealand Electoral Survey populism, authoritarianism and outgroups items

	Authoritarian	Populist	Immigration	Nativism	Cultural Conformity
Strong leader bends rules	**0.6834**	−0.1153	−0.0155	0.1566	−0.0672
Young need strong discipline	**0.6575**	0.116	0.1009	0.1774	0.1067
Strong leaders better	**0.6463**	0.183	0.0528	0.2406	−0.0637
Majority overrules minority	**0.5646**	−0.0461	0.3329	−0.101	0.3466
Death penalty	**0.5603**	0.1084	0.251	0.114	0.0382
Minorities should adapt	**0.4662**	0.0042	0.2506	−0.2545	0.4892
Politicians care for rich	−0.0141	**0.7907**	0.1443	0.0349	−0.005
Government run big interests	−0.0176	**0.7404**	0.1212	0.0725	0.0094
People decide	0.0995	**0.6709**	0.0516	0.0325	0.0883
Politicians corrupt	0.0655	**0.5638**	0.3176	0.1734	−0.152
Public not experts	0.2801	**0.4568**	0.046	0.1838	0.0992
Compromise a sell-out	0.3477	**0.4236**	0.1302	0.0479	0.0861
Immigrants increase crime	0.2154	0.1203	**0.7645**	0.1272	0.1054
Immigrants good for economy	−0.1004	0.1614	**0.755**	0.1781	−0.121
Immigrants harm culture	0.1725	0.1332	**0.7539**	0.2062	0.1562
Important New Zealand grandparents	0.1842	0.0518	0.241	**0.7862**	0.1477
Important New Zealand-born	0.1865	0.0049	0.257	**0.7504**	0.2109
Important Māori ancestry	−0.0844	0.1777	0.0185	**0.7293**	0.0895
Follow New Zealand customs	0.1434	0.0187	0.0085	0.3172	**0.7172**
Speak English or Māori	−0.1051	0.0157	0.0442	0.27	**0.7452**

Note: Principal components, Varimax Rotation.

Source: New Zealand Election Study (2017).

Table A3.3: Social and demographic correlates of populism and authoritarianism

	Populist	Authoritarian
(Post-war)		
Boomer	0.033***	−0.074***
	(0.012)	(0.012)
Generation X	0.045***	−0.052***
	(0.014)	(0.016)
Millennial	0.067***	−0.055***
	(0.018)	(0.016)
Generation Z	0.025	−0.135***
	(0.024)	(0.037)
Female (Male)	0.017*	−0.047***
	(0.009)	(0.009)
LGBT	0.015	−0.033
	(0.025)	(0.023)
Māori	0.056***	−0.006
	(0.011)	(0.013)
Pasifika	0.073***	0.078**
	(0.025)	(0.037)
Asian	0.018	0.104***
	(0.016)	(0.019)
(No assets)		
Low-risk assets	−0.032	−0.008
	(0.021)	(0.024)
High risk assets	−0.060***	−0.016
	(0.022)	(0.024)
Household income	−0.025***	−0.007**
	(0.004)	(0.004)
Religious	0.008	0.051***
	(0.010)	(0.010)
Major urban	−0.012	−0.042***
	(0.009)	(0.010)
(Non-manual)		
Manual	0.046***	0.028**
	(0.011)	(0.011)

	Populist	Authoritarian
Farmer	−0.008	0.028
	(0.021)	(0.021)
No Job	0.047**	0.018
	(0.021)	(0.028)
University degree	−0.064***	−0.137***
	(0.011)	(0.012)
Constant	0.566***	0.617***
	(0.025)	(0.024)
Observations	3,229.000	3,229.000
R-squared	0.172	0.194

Note: Robust standard errors are given in parentheses.

*** $p < 0.01$, ** $p < 0.05$, * $p < 0.1$

Source: New Zealand Election Study (2017).

4

POPULISM, AUTHORITARIANISM, VOTE CHOICE AND DEMOCRACY

Jack Vowles

Jacinda Ardern's responses to the terrorist attack on Islamic worshippers in Christchurch, on 15 March 2019, coined a phrase that was used repeatedly in the following days: 'they are us' (Ardern, 2019). She also articulated a vision of a nation united in its support for those who had died and those who survived to mourn them: 'we are one'. This presented an exemplary rejection of exclusionary political rhetoric (see also Chapter 6). In contrast, Winston Peters' words emphasised what he, and many others, now consider to be the core values of a New Zealander, the defining characteristics of the New Zealand people and a consequent source of national pride: giving people a 'fair go', practicality and tolerance (Peters, 2019). Unlike Ardern, he did not acknowledge difference by way of a collective 'they', other than through the principle of freedom of religion: an individual freedom. Arden used the word 'nation', whereas Peters used 'New Zealand people'—a key signifier of populism. These represent subtle but significant differences.

At the end of 2018, New Zealand signed the United Nations Migration Compact, an agreement on common principles to apply to immigration policies. The United States and Australia refused to sign, claiming that the compact could abrogate national sovereignty. The New Zealand

Government received legal advice confirming that the compact would have no binding effect on immigration and foreign policy. The Deputy Prime Minister and Minister of Foreign Affairs, Winston Peters, agreed; however, the National Party and its leader, Simon Bridges, opposed the pact on sovereignty grounds, despite the previous National-led government's apparent support for the agreement (Bridges, 2018). A petition for withdrawal was launched, only to be removed in somewhat mysterious circumstances from the National Party's website in the aftermath of the Christchurch mosque attack. A few weeks before the mosque attack, death threats had been made against Winston Peters at a far-right rally in Christchurch (Gower, 2019). Elements associated with the various varieties of populism, as defined in the literature, are found in virtually all New Zealand political parties—and not always in the expected places.

First, this chapter examines the association between populism and authoritarianism in the language of New Zealand's political parties. Next, it examines the relationship between populist and authoritarian attitudes and left and right policy dimensions, to determine whether populism is predominantly a left-wing or right-wing phenomenon in New Zealand. In terms of vote choices, it is expected that both populism and authoritarianism will be associated with votes for New Zealand First. Considering further implications for the condition of democracy in New Zealand, the next step is analysis of the extent to which populism and authoritarianism can be linked to both satisfaction with, and support for, democracy. Initial expectations follow from theory: populists will be unsatisfied with, but supportive of, democracy. Because of the potential overlap between low political efficacy and populist attitudes as operationalised in our data, a combination of low political efficacy and anti-pluralism might shift populists towards apparently lower support for democracy. In theory, authoritarians should be more likely to be both unsatisfied and unsupportive—in the New Zealand case in particular, this is because they are likely to be less enamoured of proportional representation than liberals. However, the New Zealand Government continues to be based on concentrated power in a unitary state and still lacks constitutional restraints on legislative and executive authority—an institutional framework that should be appealing both to authoritarians and populists.

Party Positions and Discourses

Party positions are best estimated from the statements they make with the widest public currency—the kind of statements that were used to introduce this chapter. The extent to which parties across the globe employ populist discourse in their manifestos has formed the focus of much recent research. An excellent source of data on political party discourse regarding populism is the Chapel Hill Expert Survey (see Polk et al., 2017); however, this is largely confined to European countries. A 2019 paper includes analysis of recent New Zealand political party manifestos among 119 others from the United States, Canada, the United Kingdom, Ireland, South Africa and Australia (Dai, 2018). Consistent with interpretations of the populist nature of New Zealand political culture, Dai found that the most populist example was that of New Zealand First in 2011 and the fourth that of the New Zealand Labour Party in 2011. The 2008 New Zealand National Party manifesto ranked eighth. Across different election years, however, indicators of populism have waxed and waned, even among parties (e.g. New Zealand First) that are widely understood to be populist.

Dai employs a sophisticated methodology that matches phrases and combinations of words but also operationalises populism according to the Mudde model; that is, it is assumed to be anti-pluralist, moralist and the antithesis of liberal pluralism—the conflation of populism with authoritarianism discussed in previous chapters. It is worth noting that the election years 2008 and 2011 took place during, and immediately after, the global financial crisis, providing ample ammunition for anti-elite discourse; further, the three-party programmes in question were from opposition parties. Dai's dataset does not include 2017 New Zealand political party statements. We now focus our attention on these. Like Dai, we searched for key words and phrases reflecting possible populism and authoritarianism; however, the quantity of text to be analysed is small enough not to require electronic processing.

Table 4.1 comprises several sections. The first contains populist words and phrases drawn from New Zealand First's 2011 leader's speech, probably the most populist document in New Zealand politics in recent history (Peters, 2011). Following this are similar phrases drawn from the 2017 New Zealand First, Labour, National and Green Party policy statements.

In 2017, the central focus of New Zealand First policy was 'the regions'—
that is, provincial areas falling behind in growth, living standards and
infrastructure development. However, beneath this overall theme, populist
language emerged, mostly directed at foreign ownership of New Zealand
assets and New Zealand First's perception of excessive recent immigration
to New Zealand (Peters, 2017).[1]

Table 4.1: Populist words and phrases in New Zealand politics

A: New Zealand First 2011		
the few	the favoured	special interests
all New Zealanders	special treatment	the many
stand for people	welfare of all	a fair go
rich people	bosses	mates
fat cats	foreign	rich person
multi-millionaires	government's mates	all the people
select few	secret deals	people no say
foreign ownership	New Zealand ... great again	unite the nation
closed doors	crooks	bankers
financial wheeler-dealers	ordinary people	New Zealand ownership
one law for all	voice of the people	people power
not just the few		

Source: Peters, 2011.

B: New Zealand First 2017		
corrupt	all of New Zealand	open door immigration
queen street farmers	financial speculators	overseas owners
sell-off of our country	foreign buyers	
foreign ownership	foreign companies	
banana republic	record net immigration	

Source: Peters, 2017.

C: Labour 2017		
speculators' unfair tax advantages	gap between rich and poor	what New Zealand meant to be
ban foreign buyers/ speculators	take a breather on immigration	

Source: Ardern, 2017.

---

1   Before the 2017 election, New Zealand First considered (but rejected on grounds of possible racist implications) a placard with the slogan: 'It's About You, Not Them' (Cook & Manch, 2019).

D: National 2017		
back New Zealanders	Kiwi character	all New Zealanders

Source: English, 2017.

E: Green 2017		
policies decided by our members	a movement of New Zealanders	choose whose side we are on
take our country back	people that really represent them	a country that works for and includes everyone, that excludes no one
we are only great, when we are great together		

Source: Shaw (2017); Turei (2017).

The central theme of the Labour Party's main campaign speech was its new leader—Jacinda Ardern. Her immediate background before becoming a member of parliament was as a party policy advisor, including working for the Blair government in the United Kingdom. However, she drew on her childhood and youth to successfully present herself as a small-town person with deep roots in everyday New Zealand. Labour language approached populism via use of 'rich and poor'. Labour expressed intentions to reduce the tax advantages of speculators in the housing market, particularly those from overseas, and to 'take a breather' on immigration. Meanwhile, significant sections of Labour policy also promoted multiculturalism (New Zealand Labour Party, 2017).

National's principal policy statement, delivered in its campaign opening speech, stressed the importance of governing in the interests of those who 'work hard and back themselves' with 'ambition for the future'. National proposed to back New Zealanders in those entrepreneurial terms and praised the 'Kiwi character', as so defined. However, the discourse is otherwise lacking in populist rhetoric (English, 2017). The two Green Party speeches could be described as containing 'populism-lite', referring to internal party democracy, our country, representation of all and New Zealanders being 'great together'—this slogan had to be replaced during the campaign when co-leader Metiria Turei was forced to resign following her disastrous speech and two members of parliament left the party due to their premature demand for her departure (Shaw, 2017; Turei, 2017). We conclude that populist 'frames' were present in New Zealand politics in 2017; however, these were not dominant or central. Concerns regarding foreign ownership and immigration were present but expressed in relatively moderate language. Labour's immigration policies were motivated by economic and social factors, most notably in the context of a highly inflated housing market combined with a housing shortage, for which high levels of recent immigration, foreign buyers and speculation in general were claimed to be responsible (a claim for which there was some evidence).

Data and Operationalisation

The authoritarian and populist attitudinal scales (defined in Chapter 3), as applied to New Zealand voters, correlate quite strongly with how people rate themselves on the left and right scale. Figure 4.1 demonstrates this using simple regressions of authoritarianism and populism together, against left–right position (details of this can be found in Table A4.1). New Zealand authoritarians tend to the right and populists to the left. A control for external political efficacy in Table A4.1 makes little or no difference to the strength of the relationship, for either populism or authoritarianism. Populism, in the New Zealand context, is a phenomenon generally found on the left rather than the right.

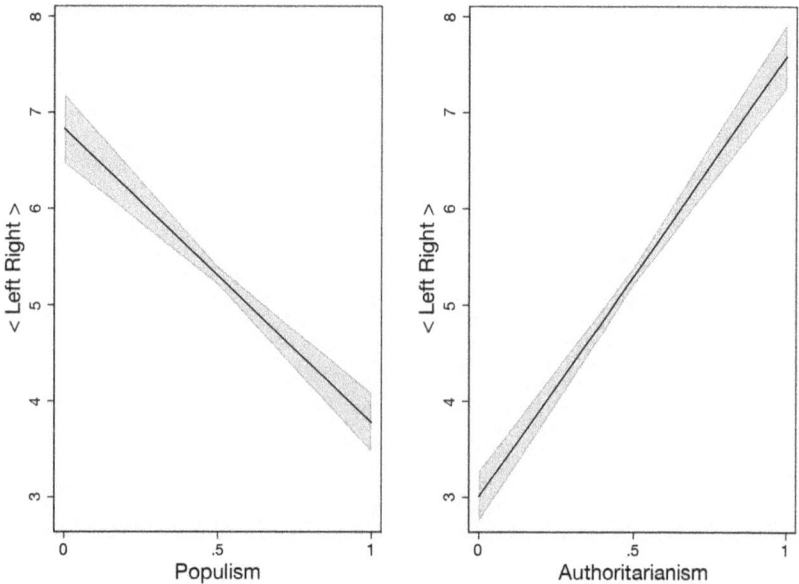

Figure 4.1: Populism, authoritarianism and the left–right scale.
Source: New Zealand Election Study (2017) (see Table A4.1 [Model 1]).

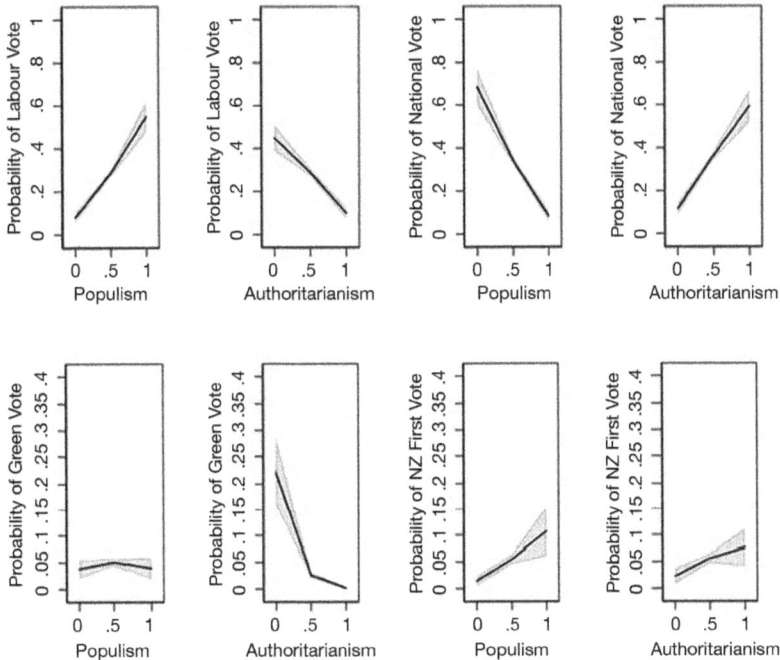

Figure 4.2: Populism, authoritarianism and vote choice in 2017.
Source: New Zealand Election Study (2017) (see Table A4.2 [Model 1]).

The next factor for consideration is party vote choice. Figure 4.2 shows that the two major parties—National and Labour—sit on different sides of the coin regarding both dimensions (see the estimates in Table A4.2). The Labour vote is associated with populism and liberal social attitudes and the National vote with elitism and authoritarianism; these associations are quite strong. The Green vote has a weak relationship with populism but a very strong relationship with liberal social attitudes. As expected, those who vote for New Zealand First tend to combine populism with authoritarianism.[2] A second model, augmented with social structure controls and an estimate of respondents' political efficacy, shows that the association between these dimensions and vote choice is almost completely unaffected by accounting for these factors (see Table A4.3). The association between populism and a desire to reduce immigration is partly explained by party policy positions. The Labour Party stated that New Zealand should 'take a breather' on immigration, whereas National made no statements on immigration in its major policy presentations.

---

2   The negative sign for authoritarianism in Table A4.2 is relative to the National vote reference category.

A third model somewhat qualifies these findings. Populism might be associated with voting for the left in New Zealand in 2017 simply because the left had not occupied office since 2008; therefore, left-leaning voters may have felt less efficacious than under different circumstances. Although we employ a control for political efficacy, one's party being out of government may still encourage apparent populist attitudes. The sample data enable investigation of this possibility, to some extent. The election was quite close; therefore, it was unknown for some time which major party would form the government. As the National Party won the most votes, until 17 October, the most probable outcome was that National would win negotiations with New Zealand First. However, post-October, it became clear that Labour would govern. Two-thirds of the sample responded before the announcement and one-third after. We created a dichotomous variable based on this distribution and further weighted the sample to ensure party vote distributions were the same in each set of respondents;[3] the coalition formation dummy was then interacted with the populism scale (see Figure 4.3).

In Table A4.3, no interactions appear significant; however, the 'after government formation' variable is significant for both Labour and the Green Party. Plotting the interaction effects, a more robust approach, the two slope lines for the National Party were almost identical (and, for this reason, not displayed in Figure 4.3). The interaction is not significant for the Green Party vote and confidence intervals also overlap; however, we note that the weak association between populist attitudes reverses between pre- and post-government formation. Populism becomes a little less associated with the Labour vote following the government announcement. The vote probability gap is substantial and just outside confidence intervals. For New Zealand First, there emerges no difference. A change of government in favour of the left may reduce agreement with left populist statements; however, there still exists a strong association between populism and Labour vote choice. Models 3 and 4 in Table A4.1 confirm the same effect for the relationship between populism and left–right placements; it was a little weaker, although still strong, after the change of government was announced. Again, this was well within confidence intervals; however, in this case, the interaction effect is statistically significant.

---

3 Chapter 8 explains the rationale and details of this weighting.

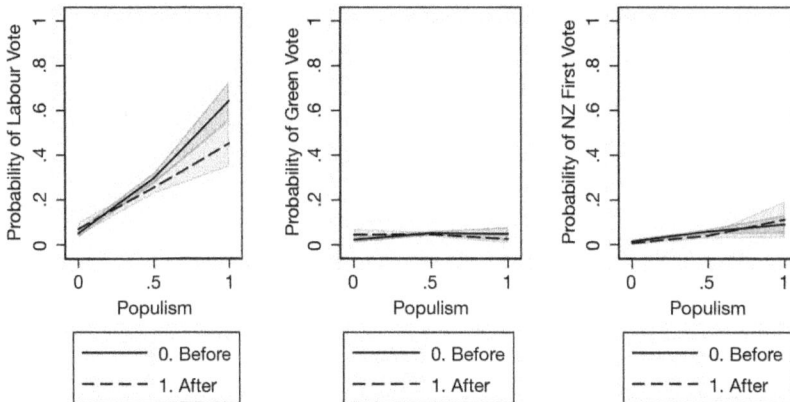

Figure 4.3: Populism conditioned by time of government formation.
Source: New Zealand Election Study (2017) (see Table A4.2 [Model 3]).

Democracy: Satisfaction and Support?

The main current of populist-inspired voting in New Zealand tends towards Labour, a party of the mainstream centre-left, while authoritarianism is more strongly associated with voting for the mainstream centre-right National Party. New Zealand First, the only party whose voters combine populism and authoritarianism, is a minor (albeit pivotal) party. However, further analysis is required to probe more deeply into this issue—both attitudinal dispositions are relatively prevalent in New Zealand and there may be additional consequences.

Concern regarding the future of democracy is currently a major theme in comparative political science. Examples of creeping authoritarianism in countries such as Poland, Hungary and Turkey garner much attention. Of even greater concern is a claim that support for democracy is declining among mass publics in the most apparently secure and stable democracies, such as New Zealand (Ferrin & Kriesi, 2016). Populist and authoritarian attitudes could underpin or at least reinforce this trend. Indeed, there is strong behavioural evidence that political participation of most kinds is declining in established democracies. Until recently, such fears were confined to electoral turnout; however, they have now moved further afield and are found in, for example, so-called unconventional forms of participation such as protest (Grasso, 2016). A long-term trend of turnout decline has been well documented in New Zealand (Vowles, 2014), although turnout recovered somewhat in 2014 and again in 2017, albeit from a low base. The greatest concern is that these trends are shaped by age differences that are generational, rather than simply reflecting change over the life cycle, as seems to be the case for turnout in New Zealand and many other countries (Franklin, 2004; Vowles, 2010).

Behavioural change does not necessarily signify wholesale attitudinal change. People may continue to support democracy without feeling the need to participate themselves—a phenomenon labelled 'stealth democracy' (Hibbing & Theiss-Morse, 2003). Two instruments are available from the 2017 New Zealand Election Study (NZES) to test the relevant attitudes. First is a standard question eliciting satisfaction with 'how democracy works' in New Zealand (with options of 'very satisfied', 'fairly satisfied', 'not very satisfied', 'not at all satisfied' and 'don't know'). 'Satisfaction with democracy' is one of the most widely used estimates in the literature to assess both the accountability and responsiveness of democracies. However, this does not escape criticism—it taps into a wide range of sentiments and may confuse evaluations of democracies in principle and in practice (Thomas, 2016). Nonetheless, it has value as a summary measure; its wide use in the literature attests to its worth, subject to caution (Anderson, 2002). Democratic dissatisfaction may represent 'a felt discrepancy between democratic norms and the actual democratic process' (Thomassen, 1995, p. 383).

Democratic satisfaction has been measured in New Zealand since 1996. Unfortunately, we lack a time series prior to electoral system change. Two mid-term election datasets illustrate the picture in both 1998 and 2001. Data collection in 1998 was fortunately timed to capture the collapse of the first coalition government under the mixed member proportional (MMP) system and the following fallout (Karp & Bowler, 2001). Figure 4.4 shows that, at the first MMP election, the level of democratic satisfaction was only a little below 70 per cent. Disillusion followed but satisfaction had returned almost to the 1996 level by 2002. Since 2005, democratic satisfaction has remained steady at approximately 65 per cent, which is somewhat better than average, in international terms, but not outstanding (Aarts & Thomassen, 2008, p. 12; Thomas, 2016, p. 219). In 2017, a slight drop may be observed; however, this is within confidence intervals when compared to 2014. We elucidate the possible reason for this apparent change in Chapter 8.

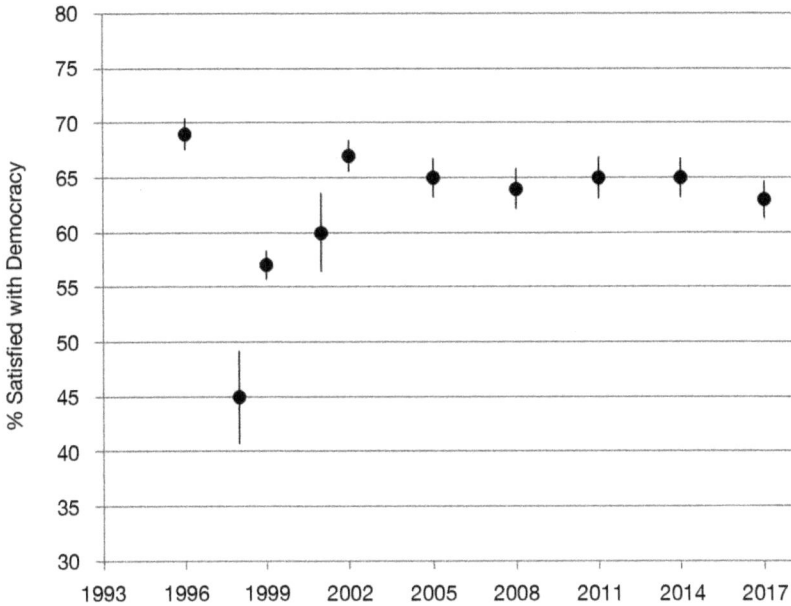

Figure 4.4: Satisfaction with democracy in New Zealand (1996–2017).
Source: New Zealand Election Study (2017).

Unless New Zealand democracy fully meets their expectations, which is
unlikely, one would expect populists to be less satisfied with democracy
than non-populists. For authoritarians, more ambiguity is likely—
dissatisfaction with the performance of democracy does not necessarily
imply dissatisfaction with democracy, as such, or that people would
prefer some authoritarian alternative. Alternatively, an authoritarian
might be satisfied with democracy when things are going well but prefer
authoritarian government when things go badly (Linde & Ekman, 2003).

The second question available in the 2017 NZES is a five-point scale
measuring agreement or disagreement with the statement: 'Democracy
may have problems but it's better than any other form of government'.
This question implicitly references Winston Churchill's famous words,
a rueful comment on his rejection by the British electorate in 1945.
The same question was also asked in the 2002 NZES, thereby providing
a useful comparison across 15 years. Concern regarding declining support
for democracy in established democracies has been widely expressed and
younger generations have been identified as those most susceptible (Foa
& Mounk, 2017). However, this finding appears driven largely by the
United States. Elsewhere, including New Zealand, over the last 20 years,

across a range of questions, overall support for democracy remains high, evidencing little change (Voeten, 2017). NZES comparison between 2002 and 2007, setting the five-point scale at minimum 0 and maximum 1 confirms this, demonstrating no significant difference in agreement with the question—the mean is 0.8, indicating a relatively high level of support. Nonetheless, changes within the electorate, particularly among and across generations, may still constitute cause for concern.

Figure 4.5 displays two sets of estimates derived from two linear regression models, one on satisfaction with democracy, the other on 'democracy is better'; each use five-point scales with minimum set at 0 and maximum at 1 (see Tables A4.3 and A4.4). The figure shows the probability shifts of the categorical variables from their minimum to maximum values. Figures for the continuous variables—populism, authoritarianism, income and political efficacy—are found below. The models were also run using ordinal logit, which returned almost identical results. Our use of linear regression provides results that are easier to interpret.

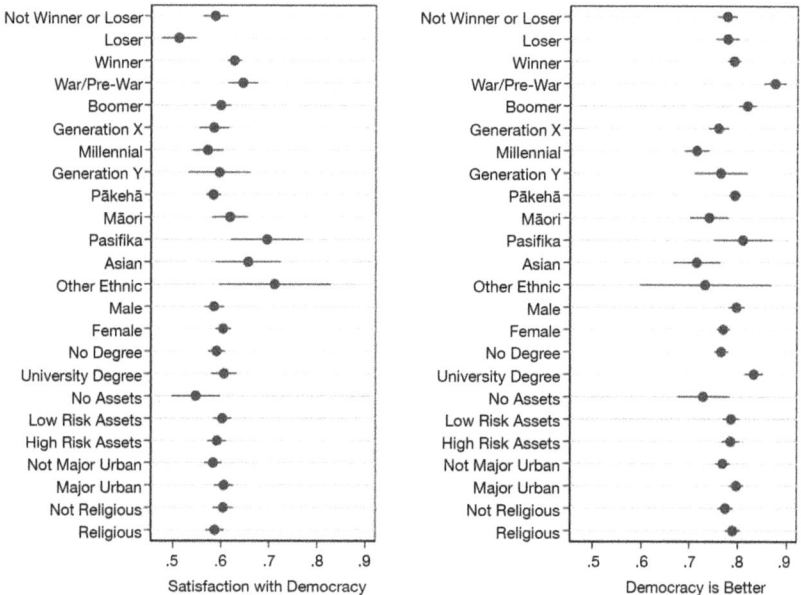

Figure 4.5: Satisfaction with and support for democracy in New Zealand.

Note: Dots and 95 per cent confidence intervals indicate the comparative positions of each group on the two scales, with satisfaction/support at a maximum of 1 and dissatisfaction/opposition at a maximum of 0.

Source: New Zealand Election Study (2017) (see Table A4.3 [Model 4] and Table A4.4 [Model 4]).

The model contains controls for 'winner' and 'loser' to estimate short-term effects. It is expected that winners will be more satisfied and supportive, losers less so. The election result and the delay in deciding which parties would govern complicate the coding of this question. 'Winners' are defined as government parties; however, prior to Winston Peters' announcement, most people expected that National and New Zealand First would govern. Therefore, 'winners' were coded as National and New Zealand First before the announcement of the government, and Labour, New Zealand First and Green afterward. 'Losers' were defined as parties who moved out of government—this applied to Māori Party and ACT voters throughout, because a National–New Zealand First coalition would have been very unlikely to include them, and also to National following the formation of the Labour-led coalition (and Labour before it). The group in the middle are non-voters and those voting for parties not in the government either before or after the election. Figure 4.5 shows the expected effects for winners and losers under satisfaction; however, little of note emerges under 'democracy is best'. The questions appear to effectively separate short-term and long-term perspectives.

We defined generational cohorts as in Chapter 3. Compared to war and pre-war generations, successive generations become less satisfied with democracy until generation Z, whose score reverts in the other direction. The same pattern, albeit stronger, emerges for support. Younger generations, or age groups, show declining levels of support and satisfaction, consistent with fears expressed concerning generational decline in support in established democracies.

The use of the words 'generations' or 'age groups' as alternatives highlights a key point. The differences may not be generational but instead reflect the life cycle; support for and satisfaction with democracy is lower among the young but rises as people age and become more satisfied and supportive. In the wider international debate (in contrast to the debate regarding electoral turnout), the life cycle interpretation has the best evidence (Norris, 2017; Voeten, 2017). Shorn of all controls, Figure 4.6 displays the 'generational' probabilities of supporting democracy in 2002 and 2017, with the generations pinned to birth years, rather than age at any one time. The older generation becomes significantly more likely to support democracy. In 2017, this is a smaller group, excluding those who have died in the intervening years. Boomers remain in the same position; however, generation X shifts towards a higher level of democratic support. Millennials (only slightly represented in 2002 compared to 2017) may also have shifted upward; however, the confidence intervals overlap. Generation Z could not vote in 2002 and their slightly higher level than that of millennials in 2017 is not statistically significant. On balance, the evidence from this analysis best supports the life cycle interpretation.

Returning to Figure 4.5, Pākehā are, surprisingly, the least satisfied with democracy. Māori are more satisfied, but still within confidence intervals. Pasifika stand out as the most satisfied group. The Māori finding is surprising and presumably results from other variables in the model. With ethnic groups alone, in an alternative model, the picture changes: Māori are the least satisfied (although, again, they are not statistically different from Pākehā: the difference is only 0.03). All immigrant minority groups are more satisfied than the rest; however, according to the confidence intervals, the difference is only robust between Pākehā and Pasifika. Regarding the rest of the variables, confidence intervals tend to overlap or are quite close.

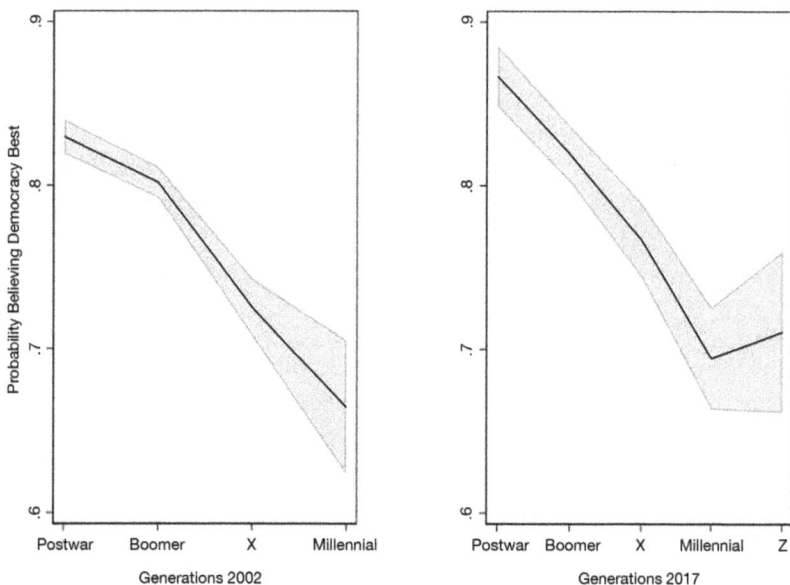

Figure 4.6: Generational comparisons of support for democracy.

Note: Lines and 95 per cent confidence intervals indicate the comparative positions of each group on the two scales, with satisfaction/support at a maximum of 1 and dissatisfaction/opposition at a maximum of 0.

Source: New Zealand Election Study (2002, 2017).

As expected, the ethnic groups divide more on 'democracy is best'. Pākehā and Pasifika are most likely to agree; Māori, Asians and 'others' are less likely to agree. Given their experience as a colonised minority, the Māori position is to be expected. Asian and 'other' ethnic groups, most of whom are likely to be recent immigrants, are also more likely to have been born in countries less democratic than New Zealand. There exist more differences between the remaining groups for 'democracy is best'. Men, those with university degrees and major urban dwellers are somewhat more pro-democracy than women, those without degrees and those living outside major urban areas.

Figure 4.7 shows that authoritarians are less satisfied with democracy, as expected, but are only marginally less likely to support democracy than liberals—the difference is, statistically, nothing to speak of. This is an unexpected but notable finding—it appears that New Zealand authoritarians do not desire non-democratic alternatives.

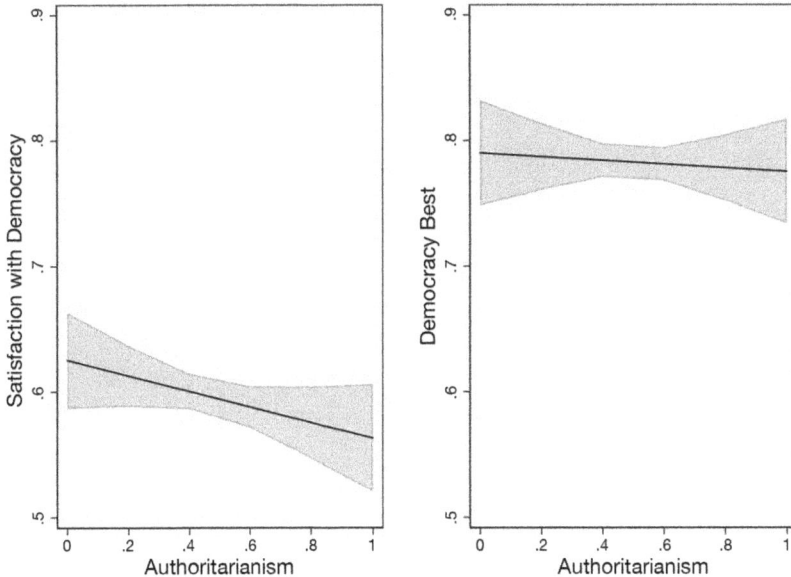

Figure 4.7: Satisfaction with democracy, support for democracy and authoritarianism.

Source: New Zealand Election Study (2017) (see Table A4.3 [Model 4] and Table A4.4 [Model 4]).

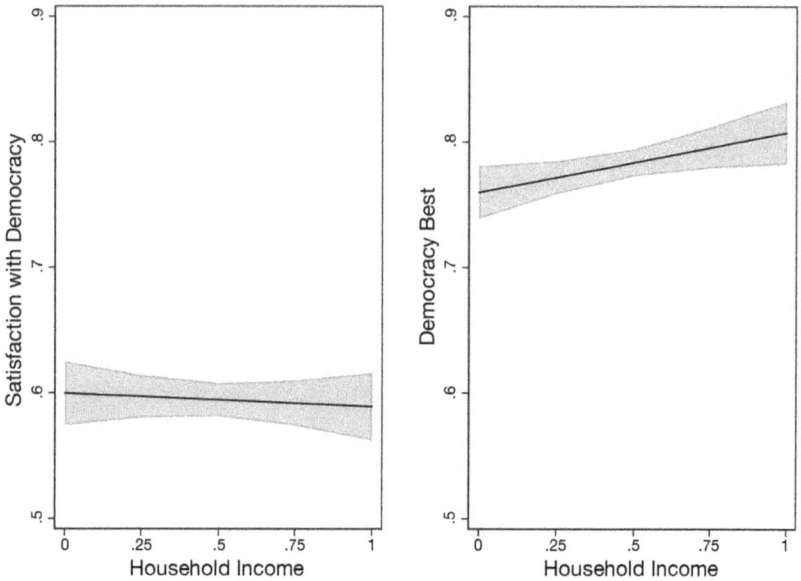

Figure 4.8: Satisfaction with democracy, support for democracy and income.

Source: New Zealand Election Study (2017) (see Table A4.4 [Model 3] and Table A4.4 [Model 3]).

As noted earlier, despite a proportional electoral system, governmental authority in New Zealand is concentrated in a unitary state, with no fundamental law to constrain the power of the legislature and executive. However, we might expect authoritarians to resist proposals for the introduction of binding constitutional law (see e.g. Palmer & Butler, 2019) or for devolution of central government authority to regional and local authorities. Figure 4.8 shows that income has no effect on satisfaction with democracy but demonstrates a significant association with democratic support—those with higher incomes are more likely to support democracy against alternatives.

Figure 4.9 shows that external political efficacy is strongly associated with both satisfaction with and support for democracy (but most strongly with the latter). Figure 4.10 displays the relationship between populist attitudes, satisfaction with democracy and support for democracy. As expected, populists are much less satisfied with democracy than non-populists. By contrast, regarding democratic support, although the slope of the probability estimate is in the same direction, the confidence intervals overlap and the coefficient is insignificant in Model 3 (Table A4.4). In the first two models of that table, populism appears strongly negatively associated with democratic support; the addition of efficacy to Model 3 reduces populism to statistical insignificance. If efficacy is a short-term perception of government responsiveness and populism is representative of more deep-seated preferences regarding government, we may conclude that populists in New Zealand are not anti-democratic. However, the relationship may not be so straightforward—populists may be generally prone to feelings of low external efficacy.

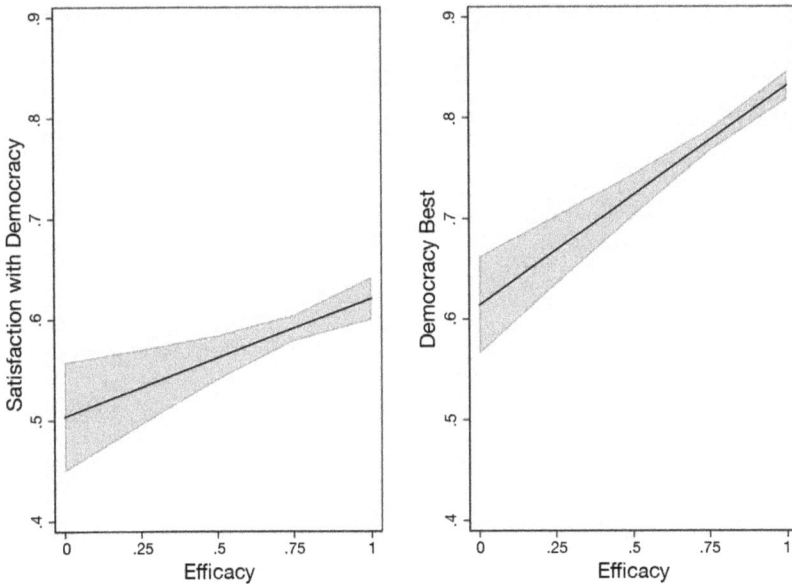

Figure 4.9: Democratic satisfaction, support for democracy and external efficacy.

Source: New Zealand Election Study (2017) (see Table A4.4 [Model 3] and Table A4.4 [Model 3]).

Figure 4.11 returns the focus to age, this time included by year rather than by generational cohort. The figure is derived from Model 5 on democratic support. To give a more robust estimate, the points at which populism is measured are somewhat estimated slightly short of the extreme values of the scale (which are 0 or 1). It shows that a significant proportion of age difference in support for democracy can be attributed to populists, who become more supportive of democracy as they grow older, perhaps as their expectations of democracy become more modest. This model includes the control for efficacy—without this, there exists a somewhat stronger effect, indicating the effect of increasing efficacy as people age. However, this figure controls for this effect.

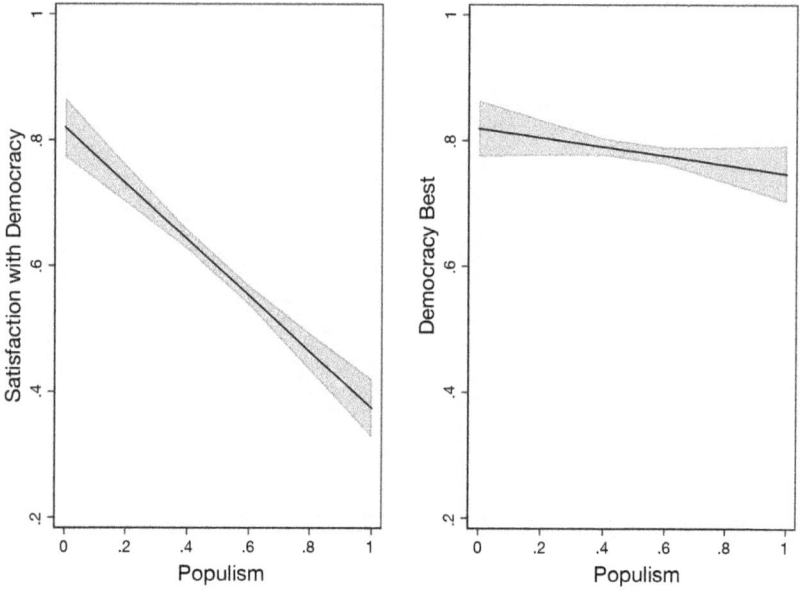

Figure 4.10: Democratic satisfaction, support for democracy and populism.

Source: New Zealand Election Study (2017) (Table A4.3 [Model 4] and Table A4.4 [Model 4]).

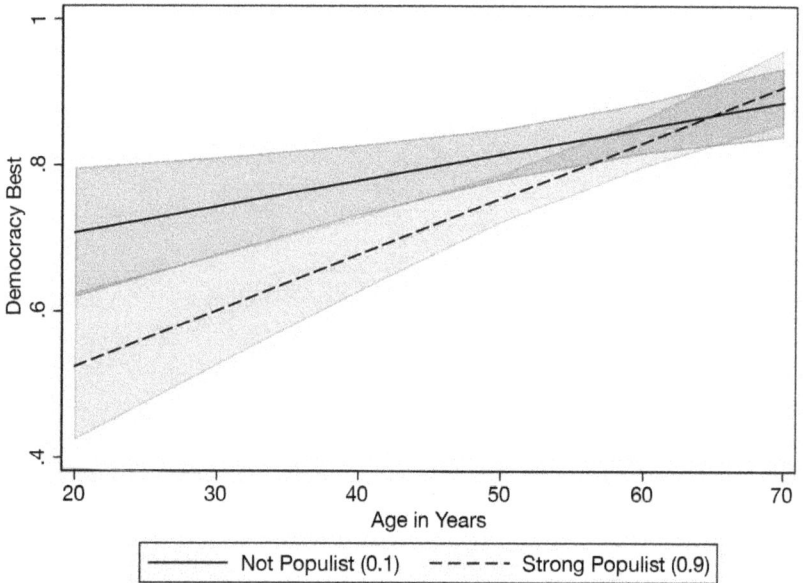

Figure 4.11: How populism and age affect democratic support.

Source: New Zealand Election Study (2017) (see Table A4.5 [Model 5]).

Discussion and Conclusions

In New Zealand, populism is predominantly an attribute of those who lean left, rather than right. In part, this may be attributed to the effect of a centre-right government who have been in office since 2008. Left populist sentiments may be less associated with vote choice when the left is in power—populism did become somewhat less associated with Labour vote choice after the outcome of the election gave power to their party; consequently, some Labour voters became a little less populist. Over the longer term, an even stronger effect may be expected. Therefore, replication of this analysis with 2020 election data should be a strong priority. The separation between the two dimensions of populism and authoritarianism means that Labour may appeal to populists, but not so much to authoritarians, and National may appeal to authoritarians, but not so much to populists. The combination of populism and authoritarianism occurs among those who vote for New Zealand First; otherwise populists tend to vote Labour, authoritarians National and left–right positions display the same pattern.

As might be expected, populists are less satisfied with New Zealand democracy than non-populists. After controlling for political efficacy, populists demonstrate a high level of support for democracy; however, the level is not significantly higher than that of the population in general and is, perhaps, marginally lower. This is more likely a reflection of disappointment with, rather than a rejection of, democracy. Authoritarians are also no less satisfied with or supportive of New Zealand democracy than liberals. These findings are reassuring for democrats, as are the indications that support for democracy in New Zealand is not declining over time. If the young are less supportive of democracy than the old, this is most likely a life cycle rather than a generational effect. As people age, and tend to become more secure and integrated into society, they become more supportive of democracy. Higher incomes, higher education and, to a lesser extent, accumulation of assets also generate greater support. Populists, more so than non-populists, appear to be most responsible for this ageing effect.

There are several key implications for New Zealand politics. A greater degree of both populism and authoritarianism is clearly possible in New Zealand politics. Social and economic inequalities remain relatively high and demonstrate a strong association with social and political cleavage structures (Vowles, Coffé & Curtin, 2017). Māori, Pasifika and all those on low incomes and with insecure employment are generally less satisfied and less supportive of the democratic status quo. New Zealanders were lucky that their experiences of the global financial crisis and the following recession were mild, compared to those in many other countries. Immigration surged significantly after 2013; however, this occurred in a context of economic recovery and labour shortages. New Zealand is advantaged by moderate mainstream party elites and a conservative, but not politically manipulative, traditional media—extremist voices receive little traction; however, social media give them more opportunities than in the past. In the aftermath of the Christchurch attack on Islamic worshippers, political elites and traditional media uniformly broadcasted a message of social inclusion and cultural tolerance.

A historian coined the phrase 'a lucky country' to describe Australia in the 1960s (Horne, 1964). The description stuck, despite being ironic. Australians have demonstrated a habit of co-opting New Zealand's achievements—perhaps it is time to return the favour? Crucially, this luck is only relative—in comparison to the darker pathways being followed in other countries. Despite widely acknowledged contemporary flaws in its politics and society, New Zealand's moderately populist democracy better fits the 'lucky' label in the early 21st century. However, given historical experience, social inequalities and injustice, the ambitions of opposition politicians, unstable global politics and the possibility of a domestic spillover in relation to an external shock or global recession, no one can be sure that this relatively happy state of affairs will last.

References

Aarts, K. & Thomassen, J. (2008). Satisfaction with democracy: Do institutions matter? *Electoral Studies, 7*, 5–18. doi.org/10.1016/j.electstud.2007.11.005

Anderson, C. J. (2002). Good questions, dubious inferences and bad solutions: Some further thoughts on satisfaction with democracy (Unpublished manuscript). Retrieved from www.researchgate.net/publication/251498295_Good_Questions_Dubious_Inferences_and_Bad_Solutions_Some_Further_Thoughts_on_Satisfaction_with_Democracy/link/02e7e53199893ba764000000/download

Ardern, J. (2017). Jacinda's speech to campaign launch. *New Zealand Labour Party*. Retrieved from www.labour.org.nz/jacindas_speech_to_campaign_launch

Ardern, J. (2019). *Full statement: Jacinda Ardern addresses Parliament on Christchurch terror attack*. Retrieved from www.tvnz.co.nz/one-news/new-zealand/full-statement-jacinda-ardern-addresses-parliament-christchurch-terror-attack

Bridges, S. (2018). New Zealand National party: Pull NZ out of the UN migration pact. *Facebook*. Retrieved from www.national.org.nz/national_would_pull_nz_out_of_un_migration_pact

Cook, H. & Manch, T. (2019). Major leak of NZ First membership database exposes personal details, Winston Peters refers to police. *Stuff*. Retrieved from www.stuff.co.nz/national/politics/116409225/major-leak-of-nz-first-membership-database-exposes-personal-details

Dai, Y. (2018). *Measuring populism in context: A supervised approach with word embedding models*. Retrieved from sites.psu.edu/yaoyaodai/files/2018/09/Dai_paper_populism-2bj779b.pdf

English, B. (2017). Speech to the National Party campaign launch 2017. *New Zealand National Party*. Retrieved from www.national.org.nz/speech_to_the_national_party_campaign_launch

Ferrin, M. & Kriesi, H. (2016). *How Europeans view and evaluate democracy*. Oxford, United Kingdom: Oxford University Press.

Foa, R. S. & Mounk, Y. (2017). The signs of deconsolidation. *Journal of Democracy*, *28*(1), 5–15.

Franklin, M. N. (2004). *Voter turnout and the dynamics of electoral competition in established democracies since 1945*. Cambridge, United Kingdom: Cambridge University Press.

Gower, P. (2019). Police investigating white supremacists' death threats against Winston Peters. *Newshub*. Retrieved from www.newshub.co.nz/home/new-zealand/2019/06/exclusive-police-investigating-white-supremacists-death-threats-against-winston-peters.html

Grasso, M. T. (2016). *Generations, political participation and social change in Western Europe*. London, United Kingdom: Routledge.

Hibbing, J. & Theiss-Morse, E. (2003). *Stealth democracy: Americans' beliefs about how government should work*. Cambridge, United Kingdom: Cambridge University Press.

Horne, D. (1964). *The lucky country?* Hawthorne, Australia: Penguin Australia.

Karp, J. A. & Bowler, S. (2001). Coalition politics and satisfaction with democracy: Explaining New Zealand's reaction to proportional representation. *European Journal of Political Research, 40*(1), 57–79. doi.org/10.1111/1475-6765.00589

Linde, J. & Ekman, J. (2003). Satisfaction with democracy: A note on a frequently used indicator in comparative politics. *European Journal of Political Research, 42*, 391–408. doi.org/10.1111/1475-6765.00089

Norris, P. (2017). *Is Western democracy backsliding? Diagnosing the risks.* Retrieved from www.journalofdemocracy.org/wp-content/uploads/2018/12/Journal-of-Democracy-Web-Exchange-Norris_0.pdf

New Zealand Election Study. (2002). New Zealand Election Study [dataset]. Retrieved from www.nzes.org/exec/show/data

New Zealand Election Study. (2017). *New Zealand Election Study* [dataset]. Retrieved from www.nzes.org/exec/show/data

New Zealand Labour Party. (2017). *Think Labour's got no policies? Think again.* Retrieved from www.labour.org.nz/thelonglist

Palmer, G. & Butler, A. (2019). *Towards democratic renewal: Ideas for constitutional change in New Zealand.* Wellington, New Zealand: Victoria University Press.

Peters, W. (2011). For a fair go. *Scoop.* Retrieved from www.scoop.co.nz/stories/PO1110/S00543/rt-hon-winston-peters-for-a-fair-go.htm

Peters, W. (2017). NZ First campaign launch speech. *New Zealand First.* Retrieved from yournz.org/2017/06/26/nz-first-campaign-launch-speech/

Peters, W. (2019). Winston Peters speech to commemorate the Christchurch Mosque. *Scoop.* retrieved from www.scoop.co.nz/stories/PA1903/S00133/winston-peters-speech-to-commemorate-the-christchurch-mosque.htm

Polk, J., Rovny, J., Bakker, R., Edwards, E., Hooghe, L., Jolly, S., … Zilovic, M. (2017). Explaining the salience of anti-elitism and reducing political corruption for political parties in Europe with the 2014 Chapel Hill expert survey data. *Research and Politics, 4*(1), 1–9. doi.org/10.1177/2053168016686915

Shaw, J. (2017). Green Party campaign launch—Nelson 2017. *Green Party.* Retrieved from www.greens.org.nz/news/speech/james-shaw-green-party-campaign-launch-nelson-2017

Thomas, K. (2016). Democratic support and globalisation. In J. Vowles & G. Xezonakis (Eds), *Globalisation and domestic politics: Parties, elections and public opinion* (pp. 209–230). Oxford, United Kingdom: Oxford University Press. doi.org/10.1093/acprof:oso/9780198757986.003.0011

Thomassen, J. (1995). Support for democratic values. In H-D Klingemann & D. Fuchs (Eds), *Citizens and the state* (pp. 383–415). Oxford, United Kingdom: Oxford University Press. doi.org/10.1093/0198294735.003.0013

Turei, M. (2017). Green Party campaign launch—Nelson 2017. *Green Party*. Retrieved from www.greens.org.nz/news/speech/metiria-turei-green-party-campaign-launch-nelson-2017

Voeten, E. (2017). Are people really turning away from democracy? Retrieved from www.journalofdemocracy.org/online-exchange-democratic-deconsolidation/

Vowles, J. (2010). Electoral system change, generations, competitiveness and turnout in New Zealand, 1963–2005. *British Journal of Political Science, 40*(4), 875–895. doi.org/10.1017/S0007123409990342

Vowles, J. (2014). Down, down, down: Turnout from 1946 to 2011. In J. Vowles (Ed.), *The new electoral politics in New Zealand: The significance of the 2011 Election* (pp. 53–73). Wellington, New Zealand: Institute for Governance and Policy Studies.

Vowles, J., Coffé, H. & Curtin, J. (2017). *A bark but no bite: Inequality and the 2014 New Zealand general election.* Canberra, Australia: ANU Press. doi.org/10.22459/BBNB.08.2017

Appendices

Table A4.1: Populism, authoritarianism and the self-assigned left (0)–right (10) position

Ordinary Least Squares	Model 1	Model 2	Model 3	Model 4
Populism	−3.053***	−2.978***	−3.478***	−3.408***
	(0.326)	(0.320)	(0.434)	(0.426)
After government (AG)			−0.660**	−0.658**
			(0.298)	(0.298)
Populism* AG			1.232**	1.253**
			(0.547)	(0.548)
Authoritarianism	4.576***	4.546***	4.520***	4.486***
	(0.293)	(0.290)	(0.293)	(0.291)

Ordinary Least Squares	Model 1	Model 2	Model 3	Model 4
Efficacy		0.342*		0.369*
		(0.206)		(0.205)
Constant	4.566***	4.279***	4.803***	4.494***
	(0.154)	(0.209)	(0.206)	(0.239)
Observations	3,455.000	3,455.000	3,455.000	3,455.000
R-squared	0.192	0.193	0.192	0.193

Note: Robust standard errors in parentheses.
*** p < 0.01, ** p < 0.05, * p < 0.1.
Source: New Zealand Election Study (2017).

Table A4.2: Populism, authoritarianism and party vote in 2017

Model 1					
Multinomial Logit	(1) Non-vote	(2) Labour	(4) Green	(5) New Zealand First	(6) Other
Populism	4.065***	5.293***	3.835***	4.974***	3.659***
	(0.702)	(0.400)	(0.597)	(0.604)	(0.532)
Authoritarianism	−1.668***	−3.980***	−8.071***	−0.313	−3.092***
	(0.547)	(0.365)	(0.553)	(0.584)	(0.430)
Constant	−1.15***	−0.846***	−0.416	−4.200***	−1.695***
	(0.324)	(0.190)	(0.264)	(0.357)	(0.268)
Pseudo R-squared	0.075				
Observations	3,438.000	3,438.000	3,438.000	3,438.000	3,438.000

Model 2					
Multinomial Logit	(1) Nonvote	(2) Labour	(4) Green	(5) New Zealand First	(6) Other
Populism	2.530***	4.573***	2.955***	4.306***	3.125***
	(0.784)	(0.403)	(0.658)	(0.633)	(0.594)
Authoritarianism	−1.375**	−3.687***	−7.158***	−0.780	−3.154***
	(0.649)	(0.346)	(0.612)	(0.632)	(0.541)
Age	−0.032***	−0.004	−0.033***	0.008	−0.012*
	(0.008)	(0.004)	(0.007)	(0.006)	(0.006)
Female (male)	−0.614***	−0.103	−0.387**	−0.635***	−0.635***
	(0.220)	(0.123)	(0.195)	(0.186)	(0.200)
Māori (European)	1.427***	1.363***	0.887***	1.221***	1.788***
	(0.293)	(0.231)	(0.338)	(0.300)	(0.269)

Model 2					
Multinomial Logit	**(1) Nonvote**	**(2) Labour**	**(4) Green**	**(5) New Zealand First**	**(6) Other**
Pasifika (European)	0.460	0.819*	−1.151	0.270	0.251
	(0.816)	(0.482)	(1.109)	(0.871)	(0.831)
Asian (European)	−0.088	−0.320	−1.062**	−15.182***	0.148
	(0.441)	(0.276)	(0.474)	(0.238)	(0.500)
Other (European)	−14.536***	1.852*	−0.416	−14.115***	1.378
	(1.131)	(0.950)	(1.512)	(1.115)	(1.346)
University	−0.081	0.464***	0.674***	0.087	0.340
	(0.303)	(0.143)	(0.220)	(0.266)	(0.222)
Household income	−0.181**	−0.153***	−0.311***	−0.211***	−0.142**
	(0.092)	(0.047)	(0.078)	(0.079)	(0.072)
Low-risk assets	−1.042*	−0.899***	−0.473	−0.558	−1.493***
	(0.537)	(0.314)	(0.610)	(0.523)	(0.498)
High-risk assets	−1.175**	−1.323***	−0.601	−0.525	−1.267**
	(0.545)	(0.319)	(0.621)	(0.538)	(0.509)
Religious	−0.002	−0.260**	−0.621***	0.064	0.076
	(0.240)	(0.129)	(0.205)	(0.203)	(0.205)
Major urban	−0.181	0.249**	0.254	−0.242	0.171
	(0.234)	(0.124)	(0.210)	(0.198)	(0.203)
Efficacy	−2.639***	−0.009	−0.490	−1.064***	−1.458***
	(0.477)	(0.312)	(0.540)	(0.397)	(0.411)
Constant	4.313***	0.940*	3.151***	−1.721*	1.761**
	(0.904)	(0.550)	(0.924)	(0.908)	(0.759)
Pseudo R-squared					
	3,230.000	3,230.000	3,230.000	3,230.000	3,230.000
Observations	4.313***	0.940*	3.151***	−1.721*	1.761**

Model 3					
Multinomial Logit	**(1) Nonvote**	**(2) Labour**	**(4) Green**	**(5) New Zealand First**	**(6) Other**
Populism	3.699***	5.503***	4.292***	4.644***	3.034***
	(1.163)	(0.490)	(0.780)	(0.645)	(0.633)
After government (AG)	0.909	0.896**	1.180**	−0.636	−0.103
	(0.701)	(0.370)	(0.524)	(0.717)	(0.535)

Model 3					
Multinomial Logit	**(1)** **Nonvote**	**(2)** **Labour**	**(4)** **Green**	**(5)** **New Zealand First**	**(6)** **Other**
Populism* AG	0.189	−0.929	−1.736	0.805	1.114
	(1.261)	(0.707)	(1.078)	(1.192)	(1.024)
Authoritarianism	−1.728***	−3.969***	−8.054***	−0.291	−3.121***
	(0.569)	(0.365)	(0.563)	(0.578)	(0.434)
Constant	−1.898***	−1.133***	−0.778**	−3.971***	−1.577***
	(0.533)	(0.231)	(0.338)	(0.368)	(0.326)
Pseudo R-squared	0.087				
Observations	3,438.000	3,438.000	3,438.000	3,438.000	3,438.000

Note: Bracketed categories are those for reference. Vote for National (3) is the reference category for vote choice.

Robust standard errors in parentheses.

*** p < 0.01, ** p < 0.05, * p < 0.1.

Models 1 and 2 are weighted by demographics, education and party vote. Model 3 is further weighted by party votes, both pre- and post-government formation.

Source: New Zealand Election Study (2017).

Table A4.3: Satisfaction with democracy

Ordinary Least Squares	**1**	**2**	**3**	**4**
Populism	−0.462***	−0.454***	−0.469***	−0.446***
	(0.046)	(0.046)	(0.048)	(0.046)
Authoritarianism	−0.057	−0.053	−0.055	−0.062
	(0.037)	(0.037)	(0.040)	(0.039)
Winner		0.052***	0.048***	0.039**
		(0.015)	(0.015)	(0.015)
Loser		−0.062***	−0.068***	−0.076***
		(0.022)	(0.023)	(0.023)
Boomer			−0.048***	−0.046**
			(0.018)	(0.018)
Generation X			−0.062***	−0.060**
			(0.024)	(0.024)
Millennial			−0.082***	−0.073***
			(0.024)	(0.024)
Generation Y			−0.055	−0.049
			(0.036)	(0.038)

Ordinary Least Squares	1	2	3	4
Female (male)			0.025*	0.019
			(0.013)	(0.013)
Māori			0.047**	0.034
			(0.021)	(0.021)
Pasifika			0.110***	0.112***
			(0.040)	(0.040)
Asian			0.072*	0.073**
			(0.038)	(0.036)
Other ethnic			0.144**	0.128**
			(0.058)	(0.060)
University degree			0.018	0.016
			(0.018)	(0.018)
Household income			−0.013	−0.010
			(0.024)	(0.023)
Low-risk assets			0.056**	0.055**
			(0.028)	(0.028)
High-risk assets			0.045	0.044
			(0.029)	(0.028)
Major urban			0.025*	0.022
			(0.014)	(0.014)
Religious			−0.015	−0.017
			(0.015)	(0.015)
Efficacy				0.117***
				(0.035)
Constant	0.857***	0.837***	0.825***	0.733***
	(0.021)	(0.024)	(0.042)	(0.046)
Observations	3,403.000	3,403.000	3,215.000	3,215.000
R-squared	0.105	0.123	0.148	0.156

Note: Robust standard errors in parentheses.

*** p < 0.01, ** p < 0.05, * p < 0.1.

Source: New Zealand Election Study (2017).

Table A4.4: Democracy is better

Ordinary Least Squares	1	2	3	4	5
Populism	−0.240***	−0.215***	−0.117**	−0.072	−0.336***
	(0.043)	(0.044)	(0.049)	(0.045)	(0.126)
Authoritarianism	0.018	0.002	−0.001	−0.015	−0.026
	(0.042)	(0.042)	(0.046)	(0.041)	(0.037)
Winner		0.057***	0.030**	0.015	0.014
		(0.014)	(0.013)	(0.013)	(0.012)
Loser		0.028	0.015	0.001	−0.000
		(0.018)	(0.017)	(0.017)	(0.016)
Boomer			−0.062***	−0.056***	
			(0.015)	(0.015)	
Generation X			−0.122***	−0.115***	
			(0.017)	(0.017)	
Millennial			−0.179***	−0.160***	
			(0.019)	(0.018)	
Generation Y			−0.123***	−0.111***	
			(0.028)	(0.031)	
Age					0.001
					(0.001)
Populism x age					0.005***
					(0.002)
Female (male)			−0.016	−0.027**	−0.025**
			(0.012)	(0.011)	(0.011)
Māori			−0.029	−0.053**	−0.049**
			(0.022)	(0.022)	(0.021)
Pasifika			0.011	0.017	0.023
			(0.032)	(0.031)	(0.030)
Asian			−0.079***	−0.078***	−0.076***
			(0.027)	(0.026)	(0.026)
Other ethnic			−0.030	−0.061	−0.020
			(0.067)	(0.069)	(0.060)
University degree			0.072***	0.067***	0.059***
			(0.015)	(0.013)	(0.013)
Household income			0.044**	0.048**	0.044**
			(0.022)	(0.021)	(0.020)

Ordinary Least Squares	1	2	3	4	5
Low-risk assets			0.060**	0.058**	0.059**
			(0.030)	(0.028)	(0.028)
High-risk assets			0.057*	0.057*	0.061**
			(0.032)	(0.030)	(0.030)
Major urban			0.033***	0.028***	0.026**
			(0.011)	(0.011)	(0.011)
Religious			0.020*	0.015	0.009
			(0.012)	(0.011)	(0.012)
Efficacy				0.218***	0.213***
				(0.029)	(0.028)
Constant	0.110***	0.143***	0.820***	0.648***	0.550***
	(0.016)	(0.020)	(0.038)	(0.044)	(0.067)
Observations	3,367	3,367	3,213	3,213	3,213
R-squared	0.038	0.050	0.145	0.190	0.203

Note: Robust standard errors in parentheses.

*** $p < 0.01$, ** $p < 0.05$, * $p < 0.1$.

Source: New Zealand Election Study (2017).

5

IMMIGRATION AND POPULISM IN THE NEW ZEALAND 2017 ELECTION

Kate McMillan and Matthew Gibbons

By the end of the 2010s, anti-immigration populist parties held seats in 19 national parliaments across Europe (British Broadcasting Corporation, 2019). In Hungary and Poland, such parties led their respective governments; in Italy, Sweden and Slovenia, they had received the largest proportion of votes in recent national elections. Anti-immigration parties increased their representation in the European Parliament following elections in mid-2019, and, even as some far-right parties lost support in that election, more voters from the United Kingdom, France, Slovenia, Italy and Hungary supported their respective right-wing, anti-immigration populist parties—United Kingdom Independence Party, National Rally, the Slovenian Democratic Party, Lega and Fidesz—than other parties. Moreover, railing against immigration (and the multiculturalism to which it gives rise) was not the sole province of far-right populist parties in Europe; this approach had become core politics for mainstream centre-right leaders in major liberal democracies. Donald Trump, David Cameron, Nicolas Sarkozy and every Australian Liberal prime minister since and including John Howard had all deployed anti-immigration rhetoric for electoral gain. Thus, by 2020, a kind of populism described as 'exclusionary' by Mudde and Kaltwasser (2013) was firmly established in Western liberal democracies. In this kind of populism, a virtuous 'us'—

'the people'—are defined in opposition not only to populism's traditional foe—the 'elites'—but also against immigrants, asylum seekers and ethnic and religious minorities.

The electoral success of populist anti-immigration parties has raised fears regarding a global trend away from liberal democracy and towards anti-pluralism, authoritarianism, nationalism and even fascism. In this chapter, and in line with the central theme of this book, we ask whether New Zealand is an exception to, or another example of, such a trend. We acknowledge, however, the need for a much clearer definition of this 'trend' we are examining. After all, not all parties advocating a reduction in immigration are populists and not all populists are 'exclusionary', nativistic, authoritarian or right-wing (Norris & Inglehart, 2019). Therefore, our queries focus on whether New Zealand has experienced a phenomenon in which anti-immigration sentiment is both increasing and associated with support for populism of an 'exclusionary', authoritarian or nativistic variety.

Superficially, this inquiry might be dispensed with reasonably quickly—support for New Zealand's populist anti-immigration party, New Zealand First, dropped between 2014 (9 per cent) and 2017 (7.2 per cent). Further, as Chapter 3 reports, the New Zealand Election Study (NZES) data do not demonstrate a particularly strong appetite for authoritarian populism among New Zealand voters. Combined, these statistics would suggest that, in 2017, New Zealand presented a clear exception to the phenomenon of growing support for anti-immigration exclusionary populism. Yet, almost half of NZES respondents in 2017 wanted immigration levels reduced, there was a significant increase in the proportion for whom immigration was the most important issue at the polls between 2014 and 2017, and just over 20 per cent thought immigration posed a threat to New Zealand's culture. Further, in the context of record immigration numbers in the year ahead of the election, both major parties (Labour and National) and the Green Party proposed significant cuts to immigration, breaking these three parties' support, since the early 1990s, for existing immigration policies. Then, post election, Labour entered into a coalition with New Zealand First, a party that had campaigned strongly for major reductions in immigration. These developments present a contradictory picture of New Zealand. Was it an exception only in terms of levels of support for immigration reduction and populism, or was it also an exception in terms of the relationship between immigration sentiment, populism and authoritarianism?

Populism may, of course, take many different forms, including what Norris and Inglehart (2019) call 'authoritarian populism' (Golder, 2016; Mudde & Kaltwasser, 2013). In their formulation, authoritarian populism is characterised by use of populist rhetoric to pursue values emphasising conformity and loyalty to, and security of, one's group and its leader, even at the expense of individual and minority rights. Given their emphasis on cultural conformity, those who support authoritarian values might see immigrants, particularly those who differ ethnically, culturally or racially from the native population, as challenging existing cultural and social norms. Therefore, authoritarian–populist parties frequently frame immigration as a danger to local culture, values and social norms (Norris & Inglehart, 2019), resulting in the kind of exclusionary populism discussed earlier in this book. The research presented in Chapter 3 found that populism, authoritarianism, nativism, cultural conformity and opposition to immigration all form separate dimensions of public opinion in New Zealand.

Opposition to immigration may also be based on economic grounds, from those on both the left and right of the political spectrum. For example, those on the left who value economic equality may oppose immigration because, although immigration results in a larger economy, immigrants sometimes compete for jobs with less-skilled workers, whose real incomes are being eroded by automation and globalisation (Eatwell & Goodwin, 2018). Further, immigration can place pressure on a country's public services and infrastructure and increase demand for housing (Sharpe, 2019). When housing prices increase, existing homeowners benefit; however, those renting in the public and private sector, including the children of existing homeowners, face higher housing costs. Although immigration usually has only a minor effect on wages and housing costs (Cochrane & Poot, 2019; Edo, 2019), immigrants may be perceived as driving wages down and house prices up. Further, there sometimes exist incentives for left-wing parties to support the restriction of immigration, particularly when they face strong competition for working-class voters from an authoritarian populist party (Kosiara-Pedersen, 2019; Wagner & Meyer, 2016). Such parties may employ left-wing populist rhetoric to identify immigration as a threat posed by neoliberal business interests against the interests of both native and immigrant workers. By contrast, authoritarian populist parties may use exclusionary rhetoric to conflate what they identify as the cultural and economic threats posed by immigration.

In this chapter, we examine the relationship between attitudes towards immigration, populism and other aspects of public opinion, using longitudinal data from the NZES. We focus on the demand side of electoral politics—that is, the extent to which voters display a desire for restrictive immigration policies, as measured by public opinion and voting behaviour over the past six elections in New Zealand. We also draw on comparative data, where available, from electoral studies in Australia, the United Kingdom, Ireland and the United States.

Our key finding is that the desire for reduced immigration in New Zealand in 2017 was more commonly a left-wing populist phenomenon than an authoritarian–populist phenomenon. This is not to say that exclusionary populist and authoritarian values were not present among some of those who desired the reduction of immigration. They were present, particularly among New Zealand First voters; however, our analysis shows that concern regarding inequality and support for redistribution and trade unions better explain restrictive immigration attitudes than do exclusionary populist or authoritarian views.

Given that context helps shape whether and how populism arises and succeeds (Golder, 2016; Lees-Marshment, 2009) and that the 'supply' of different types of populism can help create and shape latent demand and meet existing demand for such populism, we begin our discussion with a brief overview of New Zealand's contemporary immigration experience, its specific electoral settings and the supply side of the anti-immigration–populism equation in New Zealand ahead of the 2017 election.

New Zealand's Immigration and Electoral Settings

Immigration is core to the human experience in New Zealand. Voyagers from Eastern Polynesia first settled the landmass they called Aotearoa at the end of the 13th century (Wilson, 2005), developing over time the culture, language and traditions now known as Māori. European settlers began arriving in significant numbers from the mid-19th century and, by as early as 1858, outnumbered Māori. Until the late 20th century, the population was overwhelmingly composed of the European or Pākehā majority, predominantly from the United Kingdom, and the Māori minority, now considered indigenous. Low numbers of migrants from

China, India, the former Yugoslavia, the Netherlands, Denmark and Poland also settled in New Zealand from the mid-19th century, joined from the 1950s onwards by people from the Pacific Islands—Samoa, Tonga, Fiji, the Cook Islands, Niue and Tokelau—many of whom were recruited to work in New Zealand's expanding post-war manufacturing industries. In the 1970s, New Zealand accepted several thousand refugees from Vietnam, Laos and Cambodia. For much of the post-war period, however, New Zealand operated a restrictive immigration policy, strictly linking immigration opportunities to gaps in the labour market and exercising a statutory preference for migrants from 'traditional source countries', meaning, primarily, the United Kingdom and northern Europe.

A review of immigration policy in 1987 led to the removal of this 'traditional source country' preference. In 1991, the introduction of a points-system immigration policy paved the way for a new era of immigration into New Zealand. Since 1991, New Zealand has experienced large-scale flows of immigration from new sources, most notably China, India and the Philippines. By 2018, a little over 27 per cent of New Zealand's population was born overseas (Statistics New Zealand, 2019), one of the highest rates among OECD countries.

Nevertheless, immigration has generally been of low electoral salience for most New Zealanders, despite New Zealand First's repeated attempts to make it an election issue since the party's formation (McMillan, 2005). The low electoral salience of immigration may be explained by several factors, including the country's long history of migration and settlement; the domination of skilled migration since the early 1990s; very low levels of illegal or irregular migration; New Zealand's geographical isolation and, hence, low threat perception; low unemployment; a dominant media and political narrative that immigration is crucial to New Zealand's economy; and, for most of the time since 1987, a bipartisan agreement between the two major parties that immigration was both desirable and manageable. The free-movement agreement that New Zealand has with Australia is likewise comparatively uncontroversial, largely because many more New Zealanders take advantage of this arrangement to live in Australia than the reverse. Refugee policies have been similarly uncontroversial. Indeed, the most recent (2018) refugee-related campaign in New Zealand argued, successfully, that New Zealand ought to increase the number of refugees it should accept each year (Doing our bit, 2018).

New Zealand's electoral settings also contribute to its immigration politics. Resident non-citizens have possessed national voting rights since the 1970s (Barker & McMillan, 2014) and the proportional electoral system has facilitated the representation of ethnic and immigrant minorities (McMillan, 2019). The enfranchisement of rapidly growing immigrant and ethnic minority populations has caused all major parties to expend considerable energy on wooing the Chinese, Indian, Pasifika and Filipino votes; alienation of these groups has the potential to inflict considerable electoral cost.

New Zealand's media landscape is also important, which, while highly commercialised and concentrated, does not include any locally produced 24-hour cable news networks. Such networks (e.g. FOX in the United States and SKY in Australia) tend towards highly combative and polarising programming that deliberately amplifies conservative populist politicians' exclusionary messages. News Corporation, which created both of those networks, in addition to owning various conservative newspapers in Australia, the United Kingdom and the United States, no longer has a stake in the New Zealand media market. Talkback radio in New Zealand tends to be right wing; however, no host can claim the influence of their counterparts in Australia and the United States. The territorial monopoly enjoyed by all the metropolitan newspapers has caused these titles to strive for internal diversity in an attempt to reach the largest possible audience. Crucially, all major newspapers, in addition to the websites of mainstream commercial broadcasters, have signed the Media Council's Statement of Principles, which requires signatories to be bound by principles of fairness, balance and accuracy, and provide that 'in articles of controversy or disagreement, a fair voice ... be given to the opposition view' (New Zealand Media Council, 2020). Broadcast media are statutorily bound to fairness, balance and accuracy by the 1989 *Broadcasting Act*. Audiences from both sides of the political spectrum will inevitably see partisan bias in New Zealand's news coverage. However, detailed content analysis of the three major metropolitan newspapers (*The NZ Herald*, *The Dominion Post* and the *Christchurch Press*) and the two main television channels (*TV ONE* and *TV3*), across three elections between 2008 and 2014, found no sustained bias towards for or against either of the two major parties (Bahador, Boyd & Roff, 2016).

Immigration and Party Positioning on Immigration in 2017

Net migration into New Zealand was at an all-time high during the year prior to the 2017 election, driven largely by New Zealanders returning from Australia following a downturn in the Australian economy but also by the number of people entering on temporary work visas (Statistics New Zealand, 2017). Net permanent and long-term migration had risen to 72,000 in June (1.2 per cent of New Zealand's total population of 4.5 million), 15 times the net migration of 4,700 when National had taken office nine years earlier (Barker, 2018).

Considerable media attention was given to this dramatic increase in migration (New Zealand Herald Business Desk, 2017; McKenzie, 2017; Rutherford, 2017; Tan, 2017). Media also reported on various forms of immigration fraud and immigrant exploitation. The high number of international student numbers in New Zealand's tertiary education sector, some of whom had been revealed to be on fraudulently acquired visas, also drew attention (Speedy & Bryant, 2016). Other international students were reportedly enrolled in sham or low-quality, non-university courses, only to access a post-study work visa in New Zealand (Laxon, 2016). Stories of migrant labour exploitation, particularly among international students seeking to transition to permanent visas, also began to emerge with greater frequency (Dozens of employers under Immigration NZ investigation for alleged immigration fraud, 2017; Tupou, 2017). This reporting followed in the wake of claims by New Zealand's trade union movement that migrants were being employed in industries such as farming and hospitality for less than the minimum wage, thus reducing wages for New Zealand workers (Concern over migrant 'exploitation' in Queenstown, 2015; Towle, 2016).

Simultaneously, media discourse increasingly linked record immigration with other salient concerns, such as growing inequality, homelessness, the unaffordability of housing and pressure on the country's social and roading infrastructure (Barker, 2018). Housing costs had increased for all income quintiles and, by 2017, had more than doubled (since 1990) as a percentage of household income for the lowest income quintile (Perry, 2019, p. 72). Indeed, by 2017, high housing costs meant that, despite wage increases, the median discretionary household income in some of New Zealand's fastest growing cities, including Auckland, Hamilton and

Tauranga, had fallen sharply over the previous few years (PWC, 2019). New Zealand now had the most unaffordable house prices in the world (Global House Prices, 2017). While the media and politicians also discussed other reasons for increased housing prices, such as restrictive planning laws and the absence of a capital gains tax (Schrader, 2018), the scene was set for immigration to become a major election issue.

Five months ahead of the September election, the National-led government proposed several changes to immigration policy: raising the salary cap needed for an applicant to qualify under the skilled migrant category, a three-year visa limit for lower-skilled workers and more restrictive rules for partners and children of migrants. These changes were marketed with the tagline 'Kiwis first' (McBeth, 2017) and were announced the day after the Australian Government declared it was 'putting Australians first' with changes to its visa system (specifically, 457 visas) (Kimmorley, 2017). In the context of Trump's pronouncement of an 'America First' foreign policy, this framing had clear populist resonances for those who wished to see them. However, following significant backlash from employer groups and farmers, National retreated on the more restrictive aspects of the proposals (Davison, 2017). The watered-down policy changes did more to restrict migrants' access to permanent status than reduce the number of people entering New Zealand (Collins, 2017). By the time the election campaign began, National was no longer discussing the need to decrease immigration. Rather, discussion of immigration policy was embedded within its broader narrative about wanting to keep New Zealand 'open', particularly for business (see e.g. Woodhouse, 2017).

National had governed during the previous term with support from three other parliamentary parties: the libertarian ACT Party, the Māori Party and centrist United Future. None of these parties proposed any restrictions on immigration ahead of the 2017 election. Indeed, ACT, United Future and the Māori Party competed on openness to immigration (Jones, 2017; Maori Party, 2017).

In contrast, Labour entered the election promising to 'take a breather' on immigration (New Zealand Labour Party, 2017), aiming to cut immigration by 20,000–30,000 people per year. This was to be achieved by removing work rights for international students not studying a university-level course and by 'making sure that work visas are not being abused to fill low-skill, low-paid jobs' (New Zealand Labour Party, 2017). It was these policy goals, developed in response to concerns regarding migrant and local labour exploitation and highlighted by Labour's traditional trade union base, that led some commentators to accuse Labour of 'choosing to play the anti-immigration card' (Campbell, 2017). The *Wall Street Journal* even compared Labour's leader, Jacinda Ardern, to Donald Trump on immigration (Pasley, 2017). Ardern vociferously rejected such comparisons (Burr & Gower, 2017) and Labour assiduously attempted to demonstrate that they were not anti-immigration. Their proposed policy changes were introduced with the statement that 'New Zealand is a country built on immigration. Migrants bring to New Zealand the skills we require to grow our economy and vibrant cultures that enrich our society' (New Zealand Labour Party, 2017), a refrain that prefaced all its speeches or public statements concerning immigration policy changes (McMillan, 2017b). Labour repeatedly attempted to emphasise its policies' continuity with New Zealand's post-1991 openness to immigration and the value that immigrants brought to the country, while simultaneously identifying the negative effects on housing, social services and infrastructure of existing levels and types of immigration:

> We have always welcomed migrants to our country and will continue to do so. But, in recent years, our population has been growing rapidly as record numbers of migrants arrive here … Labour will invest in housing, infrastructure, public services and in training New Zealanders to fill skills shortages. At the same time, we will take a breather on immigration. We will do this by making sure that work visas are not being abused to fill low-skill, low-paid jobs, while ensuring that businesses can get the skilled workers they need. (Labour Party of New Zealand, 2017)

In their speeches and press releases in the months leading up to the election, Labour avoided mentioning difficulties with immigrant acculturation, or employing other ethnically or religiously focused frames that might be understood as culturally exclusionary, at least according to the news reports of their speeches, campaign events and website (McMillan, 2017a). Regarding the immigration debate during the campaign, Deputy Labour Leader Grant Robertson said that 'Anyone who makes it about immigrants, or indeed about their race … must be called out for what they are doing as being wrong and against the values of Labour and of New Zealanders' (Edwards, 2017). This did not stop commentators in New Zealand accusing Labour of dog-whistling on immigration (Edwards, 2017; Jayasinghe & Ratnayake, 2017; Spoonley, 2017). These accusations were often made with reference to Labour's disastrous attempt in 2015 (under a different leader) to highlight the issue of foreign buyers speculating in the New Zealand housing market by identifying how many of those buyers had 'Chinese-sounding names' (McCrow-Young, 2017; Rutherford, 2015).

The Green Party was similarly concerned about the potential for their immigration policy to be perceived as xenophobic, in the context of anti-immigration politics internationally. In 2016, the party had suggested that New Zealand limit immigration so that population growth stayed within 1 per cent, citing concerns regarding New Zealand's capacity to grow more quickly than this. However, during the 2017 election campaign, Green co-leader James Shaw apologised to ethnic communities for his earlier comments, saying:

> Because the background terms of the debate are now so dominated by anti-immigrant rhetoric, when I dived into numbers and data, a lot of people interpreted that as pandering to the rhetoric, rather than trying to elevate the debate and pull it in a different direction. We were mortified by that because, in fact, the Greens have the ambition of being the most migrant-friendly party in parliament. And I am sorry for any effect it may have had on your communities. (James Shaw 'sorry' after immigration policy slammed as racist, 2017)

With Labour's proposals to cut immigration, New Zealand First no longer had sole ownership of the anti-immigration space. It continued, however, to distinguish itself from the other parliamentary parties' approach to immigration by its leader's willingness to criticise immigration and asylum policies on ethnic, religious and cultural grounds. Winston Peters' speech on 6 June 2017, given in parliament to mark terror attacks in London the previous week, was illustrative of the party's positioning on immigration vis-à-vis the other parties. In this speech, Peters suggested that the families of those who carried out the attacks would have known of the terrorists' intentions and kept silent. 'What is happening', he said:

> [Is] that families, friends, and confidants are choosing to turn the other cheek, choosing silence, rather than turn these monsters in. That may be the culture of Damascus, but it is not ours. It may be acceptable in Tripoli, but it most certainly is not acceptable in New Zealand. While the Islamic community must clean house by turning these monsters in, it starts with their own families. (2017)

The lesson for New Zealand, he argued, must be that:

> [It] avoid the same politically correct trap that has allowed such communities apart to form—that is, it is we who must change as a society, they say, to accommodate the cultural practices and traditions of others; that, in some twisted spirit of inclusiveness, it is we who must change, and not them. No longer. We must stop the slide—as a people, as a culture in the West, as people who believe in freedom and liberty, and, indeed, as a country—before we see in this country, in a New Zealand locality, a repeat of these events. (2017)

These comments are consistent with other comments Peters had made over the years (see e.g. Peters, 2005). Speeches made by the other parliamentary parties following the attacks, by contrast, emphasised unity and solidarity. National's Deputy Leader Paula Bennett condemned the attack, saying 'we stand united with London'.[1] The Labour Party's finance spokesperson, Grant Robertson, explicitly evoked solidarity with Muslim communities, saying:

> We should also show our support to the Muslim community here in New Zealand, who are as appalled and disgusted by the actions of these terrorists as anyone else. We can defeat these extremists through our unity, our acceptance of diversity, and our resolve to not allow hatred and intolerance to grow.

United Future's Peter Dunne also referenced the New Zealand Muslim community, who had, he said, come together the previous week to celebrate Ramadan 'in peace and goodwill and tolerance and openness'. We needed, he said, 'to be working with people of like mind to achieve positive outcomes, not simply fuelling the fires of bigotry'. Marama Fox, co-leader of the Māori Party, said 'the terrorists and extremists who perpetuated this despicable act seek to drive a wedge between communities, but they will not succeed, and now, like many times before in its history, London stands united against a threat'. James Shaw, co-leader of the Green Party, recalled earlier terrorist attacks in London, each of which he said had attempted to drive particular minority communities 'into the ocean', offering, instead, solidarity: 'To the mayor, Sadiq Khan, and to the people of London, we want to say: we are with you. Kia kaha (*Be strong)*'. ACT's David Seymour, perhaps more ambiguously, called out Peters'

1   All quotes responding to the Christchurch massacre are from New Zealand Government [*Hansard*] (2017), unless otherwise noted.

response as 'naked political opportunism', while also identifying a need for a 'wider and more serious debate about when and whether such an event can happen here … without naivety' (New Zealand Government [*Hansard*], 2017).

To summarise, in the year preceding the election, the four largest parliamentary parties—National, Labour, the Greens and New Zealand First—all proposed some restrictions on immigration. This presented a significant change from the historical bipartisan pro-immigration position held by both National and Labour. National demonstrated some willingness to engage in exclusionary populist language with its later-abandoned 'Kiwi-first' language; however, Labour and the Greens were anxious not to be seen as stirring the anti-immigration pot with exclusionary rhetoric, even as they proposed significant reductions to immigration. A clear distinction between rhetoric and policy is, of course, very difficult to maintain—a political party that identifies any aspect of immigration as problematic may be interpreted as being 'anti-immigration' or even 'anti-immigrant'. Aware of this, both Labour and the Green Party took pains to pre-empt such accusations by repeatedly stating their strong support for both immigration and immigrants, in addition to both explaining and criticising 'dog-whistle'-type anti-immigration tactics. Arguably (some alternative interpretations are reported below), the Labour Party's proposals for immigration restrictions may be read as a form of socio-economic populism (Kyle & Gultchin, 2018), in that they responded to public concerns regarding the labour market, economic and infrastructural consequences of immigration, while rejecting a cultural or 'exclusionary' form of populism (Golder, 2016; Mudde & Kaltwasser, 2013).

Data and Concepts

We used time series data from the NZES, between 2002 and 2017, using data collected after each three-yearly election. In 2017, the data were compiled from a random sample of 3,455 people on the New Zealand electoral roll. Surveys were posted to randomly selected, registered electors across New Zealand, immediately following each election. Questions focus on voting choices, political opinions and the social and demographic characteristics of respondents. New Zealand's indigenous

Māori population and young voters are usually oversampled, to ensure that the sample better matches New Zealand's population. Further, the data are weighted by gender, age, Māori ethnicity and how and whether people voted. NZES data are available for analysis and can be downloaded from the NZES webpage (www.nzes.org/exec/show/data).

Where available, comparative data from national election studies in the United Kingdom, United States, Australia and Ireland were used. We also used data from Module 5 of the Comparative Study of Electoral Systems (CSES), which focuses on measurements of populism. The NZES is involved in the CSES, which ensures some New Zealand questions on migration are the same as those asked in other countries.

New Zealanders' Attitudes towards Immigration

Various previous studies have examined New Zealanders' attitudes towards immigration and immigrants (Ipsos, 2018; Ward et al., 2011). Some have mapped New Zealanders' attitudes towards immigration to their electoral behaviour. For example, Vowles, Coffé and Curtin (2017) used NZES data to examine attitudes to immigration by party support in 2014, as did Crothers (2014) for the 2011 and 2014 general election, and Donovan and Redlawsk (2018) for the 1996 general election. Further, there exist numerous comparative studies of 'radical right-wing', 'right-wing' populism and generic populism, which include discussion of Winston Peters and the party he established and has led since 1993—New Zealand First (Betz, 2002; Betz & Johnson, 2004; DeAngelis, 1998; Denemark & Bowler, 2002; MacDonald, 2019; Moffit, 2017). We build on the work of Vowles et al. and Crothers to examine attitudes towards immigration and how this translated into voting behaviour in the 2017 New Zealand general election campaign.

We are particularly interested in whether New Zealand is becoming more opposed to immigration and if views on immigration and populism are connected. Our first query concerns New Zealanders' support for current levels of immigration over the past 15 years and how this compares to support in other Anglo-democracies. Figure 5.1 shows the percentage of people in New Zealand, Australia and the United Kingdom who think immigration should be reduced a little or a lot. In 2017, 48 per cent of New Zealanders wanted to see immigration into the country reduced either 'a lot' or 'a little'. This figure was up slightly, but not significantly, from 2014 (46 per cent) and 2011 (45 per cent), but down from 2008 (50 per cent). The statistically significant increase occurred between 2002 (35 per cent) and 2005 (46 per cent). New Zealanders' stable attitudes towards immigration over the 12 years between 2005 and 2017 is particularly notable in light of the 15-fold increase in net migration since 2008. Attitudes to levels of immigration in New Zealand were not dissimilar to those in Australia, where the desire to see migration reduced grew between 2004 and 2010, before falling between 2010 and 2013. A lower percentage of Australians (41 per cent) wanted to see immigration reduced in 2016 than did New Zealanders in 2017. Public opinion in the United Kingdom, by contrast, has been consistently in favour of reducing immigration, with 77–79 per cent wanting a reduction between 2003 and 2011, although that figure dropped to 69 per cent in 2015.

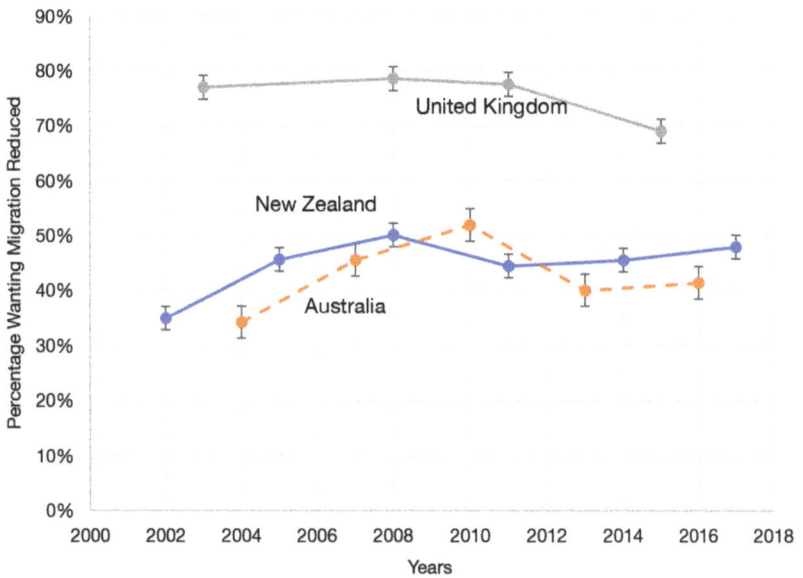

Figure 5.1: Percentage of people who want immigration reduced 'a lot' or 'a little' in New Zealand, Australia and the United Kingdom.

Source: Comparative Study of Electoral Systems (2019); New Zealand Election Study (2017).

The significance of levels of support for immigration is mediated by how important people consider the issue to be. Bartle et al. (2020) found believing immigration to be the most important issue facing their country was a significant indicator of support for authoritarian forms of populist attitudes in nine of 10 European countries (Bartle et al., 2020, p. 57). Thus, our second query concerns the salience of immigration over time in New Zealand and elsewhere, measured by responses to an open-ended question regarding the most important issue facing the country. Here, we see a significant change between 2014 and 2017 in New Zealand, with approximately 6 per cent of NZES respondents mentioning immigration or migration as part of their reply to this question, up from 1 per cent in 2014. The only time immigration has been of similar importance during the period covered was in 2005, when almost 4 per cent of respondents mentioned immigration or migration as part of their answer to the most important problem. However, even in 2017, immigration was much less important to voters than the economy, housing, health and inequality (see Chapter 2, Figure 2.2). The percentage of New Zealanders who thought immigration was the most important issue in 2017 was similar to that in Canada (2 per cent in 2015) and Australia in 2019, when 3 per cent of respondents to the Australian Election Study ranked immigration as their most important issue, although this rose to 6 per cent when combined with 'refugee and asylum-seekers' (Cameron & McAllister, 2019). Immigration was clearly a much less salient issue in either New Zealand or Australia than it was in the United Kingdom, where up to 40 per cent of voters rated it the most important issue in 2015 (Ipsos Mori, 2020). Immigration has increased in salience in the United States since the early 2010s and has become more important since Trump became President, with 23 per cent naming it their most important issue in 2019 (Jones, 2019).

Thus far, our analysis has shown that New Zealanders were less opposed to immigration than those in the United Kingdom and much less likely to think it was a highly important issue. We now investigate, in more detail, attitudes towards immigration: did people think it was good or bad for the economy, did they worry that it had harmful cultural effects (Malhotra, Margalit & Mo, 2013; Markaki & Longhi, 2013) and did they think immigration increased crime rates?

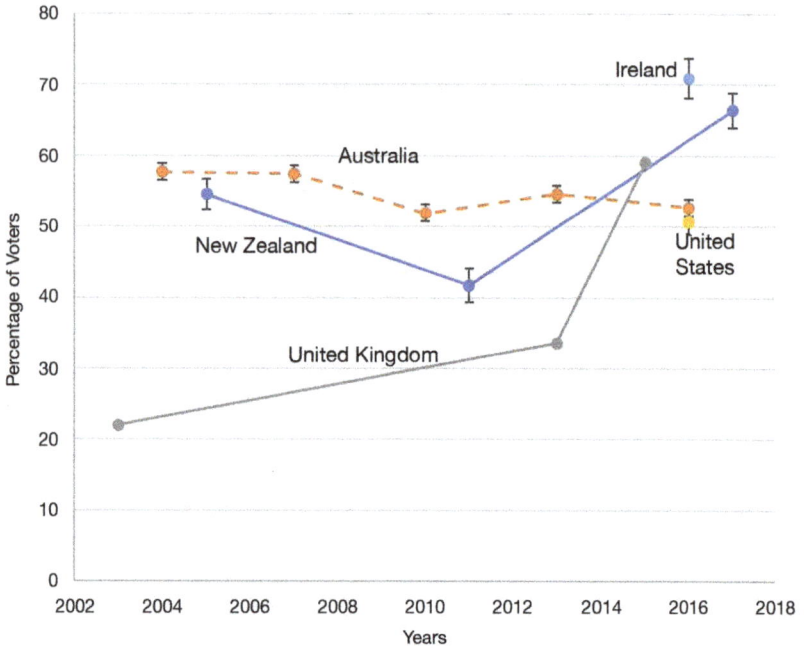

Figure 5.2: Percentage of voters who agree or strongly agree that immigration is good for the economy.

Source: Comparative Study of Electoral Systems (2019); New Zealand Election Study (2017).

Figure 5.2 shows that 66 per cent of New Zealanders in 2017 either agreed, or strongly agreed, with the statement that 'immigration is good for the economy'. This figure was up from both 2011 (42 per cent) and 2005 (55 per cent). The 2017 result for New Zealand overlaps with the confidence intervals for Ireland, where 71 per cent of people in 2016 thought migration was good for the economy. The majority of people in Australia, the United States and the United Kingdom also considered immigration to be good for the economy in recent elections; however, New Zealanders were significantly more likely to think this is the case than voters in those countries.

Views on whether migration is good for the economy are a strong predictor of the level of support people have for existing levels of migration (see Figure 5.3). Only approximately 21 per cent of the 16 per cent of New Zealanders who (in 2017) strongly agreed that migration was good for the economy were in favour of reducing migration 'a little' or 'a lot'. Indeed, people who strongly agreed that immigration is good for the economy were the only group who wanted immigration increased.

However, the 51 per cent of New Zealanders who simply agreed that migration had economic benefits and the 18 per cent of New Zealanders who were neutral or did not know were more than twice as likely to want migration reduced as those who strongly agreed that there are economic benefits. Even for the neutral group, the point estimate of 48 per cent meant than less than half of this group wanted migration reduced. In contrast, of the 12 per cent of New Zealanders who disagreed that migration had economic benefits, 83 per cent wanted migration reduced. Similarly, of the 3 per cent who strongly disagreed that migration had economic benefits, 89 per cent wanted migration reduced.

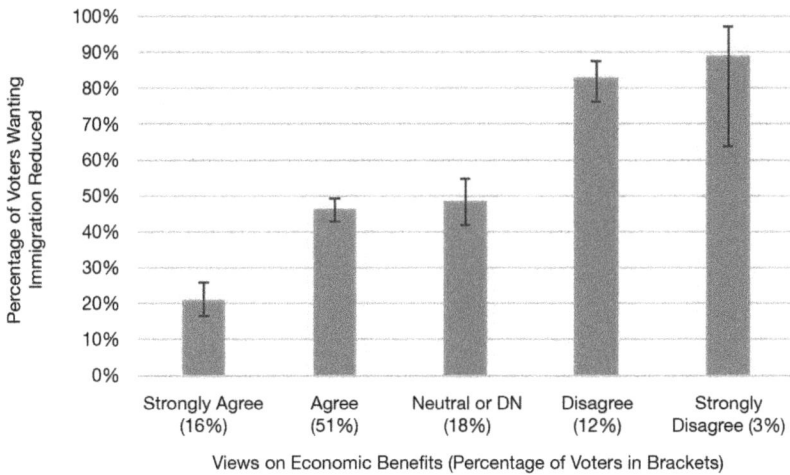

Figure 5.3: Percentage wanting immigration reduced by views on economic benefits.

Source: New Zealand Election Study (2017).

Our second, more detailed query, regarding attitudes towards immigration, asks whether people see immigration as a threat to culture. In 2017, when people were asked whether New Zealand culture is generally harmed by immigration, 5 per cent strongly agreed, 17 per cent agreed, 19 per cent were neutral or did not know, 34 per cent disagreed and 25 per cent strongly disagreed. People were less likely to think immigrants harmed New Zealand culture in 2017 than in 2011, 2008 or 2005 (see Figure 5.4). The percentage who saw migrants as a cultural threat was very similar to the percentage in Ireland and the United States. Equivalent questions have not been asked in Australia and in the United Kingdom.

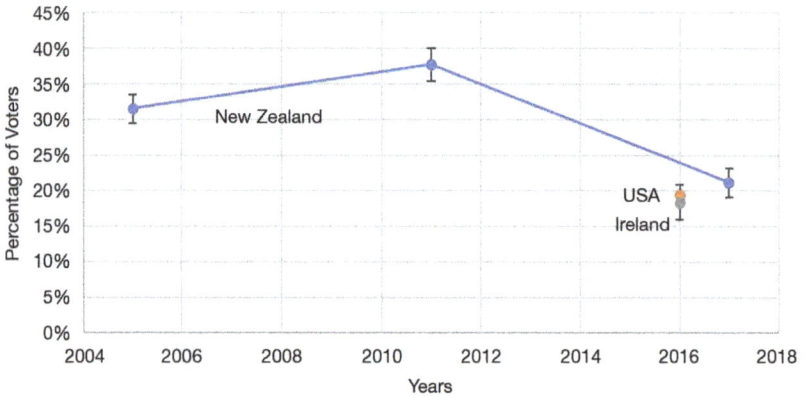

Figure 5.4: Percentage of voters who agree or strongly agree that migration is a threat to their country's culture.

Source: Comparative Study of Electoral Systems (2019); New Zealand Election Study (2017).

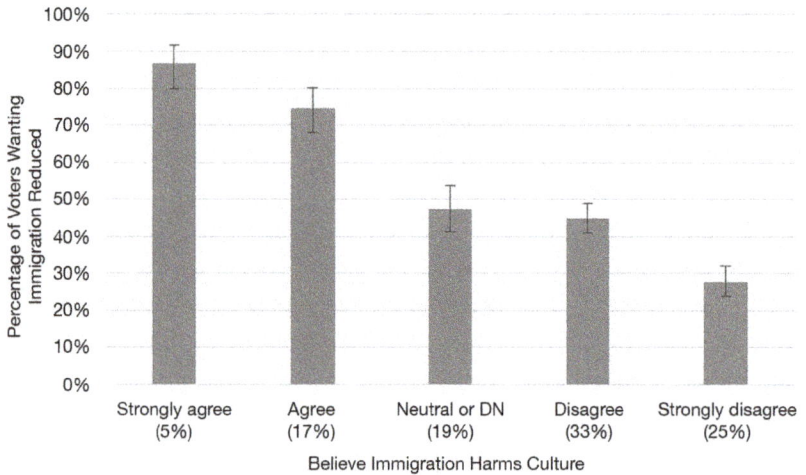

Figure 5.5: Percentage wanting immigration reduced by views on whether immigration harms culture.

Source: New Zealand Election Study (2017).

Unsurprisingly, New Zealanders who saw immigration as having negative cultural effects were those most strongly against increased immigration in 2017. Indeed, 87 per cent of the 5 per cent of New Zealanders who strongly agreed immigration had negative cultural effects wanted immigration reduced, while 75 per cent of the 17 per cent who agreed wanted immigration reduced (see Figure 5.5). Those who were neutral or disagreed that immigration had negative cultural consequences were relatively evenly divided on whether immigration should be reduced. In contrast, of the quarter of New Zealanders who strongly disagreed that migration had negative cultural effects, only 28 per cent wanted immigration reduced.

New Zealanders (15 per cent) were also much less likely than voters in the United States (28 per cent), Australia (33 per cent) and the United Kingdom (36 per cent) to think that immigrants increase crime (see Figure 5.6).

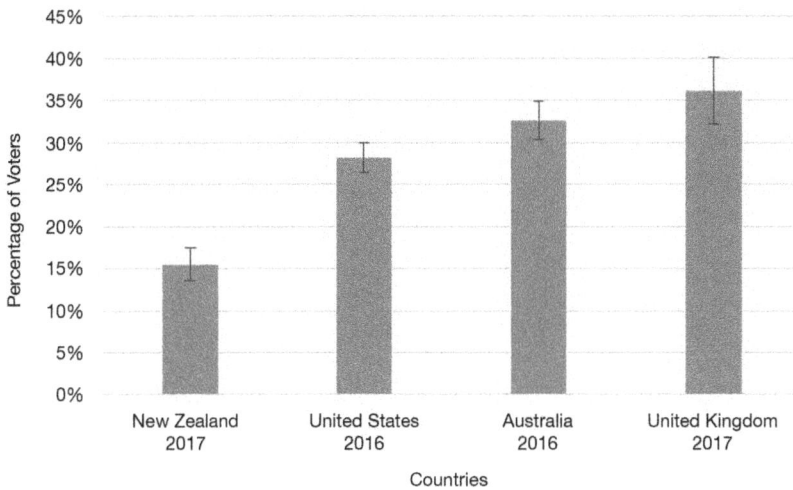

Figure 5.6: Percentage of voters who think immigrants increase crime rates.
Source: Comparative Study of Electoral Systems (2019); New Zealand Election Study (2017).

The data above provide some support for an 'exceptionalist' hypothesis; although just under half of New Zealanders wanted immigration reduced, this proportion had not increased significantly since 2005, even in the face of enormous increases in migration. Immigration had become more salient to New Zealanders, but only for a very low proportion of people, and was much, much less likely to be considered the most important issue than it was in the United Kingdom or the United States. In 2017, New Zealanders were also less likely to perceive immigrants as a threat to the economy or to law and order than people in Australia, the United Kingdom and the United States (at the time of their most recent elections). This suggests that New Zealand differs from each of these countries in terms of the demand for anti-immigration populism exhibited by its voters.

The next section seeks to understand whether the quality of anti-immigration sentiment is similar to that found in our comparator countries. Here, we are interested in whether the same kinds of variables help to explain New Zealanders' feelings regarding immigration as have been found to explain them elsewhere. We are also interested in how views regarding immigration interact with populism, authoritarianism and other aspects of public opinion. Using the measures of public opinion developed by Greaves and Vowles (see Chapter 3), we attempt to tease out opposition to current levels of immigration in New Zealand influenced by populist values (defined here by support for views that position 'the people' as the legitimate source of power, in contrast to 'elites') from those influenced by authoritarian values (defined by 'prioritising group cohesion and seeking collective security over individual and minority rights and freedoms') or nativism (understood here as 'in-group exclusivity') (Greaves & Vowles; see Chapter 3). Further, we investigate how views on left–right economic policy and trade unions affect attitudes towards immigration.

Attitudes towards Migration and Demographic and Educational Characteristics

Consistent with findings elsewhere (Card, Dustmann & Preston, 2005; Vowles et al., 2017), our analysis suggests that ethnicity, education levels, age, gender and income influence attitudes to immigration. To better understand the significance of each of these demographic factors, we used logistic regression (see Table A5.1) to test the relationship between support for reducing immigration (operationalised as indicating that immigration should be reduced a little or a lot); thinking immigrants are good for the economy, bad for New Zealand culture and cause crime (strongly agree, or slightly, for the latter three); and background characteristics. The background characteristics explain more of the variance in individual beliefs than for wanting to reduce immigration; however, all the results explain relatively little variance. Māori ethnicity was statistically significantly associated with wanting immigration reduced and thinking immigration was bad for New Zealand culture. The age and age squared variables were usually significant and work in opposite directions. The youngest voters are most in favour of immigration; opposition to immigration then increases with age, but at a decreasing rate. This also occurs in other countries and may reflect unmeasured cultural effects or perhaps older voters realising that, by increasing the size of the tax base, immigration improves the sustainability of New Zealand's universal superannuation scheme (O'Rourke & Sinnott, 2006, p. 850). Women were less likely to think immigration was bad for New Zealand culture or caused crime.

Those with a university degree were more positive regarding immigration, which frequently reflected cultural values and beliefs associated with higher education (Hainmueller & Hiscox, 2007, p. 399). People who believed they had good future economic prospects were more likely to think that immigration benefited the economy and to disagree with the idea that it threatened New Zealand culture. Despite rural areas economically benefiting from an inflow of farm workers, urban people were more likely to see immigration as having economic benefits. Those in public housing or living with relatives were less likely than other New Zealanders to believe immigration had economic benefits. National had reduced and more tightly targeted state housing entitlements while in government and people living in public housing may believe that immigrants, and particularly refugees, increase competition for public housing. Being part of a family that rented was associated with wanting immigration reduced, albeit at a 10 per cent level of statistical significance. For many in this group, achieving home ownership is an elusive goal and the 'perfect storm' of low outward immigration and high inward immigration between 2014 and 2017 had increased their housing costs (Cochrane & Poot, 2019, p. 16).

Attitudes towards Migration and Beliefs and Values

We now test the effects of populism and authoritarianism on wanting immigration reduced by adding control variables. By doing so, and as displayed in Figures 5.7 and 5.8, we find that neither populism nor authoritarianism have direct effects on immigration preferences. The effects of populism are channelled through 'immigration prejudice' (based on the three questions regarding effects on crime, culture and the economy) and socio-economic attitudes (principally, support for unions and income redistribution). By contrast, the effects of authoritarianism are channelled through immigration prejudice alone. Therefore, in Model 1, without controls, populism, authoritarianism and efficacy are all associated with wanting immigration reduced (see Table A5.2). The effects of populism on views regarding immigration are clearly not just a reflection of low efficacy, which is operationalised in terms of believing that voting and who is in power makes a difference. With controls for views on the effects of immigration on the economy, culture and crime, only populism and efficacy remain statistically significant in explaining opposition to immigration (Model 2). As Table A5.2 and Figures 5.7 and 5.8 show, the effects of populism have been more than halved, while the effects of authoritarianism are now a small fraction of their previous size, although the coefficient for efficacy has increased in size. Views regarding the effects of migrants on crime, culture and the economy more directly measure prejudice against immigrants than populism and authoritarianism.

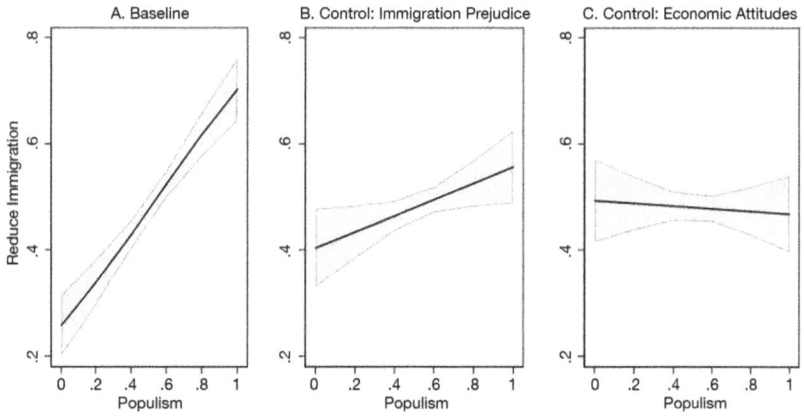

Figure 5.7: Decomposing the effects of populist attitudes on preference to reduce immigration.

Source: New Zealand Election Study (2017).

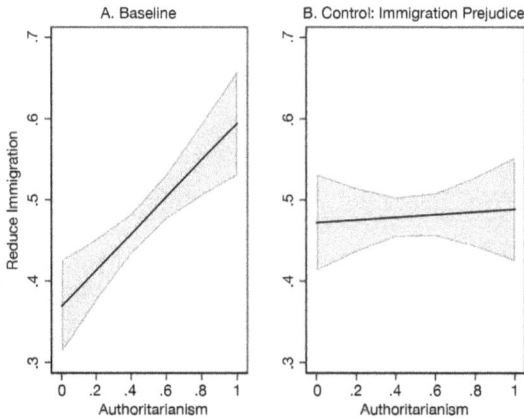

Figure 5.8: Decomposing the effects of authoritarian attitudes on preferences to reduce immigration.

Source: New Zealand Election Study (2017).

Adding variables for cultural conformity and nativism views reduces the size of the efficacy coefficient; however, the effects on the populism coefficient are minimal (see Table A5.2, Model 3). Cultural conformity has been constructed from variables for the importance of language and customs to being a New Zealander and is statistically significantly associated with wanting immigration reduced. Nativist views have been constructed from variables for the importance of being born in New Zealand, having grandparents born in New Zealand and Māori ancestry (see Chapter 3). Although nativist views are associated with wanting immigration reduced, the coefficient is small and not statistically significant when variables for specific views on immigration are included. When the variables for specific views on immigration were dropped (results not included here), the coefficient for nativism was larger and statistically significant.

With variables for views on union membership and economic inequality (see Table A5.2, Model 4), the effects of populism become negative; however, Figure 5.7 shows that the effects are no longer statistically significant. Authoritarianism is more strongly associated with wanting immigration reduced than in Models 2 and 3, but the effects are not statistically significant in Model 5 when cultural conformity and nativism are added back to the model (see Table A5.2). Conversely, efficacy, views on specific aspects of immigration, cultural conformity and left-wing views on union membership and inequality are all statistically significant predictors of wanting immigration reduced (see Figure 5.9). Indeed, opposition to immigration is better explained by specific views on immigration and left-wing economic views than by populist or authoritarian views. High immigration has been perceived by New Zealand's trade union movement as detrimental to the interests of workers, and voters who support trade unions tend to share this view. Similarly, reducing immigration seems to be perceived by some voters as another way of reducing income inequality in New Zealand. Those who want more public housing favour less immigration, probably because larger immigrant populations increase pressure on the state housing stock; however, the coefficient is not statistically significant. Other economic variables tried included opposing the Trans-Pacific Partnership Agreement, which garnered significant opposition among voters in New Zealand between the 2014 and 2017 elections (Thousands turn out to protest TPP, 2015).

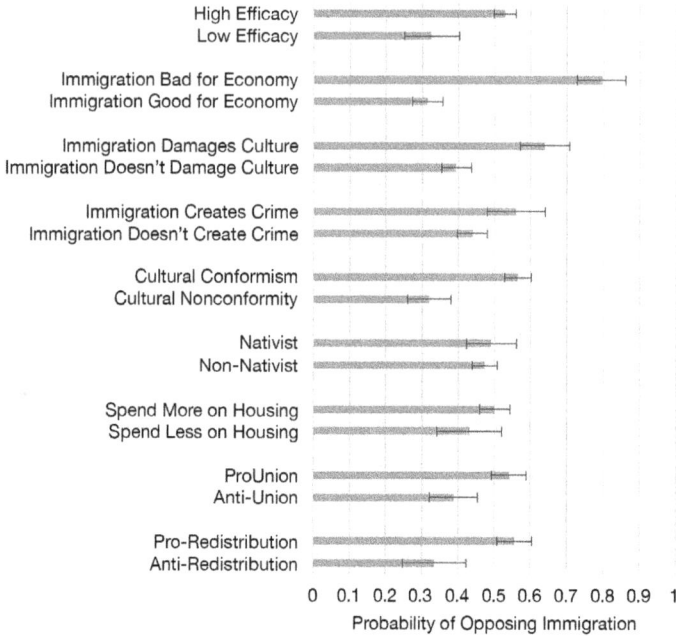

Figure 5.9: Probabilities of wanting migration reduced.
Source: New Zealand Election Study (2017) (see Table A5.2 [Model 5]).

Our findings in this section provide evidence both for and against the hypothesis that New Zealand is an exception to a trend towards exclusionary populist anti-immigration politics. Individual characteristics associated with wanting immigration reduced resemble those found in other research: being male, less educated, worried about future economic status and occupying rental housing all correlate with being more likely to want immigration reduced. However, the connection between wanting immigration reduced and populism or authoritarianism in New Zealand is weak; opposition to immigration tends to be driven by specific concerns regarding the economic, cultural and law and order effects of immigration (although, as we have seen, while the effects of these are strong, the number that think immigration is harmful is comparatively low). Opposition to current levels of immigration is also significantly related to concerns regarding inequality and support for organised labour, suggesting that wanting immigration reduced is sometimes more of a left-wing than a right-wing phenomenon in New Zealand. Notably, however, cultural conformism remains a significant predictor of wanting immigration reduced, as does political efficacy, both of which suggest some potential demand for culturally exclusionary forms of populism.

Party Support and Attitudes towards Immigration

Having examined some of the factors influencing voters' attitudes to immigration, we now turn to the question of how these attitudes relate to partisanship. In 2017, voters for the populist New Zealand First Party showed the strongest support for reducing migration (see Figure 5.10), with 84 per cent of its voters wanting immigration reduced a little or a lot. The 95 per cent confidence intervals for New Zealand First do not overlap with those for any other party. Voters for the Green Party were least likely to want immigration reduced, with just 35 per cent of its voters favouring a reduction. Although the point estimate for National was lower than for Labour, the difference was minor and the confidence intervals overlap.

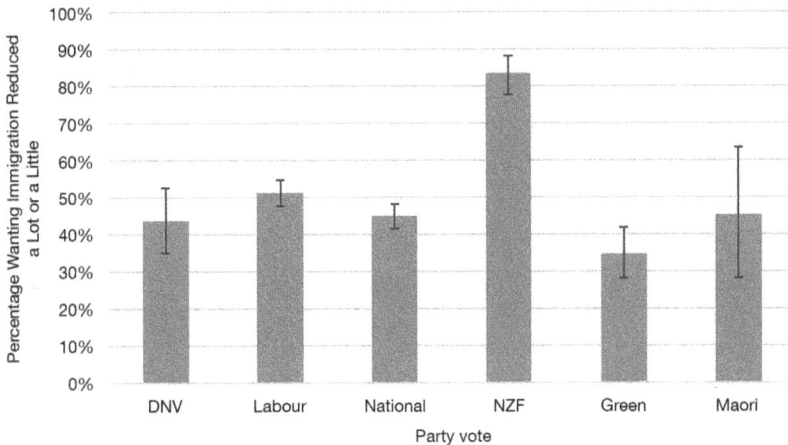

Figure 5.10: Percentage of voters wanting immigration reduced in 2017, by party vote.
Source: New Zealand Election Study (2017).

The results of other elections (see Figure 5.11) show that New Zealand First voters have shown consistently high support for wanting migration reduced a lot or a little. This has distinguished them from Labour Party and National Party voters, with the confidence intervals for New Zealand First voters never overlapping those for Labour and National voters. The point estimate for wanting migration reduced seems to have gradually increased for Labour voters over time, whereas it has trended downwards for National voters. However, the results for the two parties are similar. In addition to changes in the saliency of migration, shifts in party support mean that, at some elections shown here, parties have attracted different types of voters. Voters for the environmentalist Green Party have always been least in favour of reducing immigration. Those who have voted for the neoliberal ACT Party, which, due to falling support, are not included in the graphs, have also expressed low support for reducing immigration. Non-voters (also not shown) have, by contrast, sometimes wanted immigration reduced.

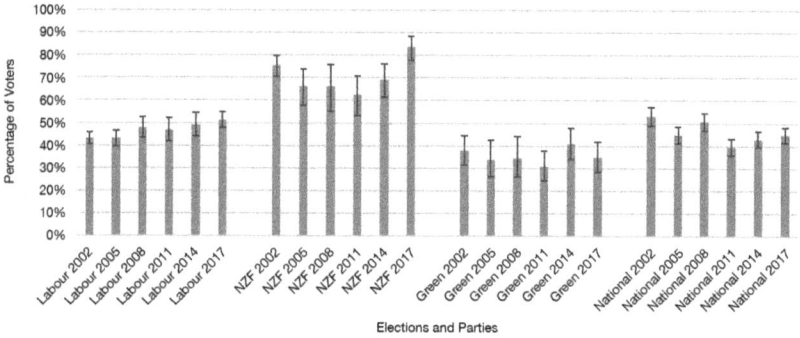

Figure 5.11: Percentage of voters wanting immigration reduced a lot or a little by party preference.
Source: New Zealand Election Study (2017).

We tested the association between people's votes and their views on immigration. With no controls, wanting lower immigration was associated with an increased probability of voting for New Zealand First rather than for National, to a lesser extent with voting for Labour rather than National and with a reduced chance of voting for the Green Party rather than National (see Table A5.3). With controls for populism, nativism, authoritarianism and a voter's left–right position added, wanting reduced immigration remained associated with voting for New Zealand First rather than National; however, the results for voting for Labour and the Green Party were no longer statistically significant (see Table A5.4). Controlling for views on immigration, populism and nativism both had statistically significant positive effects on people voting for New Zealand First, Labour and for being non-voters, rather than voting for National. Further, populism had statistically significant positive effects on whether people voted for the Green Party, rather than for National, while authoritarianism had significant negative effects on numbers voting for Labour and the Green Party rather than voting for National. The left–right control is significant for all parties, indicating the continuing significance of views regarding economic policy and redistribution on voting.

We then repeated the analysis, but with 'wanting to reduce immigration' supplemented with more specific variables regarding the effects of immigration on New Zealand's economy and culture (see Table A5.5). All four variables measuring views on immigration helped to explain voting for New Zealand First rather than National. After controlling for populism, nativism and authoritarianism, both wanting to reduce immigration and believing immigrants were bad for the economy were associated with voting for New Zealand First rather than National (see Table A5.6). Compared to those who voted for National, non-voters were also more likely to want to reduce immigration and believe that immigration was bad for the economy. Labour voters were less likely than National voters to believe that immigrants cause crime, although this variable was only significant at a 10 per cent level.

Discussion and Conclusion

Was New Zealand a 'populist exception' in 2017 in terms of immigration? On balance, we believe the results above indicate that it was, at least regarding exclusionary forms of anti-immigration populist rhetoric and policy. In terms of demand, a proportion of New Zealanders continued to respond positively to New Zealand First's brand of populism, however, that proportion has decreased rather than increased over the previous three years. In terms of supply, National, Labour, the Greens, ACT and the Māori Party all explicitly rejected rhetoric that stigmatised or sought to marginalise minorities and immigrants in 2017. This reduced the supply of anti-immigration exclusionary populism on offer for the nearly 50 per cent of New Zealanders who wanted immigration reduced.

None of this, however, is to suggest that right-wing, exclusionary or even authoritarian populism has no future in New Zealand. On the supply side, we may observe more players entering the immigration policy arena. New Zealand First's historical ownership of the immigration issue, which had been facilitated both by the bi-partisan support for immigration by the two major parties and by the absence of an anti-immigration party to the right of National, was challenged by National and Labour's willingness to debate immigration in 2017. While neither of the major parties seem likely to abandon their support for large-scale immigration, both offered more restrictive immigration policies in 2017. This could be read as evidence of those parties being subject to a 'contagion' effect (van Spanje, 2010) from New Zealand First, but might also be interpreted as both parties inoculating themselves and public discourse against such contagion by demonstrating receptivity to public concerns regarding immigration. After all, National and Labour have tended to exert a moderating influence on New Zealand First's approach to immigration during the periods in which they have relied on New Zealand First to govern.

However, it is not inconceivable that one or the other party will also begin to offer more exclusionary rhetoric when discussing immigration. National and ACT are both reported to have worked with political consulting firm Crosby Textor, credited with much of the Australian Liberal Party's anti-asylum rhetoric and policies and the British Conservative Party's anti-immigration messages since the early 2000s (Hager, 2006; Lees-Marshment, 2009). Under Don Brash's leadership (2003–2006), National demonstrated its willingness to engage in racially divisive campaigning when promising to deliver votes (Brash, 2004; Hager, 2006). Nor is it impossible that a political entrepreneur might see an opportunity in National's lack of a viable coalition partner and establish a populist, anti-immigration party to its right.

On the demand side, changes in New Zealand's immigration policy settings that have, over the last couple of decades, seen temporary migration heavily outweigh settler migration, may also alter the way that New Zealanders assess the economic, social and cultural costs and benefits of immigration. A growing under-class of immigrants who are denied access to permanent residency and, thus, to voting rights, whose vulnerable visa status makes them targets of exploitative employers and landlords, and who may compete with New Zealanders for unskilled work, has the potential to undermine New Zealanders' generally positive views regarding the economic and social effects of immigration. Unaffordable housing, growing inequality and the perception that immigrants are competing for low-skilled jobs are all variables that we have seen correlate with a desire to see immigration reduced and a growing electoral salience of immigration.

Some of the institutional settings that may have contributed to New Zealand's immigration politics to date are also under strain. Most significantly, social media and digital campaigning techniques have decreased the central role that the mainstream media have traditionally played in election campaigns. As discussed, New Zealand's mainstream print and broadcast media are, either voluntarily or by statute, committed to provide fair, balanced and accurate reportage on issues of public contention. Growing use of Facebook, YouTube, WhatsApp and any number of other social media will continue to undermine the ability of the mainstream media to authoritatively shape public debate in a way that conforms to the balance, fairness and accuracy requirements placed upon them. Similarly, the replacement of traditional mass election campaigning with digital campaign techniques involving highly targeted and temporary messages to individual voters, invisible to those to whom they are not targeted, has made exclusionary, populist politics both more feasible and more profitable for parties willing to engage in them.

Immigration has proved to be a particularly volatile addition to the alchemic electoral politics of democracies. Any combination of changes to the supply and demand variables identified above, or to the institutional and international settings within which they operate, has the potential to undermine New Zealand's status as a country that has largely avoided the most virulent strains of anti-immigration exclusionary populism.

References

Bahador, B., Boyd, M. & Roff, K. (2016). Media coverage of New Zealand elections: 2008–14. In G. Kemp, B. Bahador & C. Rudd (Eds), *Politics and the media* (2nd ed.) (pp. 201–218). Auckland, New Zealand: Auckland University Press.

Barker, F. (2018). Immigration and the Key-English government. In S. Levine (Ed.), *Stardust and substance: The New Zealand general election of 2017* (pp. 265–280). Wellington, New Zealand: Victoria University Press.

Barker, F. & McMillan, K. (2014). Constituting the democratic public: New Zealand's extension of national voting rights to non-citizens. *New Zealand Journal of Public & International Law, 12*(1), 61–80.

Bartle, J., Sanders, D. & Twyman, J. (2020). Authoritarian populist opinion in Europe. In I. Crewe and D. Sanders (Eds), *Authoritarian populism and liberal democracy* (pp. 49–71). Cham, Switzerland: Palgrave Macmillan. doi.org/10.1007/978-3-030-17997-7_4

British Broadcasting Corporation. (2019). *Europe and right-wing nationalism: A country by country guide.* Retrieved from www.bbc.com/news/world-europe-36130006

Betz, H.-G. (2002). Conditions favouring the success and failure of radical right-wing populist parties in contemporary democracies. In Y Mény & Y. Surel (Eds), *Democracies and the populist challenge* (pp. 197–212). London, United Kingdom: Palgrave Macmillan. doi.org/10.1057/9781403920072_11

Betz, H.-G. & Johnson, C. (2004). Against the current—Stemming the tide: The nostalgic ideology of the contemporary radical populist right. *Journal of Political Ideologies, 9*(3), 311–27. doi.org/10.1080/1356931042000263546

Brash, D. (2004, 28 January). Nationhood (Address to the Orewa Rotary Club). *New Zealand Herald.* Retrieved from www.nzherald.co.nz/treaty-of-waitangi/news/article.cfm?c_id=350&objectid=3545950

Burr, L. & Gower, P. (2017). Jacinda Ardern rejects Trump comparison in Wall St Journal. *Newshub.* Retrieved from www.newshub.co.nz/home/election/2017/09/jacinda-ardern-rejects-trump-comparison-in-wall-street-journal.html

Cameron, S. & McAllister, I. (2019). T*he 2019 Federal Election: Results from the Australian Election Study.* Canberra: ANU College of Arts & Social Sciences, School of Politics & International Relations. Retrieved from australianelectionstudy.org/wp-content/uploads/The-2019-Australian-Federal-Election-Results-from-the-Australian-Election-Study.pdf

Campbell, G. (2017). Gordon Campbell on Labour's anti-immigration gambit and Israel. *Blog.* Retrieved from werewolf.co.nz/2017/06/gordon-campbell-on-labours-anti-immigration-gambit-and-israel/

Card, D., Dustmann, C. & Preston, I. (2005). *Understanding attitudes to immigration: The migration and minority module of the first European Social Survey.* London, United Kingdom: University College. Retrieved from davidcard.berkeley.edu/papers/euroimmig.pdf

Cochrane, B. & Poot, J. (2019). *The effects of immigration on local housing markets.* Hamilton, New Zealand: University of Waikato. Retrieved from ideas.repec.org/p/wai/econwp/19-07.html

Collins, F. (2017). We are creating a guest-worker programme. *New Zealand Herald.* Retrieved from www.nzherald.co.nz/opinion/news/article.cfm?c_id=466&objectid=11841828

Comparative Study of Electoral Systems. (2019, 21 May). *CSES Module 5 First Advance Release* [dataset and documentation]. Ann Arbor, MI: CSES. doi.org/10.7804/cses.module5.2019-05-21

Concern over migrant 'exploitation' in Queenstown. (2015). *Television New Zealand.* Retrieved from www.tvnz.co.nz/one-news/new-zealand/concern-over-migrant-exploitation-in-queenstown-6249237

Crothers, C. (2014). Immigrants and voting in New Zealand. In J. Vowles (Ed.), *The new electoral politics in New Zealand: The significance of the 2011 election* (pp. 161–183). Wellington, New Zealand: Institute of Policy Studies.

Davison, I. (2017). Government to backtrack on immigration cuts. *New Zealand Herald*. Retrieved from www.nzherald.co.nz/business/news/article.cfm?c_id= 3&objectid=11894306

DeAngelis, R. (1998). Pauline Hanson's One Nation Party: Xenophobic populism compared. *Policy, Organisation and Society, 16*(1), 1–27. doi.org/10.1080/ 10349952.1998.11876687

Denemark, D. & Bowler, S. (2002). Minor parties and protest votes in Australia and New Zealand: Locating populist politics. *Electoral Studies, 21*, 47–67. doi.org/10.1016/S0261-3794(00)00034-2

Doing our bit. (2018). *Double the quota*. Retrieved from www.doingourbit.co.nz/

Donovan, T. & D. Redlawsk. (2018). Donald Trump and right-wing populists in comparative perspective. *Journal of Elections, Public Opinion and Parties, 28*(2), 190–207. doi.org/10.1080/17457289.2018.1441844

Dozens of employers under Immigration NZ investigation for alleged immigration fraud. (2017). *New Zealand Herald*. Retrieved from www.nzherald.co.nz/nz/ news/article.cfm?c_id=1&objectid=11876111

Eatwell, R. & Goodwin, M. (2018). *National populism: The revolt against liberal democracy*. London, United Kingdom: Pelican.

Edo, A. (2019). The impact of immigration on the labour market. *Journal of Economic Surveys, 33*(3), 922–948. doi.org/10.1111/joes.12300

Edwards, B. (2017). Labour's Goldilocks immigration policy. *New Zealand Herald*. Retrieved from www.nzherald.co.nz/nz/news/article.cfm?c_id=1& objectid=11875398

Global House Prices. (2017). *Economist, 422*(9031), 76.

Golder, M. (2016). Far right parties in Europe. *Annual Review of Political Science, 19*(1), 477–497. doi.org/10.1146/annurev-polisci-042814-012441

Hager, N. (2006). *The hollow men. A study in the politics of deception*. Nelson, New Zealand: Craig Potton.

Hainmueller, J. & Hiscox, M. J. (2007). Educated preferences: Explaining attitudes toward immigration in Europe. *International Organization, 61*(2), 399–442. doi.org/10.1017/s0020818307070142

Ipsos. (2018). What New Zealanders think of refugees and immigration. *Scoop*. Retrieved from www.scoop.co.nz/stories/PO1809/S00232/what-new-zealanders-think-of-refugees-and-immigration.htm

Ipsos Mori. (2020). *Issues Index: 2007 onwards*. doi.org/10.4135/9781473969490

James Shaw 'sorry' after immigration policy slammed as racist. (2017). *Newshub*. Retrieved from www.newshub.co.nz/home/politics/2017/07/james-shaw-sorry-after-immigration-policy-slammed-as-racist.html

Jayasinghe, P. & Ratnayake, S. (2017). *Migration, opportunity and betrayal: A personal retrospective*. Retrieved from www.pantograph-punch.com/post/migration-opportunity-betrayal-personal-retrospective

Jones, J. M. (2019). New high in U.S. Say immigration most important problem. *Gallup*. Retrieved from news.gallup.com/poll/259103/new-high-say-immigration-important-problem.aspx

Jones, N. (2017). Act's David Seymour condemns national for starting 'populist bidding war' on immigration. *New Zealand Herald*. Retrieved from www.nzherald.co.nz/business/news/article.cfm?c_id=3&objectid=11842659

Kimmorley, S. (2017). Malcolm Turnbull axes 457 visa program for skilled migration, saying he's 'putting Australians first'. *Business Insider*. Retrieved from www.businessinsider.com.au/turnbull-scraps-457-visas-for-skilled-workers-2017-4

Kosiara-Pedersen, K. (2019). Stronger core, weaker fringes: The Danish General Election 2019. *West European Politics*, 1–12. doi.org/10.1080/01402382.2019.1655920

Kyle, J. & Gultchin, L. (2018). *Populists in power around the world*. Retrieved from institute.global/insight/renewing-centre/populists-power-around-world

Labour Party of New Zealand. (2017). *Making immigration work for New Zealand*. Retrieved from www.labour.org.nz/immigration

Laxon, A. (2016). Student visa fraud: 'It's not about education'. *New Zealand Herald*. Retrieved from www.nzherald.co.nz/nz/news/article.cfm?c_id=1&objectid=11759352

Lees-Marshment, J. (2009). *Political marketing: Principles and applications*. London, United Kingdom: Routledge.

MacDonald, D. B. (2019). Between populism and pluralism: Winston Peters and the international relations of New Zealand First. In F. Stengel, D. MacDonald & D. Nabers (Eds), *Populism and world politics. Global political sociology* (pp. 227–247). Cham, Switzerland: Palgrave Macmillan. doi.org/10.1007/978-3-030-04621-7_9

Malhotra, N., Margalit, Y. & Mo, C. H. (2013). Economic explanations for opposition to immigration: Distinguishing between prevalence and conditional impact. *American Journal of Political Science, 57*(2), 391–410. doi.org/10.1111/ajps.12012

Maori Party. (2017). *Immigration policy.* Retrieved from www.maoriparty.org/immigration_policy_2017

Markaki, Y. & Longhi, S. (2013). What determines attitudes to immigration in European countries? An analysis at the regional level. *Migration Studies, 1*(3), 311–337. doi.org/10.1093/migration/mnt015

McBeth, P. (2017). Woodhouse unveils 'Kiwi First' immigration policy with new work visa rules. *National Business Review.* Retrieved from www.nbr.co.nz/article/woodhouse-unveils-kiwis-first-immigration-policy-new-work-visa-rules-b-202034

McCrow-Young, A. (2017). Why I really want to vote Labour but can't. *The Spinoff.* Retrieved from thespinoff.co.nz/politics/12-09-2017/why-i-really-want-to-vote-labour-but-i-cant/

McKenzie, D. (2017). Migration hits 72,000. *Otago Daily Times.* Retrieved from www.odt.co.nz/business/migration-hits-72000-0

McMillan, K. (2005). Immigration, nationalism and citizenship debates in the 1990s. In A. Trlin, P. Spoonley & N. Watts (Eds), *New Zealand and international migration: A digest and bibliography* (pp. 70–85). Palmerston North, New Zealand: Massey University.

McMillan, K. (2017a). *Oppose, deflect, defuse, adopt? Framing immigration in the main parties. 2017 campaign speeches and press releases.* Wellington, New Zealand: Victoria University Press.

McMillan, K. (2017b, November). *Samuel Drew Lecture: Where people settle, legends unfold: Immigration and electoral politics in Aotearoa/New Zealand* (Paper presentation). Whanganui Regional Museum.

McMillan, K. (2019). The intersecting electoral politics of immigration and inequality in Aotearoa/New Zealand. In R. Simon-Kumar, F. L. Collins and W. Friesen (Eds), *Intersections of inequality, migration and diversification: The politics of mobility in Aorearoa/New Zealand* (pp. 87–108). Cham, Switzerland: Palgrave Macmillan. doi.org/10.1007/978-3-030-19099-6_5

Moffit, B. (2017). Populism in Australia and New Zealand. In C. R. Kaltwasser, P. A. Taggart, P. O. Espejo & P. Ostiguy (Eds), *The Oxford handbook of populism* (pp. 1–21). Oxford, United Kingdom: Oxford University Press. doi.org/10.1093/oxfordhb/9780198803560.013.5

Mudde, C. & Kaltwasser, C. R. (2013). Exclusionary vs. inclusionary populism: Comparing contemporary Europe and Latin America. *Government and Opposition, 48*(2), 147–174. doi.org/10.1017/gov.2012.11

New Zealand Election Study. (2017). *New Zealand Election Study* [dataset]. Retrieved from www.nzes.org/exec/show/data

New Zealand Government [*Hansard*]. (2017). *New Zealand Parliamentary Debates, official Hansard.* Retrieved from www.parliament.nz/resource/en-NZ/HansD_20170606_20170606/40bc87c280d0a0c01e84975a38087 1195be05d33

New Zealand Herald Business Desk. (2017, 21 August). New Zealand migration hits new record in July, despite more Kiwis leaving. *New Zealand Herald.* Retrieved from www.nzherald.co.nz/business/news/article.cfm?c_id=3& objectid=11908114

New Zealand Labour Party. (2017). *Immigration.* Retrieved from www.labour. org.nz/immigration

New Zealand Media Council. (2020). *Statement of principles.* Wellington, New Zealand: New Zealand Media Council. Retrieved from www.mediacouncil. org.nz/principles

Norris, P. & Inglehart, R. (2019). *Cultural backlash: Trump, Brexit and authoritarian populism.* Cambridge, United Kingdom: Cambridge University Press. doi.org/10.1017/9781108595841

O'Rourke, K. H. & Sinnott, R. (2006). The determinants of individual attitudes towards immigration. *European Journal of Political Economy, 22*(4), 838–861. doi.org/10.1016/j.ejpoleco.2005.10.005

Pasley, J. (2017). Wall Street Journal compares Labour's leader Jacinda Ardern to Donald Trump. *Stuff.* Retrieved from www.stuff.co.nz/national/politics/ 96519787/wall-street-journal-compares-labour-leader-jacinda-ardern-to-donald-trump

Perry, B. (2019). *Household incomes in New Zealand: Trends in inequality and hardship 1982 to 2018*. Wellington, New Zealand: Ministry of Social Development.

Peters, W. (2005). The end of tolerance. Speech to Far North Grey Power. *Scoop*. Retrieved from www.scoop.co.nz/stories/PA0507/S00649.htm

PWC. (2019). *Competitive cities: A decade of shifting fortunes*. Auckland, New Zealand: PWC New Zealand. Retrieved from www.pwc.co.nz/publications/2019/citiesinstitute/cities-urban-competitivesness-tech-report-4.0.pdf

Rutherford, H. (2015). Could the Chinese-sounding names stunt be Labour's Orewa? *Stuff*. Retrieved from www.stuff.co.nz/national/politics/70225493/

Rutherford, H. (2017). NZ's net migration gain still at record highs near 72,000 as numbers continue to climb. *Stuff*. Retrieved from www.stuff.co.nz/business/91921252/net-migration-gain-near-72000-as-arrivals-continue-to-climb

Schrader, B. (2018). Crisis? What crisis? An overview of the fifth National Government's housing policies. In S. Levine (Ed.), *Stardust and substance: The New Zealand general election of 2017* (pp. 281–295). Wellington, New Zealand: Victoria University Press.

Sharpe, J. (2019). Re-evaluating the impact of immigration on the US rental housing market. *Journal of Urban Economics, 111*, 14–34. doi.org/10.1016/j.jue.2019.04.001

Speedy, E. & Bryant, R. (2016). Widespread fraud found among education agents representing Indian students. *Stuff*. www.stuff.co.nz/national/education/81386128/widespread-fraud-found-among-education-agencies-representing-indian-students

Spoonley, P. (2017). Opinion immigration—Here we go again. *Massey University News*. Retrieved from www.massey.ac.nz/massey/about-massey/news/article.cfm?mnarticle_uuid=94140180-EACD-165C-A5F8-CB83EFF319CA

Statistics New Zealand. (2017). *Annual net gain reaches a record 72,400*. Retrieved from archive.stats.govt.nz/browse_for_stats/population/Migration/IntTravelAndMigration_MRJul17.aspx

Statistics New Zealand. (2019). *Birthplace and people born overseas*. Retrieved from archive.stats.govt.nz/Census/2013-census/profile-and-summary-reports/quickstats-culture-identity/birthplace.aspx

Tan, L. (2017). New Zealand migration at new record highs, arrivals on the rise. *New Zealand Herald*. Retrieved from www.nzherald.co.nz/nz/news/article.cfm?c_id=1&objectid=11845494

Thousands turn out to protest TPP. (2015, 15 August). *Radio New Zealand.* Retrieved from www.rnz.co.nz/news/political/281466/thousands-turn-out-to-protest-tpp

Towle, M. (2016). Government happy with farm conditions monitoring. *Radio New Zealand.* Retrieved from www.rnz.co.nz/news/national/293902/govt-happy-with-farm-conditions-monitoring

Tupou, L. (2017). Migrant worker describes 'modern day slavery' scam. *Radio New Zealand.* Retrieved from www.rnz.co.nz/news/national/339373/migrant-worker-describes-modern-day-slavery-scam

van Spanje, J. (2010). Contagious parties: Anti-immigration parties and their impact on other parties—Immigration stances in contemporary Western Europe. *Party Politics, 16*(5), 563–86. doi.org/10.1177/1354068809346002

Vowles, J, Coffé, H. & Curtin, J. (2017). *A bark but no bite: Inequality and the 2014 New Zealand general election* (pp. 165–188). Canberra, Australia: ANU Press. doi.org/10.22459/BBNB.08.2017

Wagner, M. & Meyer, T. M. (2016). The radical right as niche parties? The ideological landscape of party systems in Western Europe, 1980–2014. *Political Studies, 65*(1, Suppl.), 84–107. doi.org/10.1177/0032321716639065

Ward, C., Masgoret, A-M. & Vauclair, M. (2011). *Attitudes towards immigrants and immigrants' experiences: Predictive models based on regional characteristics.* Wellington, New Zealand: New Zealand Department of Labour.

Wilson, J. (2005). *History—Māori arrival and settlement.* Retrieved from www.TeAra.govt.nz/en/history/page-1

Woodhouse, M. (2017). *Speech outlining the Government's plans for immigration.* Retrieved from www.national.org.nz/speech_outlining_the_government_s_plan_for_immigration

Appendices

Table A5.1: The social and demographic correlates of immigration opinion

Variables	Model			
	(1) Reduce immigration	(2) Immigrants good Economy	(3) Immigrants bad New Zealand culture	(4) Immigrants cause crime
Māori (European)	0.388**	−0.205	0.536***	0.171
	(0.161)	(0.162)	(0.167)	(0.201)
Pasifika (European)	0.195	0.703	0.0311	0.758*
	(0.401)	(0.514)	(0.473)	(0.447)
Asian (European)	−0.255	1.155***	−0.740**	−0.675*
	(0.276)	(0.349)	(0.350)	(0.363)
Other (European)	−1.217		0.350	−0.555
	(0.785)		(0.759)	(1.181)
Age	0.0539***	−0.0448*	0.0441*	0.0531*
	(0.0203)	(0.0231)	(0.0261)	(0.0271)
Age squared	−0.000426**	0.000636***	−0.000364	−0.000486**
	(0.000187)	(0.000215)	(0.000255)	(0.000245)
Female	−0.185*	0.0420	−0.452***	−0.491***
	(0.104)	(0.118)	(0.131)	(0.152)
School qualification	−0.317**	0.139	−0.218	−0.528***
	(0.160)	(0.176)	(0.178)	(0.204)
Tertiary qualification	−0.165	0.0905	−0.394**	−0.460**
	(0.168)	(0.184)	(0.183)	(0.206)
University degree	−0.372**	0.667***	−0.648***	−1.548***
	(0.171)	(0.192)	(0.211)	(0.266)
Income quintile	−0.0926**	0.0372	−0.193***	−0.187**
	(0.0452)	(0.0509)	(0.0552)	(0.0745)
Future prospects	−0.148*	0.538***	−0.243**	−0.146
	(0.0863)	(0.0958)	(0.108)	(0.137)
Urban	0.0267	0.263**	0.189	−0.0196
	(0.114)	(0.130)	(0.138)	(0.159)
Own home with mortgage	0.121	−0.174	0.268	−0.0767
	(0.137)	(0.156)	(0.208)	(0.226)

Variables	Model			
	(1) Reduce immigration	(2) Immigrants good Economy	(3) Immigrants bad New Zealand culture	(4) Immigrants cause crime
Family renting	0.333*	−0.235	0.671***	0.394
	(0.200)	(0.213)	(0.257)	(0.301)
Public housing	−0.203	−1.734***	0.810**	0.684*
	(0.317)	(0.296)	(0.348)	(0.386)
Board or hostel	0.561	−0.554	0.831**	0.428
	(0.369)	(0.448)	(0.391)	(0.503)
Flatting with friends	−0.219	−0.229	0.437	−0.0729
	(0.336)	(0.379)	(0.386)	(0.501)
Live with family members	0.236	−0.742***	0.371	0.153
	(0.275)	(0.280)	(0.311)	(0.425)
Constant	−0.830	0.0420	−1.568**	−1.587*
	(0.633)	(0.723)	(0.726)	(0.914)
Observations	3,270	3,258	3,270	3,270
Pseudo R-squared	0.0353	0.0895	0.0700	0.0917

Note: Robust standard errors in parentheses.
*** $p < 0.01$, ** $p < 0.05$, * $p < 0.1$.
Source: New Zealand Election Study (2017).

Table A5.2: Attitudinal correlates of preferences to reduce immigration or not

Variables	Model				
	(1) Reduce immigration	(2) Reduce immigration	(3) Reduce immigration	(4) Reduce immigration	(5) Reduce immigration
Populism	1.961***	0.734**	0.696**	−0.125	−0.0851
	(0.287)	(0.335)	(0.341)	(0.370)	(0.381)
Authoritarianism	0.952***	0.0798	−0.191	0.757**	0.437
	(0.248)	(0.283)	(0.284)	(0.318)	(0.318)
Efficacy	0.890***	1.418***	1.184***	1.268***	1.062***
	(0.244)	(0.271)	(0.267)	(0.273)	(0.272)
Good for economy		−0.574***	−0.608***	−0.575***	−0.605***
		(0.0746)	(0.0769)	(0.0761)	(0.0783)
Bad for culture		0.339***	0.289***	0.343***	0.295***
		(0.0630)	(0.0606)	(0.0612)	(0.0597)

Variables	Model				
	(1) Reduce immigration	(2) Reduce immigration	(3) Reduce immigration	(4) Reduce immigration	(5) Reduce immigration
Bad for crime		0.142**	0.129*	0.165**	0.151**
		(0.0692)	(0.0693)	(0.0694)	(0.0699)
Spend more housing				0.0958	0.0886
				(0.0801)	(0.0805)
Support unions				0.800***	0.784***
				(0.289)	(0.285)
Support redistribution				1.279***	1.134***
				(0.354)	(0.354)
Cultural conformity			1.327***		1.235***
			(0.229)		(0.230)
Nativism			0.0774		0.0923
			(0.227)		(0.234)
Constant	−2.238***	−0.637	−0.937**	−2.088***	−2.256***
	(0.252)	(0.424)	(0.426)	(0.484)	(0.478)
Pseudo-R squared	0.0394	0.1353	0.1537	0.1513	0.1670
Observations	3,455.000	3,455.000	3,455.000	3,455.000	3,455.000

Note: Robust standard errors in parentheses.
*** $p < 0.01$, ** $p < 0.05$, * $p < 0.1$.
Source: New Zealand Election Study (2017).

Table A5.3: Immigration opinion and the party vote without attitudinal controls

Variables	Model				
	(1) Nonvote	(2) Labour	(4) Green	(5) NZ_First	(6) Other
Reduce immigration	−0.050	0.255**	−0.425**	1.831***	−0.036
	(0.194)	(0.099)	(0.169)	(0.206)	(0.161)
Constant	−0.483***	−0.309***	−1.790***	−3.031***	−1.490***
	(0.131)	(0.070)	(0.104)	(0.180)	(0.108)
Observations	3,438.00	3,438.00	3,438.00	3,438.00	3,438.00

Note: Robust standard errors in parentheses.
*** $p < 0.01$, ** $p < 0.05$, * $p < 0.1$, Pseudo R2 0.0123.
Source: New Zealand Election Study (2017).

Table A5.4: Immigration and the party vote with attitudinal controls

Variables	Model				
	(1) Nonvote	(2) Labour	(3) Green	(4) NZ_First	(5) Other
Reduce immigration	−0.234	0.180	−0.150	1.597***	−0.059
	(0.199)	(0.134)	(0.207)	(0.220)	(0.171)
Populism	3.272***	3.938***	2.040***	3.627***	3.199***
	(0.728)	(0.476)	(0.760)	(0.624)	(0.555)
Nativism	1.069***	0.742***	0.458	0.748**	0.232
	(0.400)	(0.273)	(0.409)	(0.325)	(0.328)
Authoritarianism	−0.752	−2.127***	−5.103***	0.219	−2.317***
	(0.574)	(0.426)	(0.624)	(0.621)	(0.470)
Left-right	−0.391***	−0.717***	−0.915***	−0.323***	−0.295***
	(0.061)	(0.061)	(0.072)	(0.052)	(0.045)
Constant	0.351	2.401***	3.569***	−3.146***	−0.143
	(0.463)	(0.363)	(0.424)	(0.417)	(0.338)
Observations	3,438.000	3,438.000	3,438.000	3,438.000	3,438.000

Note: Robust standard errors in parentheses.
*** $p < 0.01$, ** $p < 0.05$, * $p < 0.1$, Pseudo R-squared 0.1550.
Source: New Zealand Election Study (2017).

Table A5.5: Components of immigration attitudes and the party vote

Variables	Model				
	(1) Nonvote	(2) Labour	(4) Green	(5) NZ_First	(6) Other
Reduce immigration	−0.452**	0.169	−0.308*	1.411***	−0.227
	(0.220)	(0.105)	(0.169)	(0.223)	(0.172)
Immigrants good economy	−1.327***	−0.556***	−0.556***	−0.734***	−0.757***
	(0.221)	(0.118)	(0.188)	(0.190)	(0.176)
Immigrants bad culture	0.290	0.209	−0.665**	0.592***	0.174
	(0.280)	(0.151)	(0.292)	(0.217)	(0.194)
Immigrants cause crime	0.147	−0.451**	−1.088***	0.474**	−0.025
	(0.301)	(0.182)	(0.373)	(0.216)	(0.226)
Constant	0.471**	0.156	−1.256***	−2.562***	−0.894***
	(0.215)	(0.121)	(0.177)	(0.233)	(0.176)
Observations	3,438.000	3,438.000	3,438.000	3,438.000	3,438.000

Note: Robust standard errors in parentheses.
*** $p < 0.01$, ** $p < 0.05$, * $p < 0.1$, Pseudo R-squared 0.0365.
Source: New Zealand Election Study (2017).

Table A5.6: Populism, nativism, authoritarianism, components of immigration opinion and the party vote

Variables	Model				
	(1) **Nonvote**	**(2)** **Labour**	**(4)** **Green**	**(5)** **NZ_First**	**(6)** **Other**
Reduce immigration	−0.449**	0.200	−0.135	1.394***	−0.180
	(0.224)	(0.138)	(0.209)	(0.231)	(0.178)
Immigrants good economy	−0.976***	−0.073	−0.224	−0.467**	−0.448**
	(0.229)	(0.149)	(0.236)	(0.195)	(0.182)
Immigrants bad culture	0.162	0.192	−0.172	0.449*	0.258
	(0.285)	(0.205)	(0.370)	(0.234)	(0.213)
Immigrants bad crime	0.046	−0.460*	−0.445	0.278	0.065
	(0.300)	(0.253)	(0.442)	(0.245)	(0.248)
Populism	2.786***	4.047***	2.058***	3.072***	2.907***
	(0.722)	(0.479)	(0.762)	(0.617)	(0.576)
Nativism	0.847**	0.748***	0.516	0.425	0.068
	(0.405)	(0.283)	(0.417)	(0.353)	(0.337)
Authoritarianism	−0.730	−2.097***	−4.978***	−0.077	−2.377***
	(0.591)	(0.419)	(0.623)	(0.618)	(0.467)
Left-right	−0.375***	−0.705***	−0.905***	−0.315***	−0.287***
	(0.064)	(0.060)	(0.072)	(0.053)	(0.045)
Constant	1.241**	2.332***	3.653***	−2.387***	0.337
	(0.518)	(0.399)	(0.491)	(0.478)	(0.391)
Observations	3,438.000	3,438.000	3,438.000	3,438.000	3,438.000

Note: Robust standard errors in parentheses.

*** $p < 0.01$, ** $p < 0.05$, * $p < 0.1$, Pseudo R-squared 0.1672.

Source: New Zealand Election Study (2017).

6

GENDER, POPULISM AND JACINDA ARDERN

Jennifer Curtin and Lara Greaves

When Jacinda Ardern became New Zealand's third woman prime minister in October 2017, this occurred in a most unusual way. Labour came second in vote share; however, Ardern negotiated a three-party, coalition-support agreement that spanned the political spectrum from the conservative centre to the progressive left. In a sense, this constituted New Zealand's 'Borgen' moment—a reference to the Danish political drama in which the female leader of a small centrist party finds herself as a compromise candidate for the role of prime minister following a closely fought general election. While the Labour Party is not a small party, and New Zealand's mixed member proportional system theoretically has always held the potential for any leader to marshal sufficient support to form a government, the result was highly unexpected and deemed illegitimate by some on the right side of the spectrum.

In fact, Jacinda Ardern challenged several traditional political sensibilities. She was elected to the Labour leadership in a unanimous ballot just seven weeks prior to the 2017 election, pulling Labour up from opinion poll ratings of 24 per cent to a polling day vote share of 37 per cent. After becoming New Zealand's second-youngest prime minister, she went on to become only the second prime minister in the world to give birth while in office (in July 2018). Later that year, she became the first political leader to have her baby accompany her on the floor of the UN General Assembly. In March 2019, she responded to the Christchurch massacre with words of sorrow and compassion that resonated with many across the globe. Her leadership in this moment was described as unfamiliar and rare, because many governments are 'either brazenly anti-Muslim and xenophobic, or at best silent on the matter of immigration and Islam' (Malik, 2019).

In this chapter, we focus on Ardern's leadership style during the election campaign and her use of an inclusive political rhetoric that evoked the importance of care and kindness. Notions of care have tended to be associated with femininity (or feminism) in politics, complicating life for female politicians seeking to project both strength and compassion (Johnson, 2013; Trimble, 2017). However, Ardern was able to pitch her message with charisma and authenticity, which did not appear to undermine people's belief in her capacity to lead and which left little room for a populist politics of fear.

The role of charismatic leadership is critical in understanding the success or otherwise of authoritarian populist parties. However, most often these have had 'strong male leaders who are vigorous in nature, plain-spoken and authoritarian in character and style', associated with populist parties on the right (Meret, 2015, p. 82). The attraction of these male leaders lies in their capacity to rhetorically (and symbolically) appeal to the 'ordinary' people who perceive themselves as otherwise unrepresented. Voter behaviour studies indicate that these 'ordinary people' are mostly white, male manual workers with lower levels of education (Betz & Meret, 2011; Spierings et al., 2015). Although it appears most common for male political leaders to embody the alienation felt by the voters they seek to woo, there have been female leaders who have successfully taken up this mantle. Marine le Pen is perhaps the most recognisable; we may also consider Siv Jensen, leader of Norway's Progress Party, and Pia Kjærsgaard, the first woman in Western Europe to lead a populist party (the Danish Peoples Party) from its inception in 1995 until she stepped down in 2012 (Meret, 2015). Closer to home, Australia's Pauline Hanson presents another obvious example.

As with the Brexit and United States examples, the populist rhetoric employed by these women leaders challenges the legitimate authority of the 'establishment' and questions pluralism. Elites are treated as suspicious, whereas the 'people' know best—these tropes appeal to those supportive of democracy in principle but disillusioned with it in practice. Populist women leaders, like their male counterparts, argue that they alone are able to do politics differently, on behalf of the interests of the 'people', highlighting their own 'ordinariness'. In the case of Kjærsgaard, this involved invoking her own experience as a mother and carer as both oppositional and preferable to professional political elites, including feminists and academically trained female politicians (Meret, 2015, p. 96). Le Pen and other female authoritarian populist leaders have built their parties' positions on an imagined 'us versus them', underpinned by campaign and policy messages that promote a politics of fear, including Euroscepticism (Abi-Hassam, 2017; Sawer & Hindess, 2004). Thus, theirs is a clear appeal to core authoritarian cultural values, including security and threats from 'outsiders', conformity and adherence to traditional values and ways of life. The combination of these latter two often manifests in claims that social 'identities' are overtaking the collective (material) interests of the 'silent majority'.

It might appear strange to compare these examples to Jacinda Ardern, given that she ran for election on a platform of 'hope' and 'relentless positivity'. However, under Ardern, the Labour Party (for the second time in its history) formed a coalition government with New Zealand First, classified by Norris and Inglehart (2019) as one of a number of 'authoritarian-populist' parties globally that has increased its political presence. Does this then represent a paradox of sorts?

Through analysis of a range of questions from the New Zealand Election Study (NZES), we argue that Ardern's campaign and policy messages were sufficiently inclusive and convincing that there was little discursive space (or time) for an oppositional authoritarian populist rhetoric to take hold. First, we find that, in the traditions of inclusive populism, her leadership style was positive and, rhetorically, she represented the 'people' as a diverse group coming together to make New Zealand 'better' for everyone.[1] As a leader, voters found her likeable, trustworthy and competent, although women were more positive than men on these measures. Second, although Ardern presented herself as a progressive feminist on issues such as abortion, climate change and human rights, she also campaigned strongly on material issues such as economic wellbeing, housing and social policies. Voters' responses to a range of 'cultural' or 'identity politics' questions indicate minimal backlash to feminism or

1   Some scholars have referred to this as a type of 'heresthetic' device, which strategically invokes the 'people' as an inclusive majority to maintain power or to create change (Nagel, 1993). However, the rest of this chapter focuses on the extent to which Ardern's rhetoric and imagery intentionally portrayed an 'inclusive' vision of the 'people'.

environmental issues. Third, we find some differences between younger and older voters; however, these are not significant enough to suggest the emergence of a gendered generational cultural divide.

The absence of a backlash politics may be attributable to Ardern's ability to appeal to Labour's base and her attempts to reach across generations. This overarching appeal appears to have assuaged an 'us versus them' reaction (except, perhaps, among farmers). However, it is important to recognise that Labour, under Ardern's leadership, was not able to win more of the party vote than National; further, the women's vote for Labour has yet to return to the levels seen during the halcyon days under Helen Clark.

Framing Ardern's Popularity

It may be tempting to interpret Ardern's ascension to leader of the Labour Party seven weeks out from the 2017 New Zealand election as a quintessential 'glass cliff' appointment, whereby a woman is handed an executive role in times of crisis or decline when the chance of failure is highest (Ryan & Haslam, 2005). However, this would constitute an overly simplistic reading in the New Zealand context. Indeed, replacing opposition leaders when the party's popularity drops below 30 per cent is not uncommon in recent New Zealand history (Curtin, 2018). Don Brash replaced Bill English as leader in 2003, when National was polling at approximately 25 per cent, and Labour churned through three male leaders during the 2011–2016 period, when the polls looked gloomy. Nor was Ardern an outside candidate for leader. She polled at 12 per cent in a preferred deputy leader poll in 2011 (Horizon, 2011); during Andrew Little's term as leader she outperformed him in the preferred prime minister polls (Gower, 2017a) and, in 2017, she was the highest-ranked Opposition member of parliament in *The Herald*'s Mood of the Boardroom Survey of Chief Executives. Nevertheless, the handover from Little to Ardern was unanticipated because it occurred only seven weeks prior to the election.

Almost immediately, it was claimed that the media had gone 'ga-ga'— Labour had received more positive coverage in the first half hour of Ardern's leadership than it had in the past year under Little's leadership (Keall, 2017). Within 12 hours of her becoming leader, the term 'Jacinda-mania' was born. This was, at least initially, an overstatement. Mania is usually defined as an obsession, a compulsion, fixation, fetish, fascination, preoccupation, passion, craze, fad or rage. When used as a suffix in this way, it denotes extreme enthusiasm or admiration. One early political use of 'mania' was applied to Canadian Prime Minister Pierre Trudeau. Trudeau exuded a style that was new, eclectic and, at times, sexy, distinguishing him from the more ordinary politicians of the late 1960s (Litt, 2008). 'Trudeaumania' became the term used to describe the mass adulation of his supporters, in combination with the media's positive coverage (Wright, 2016, p. 175).

Such media positivity or mass admiration was not immediately forthcoming in the case of Ardern. Rather, some opinion writers questioned her experience, her record in office and her leadership abilities, given her young age (she was 37). This kind of media focus is not surprising. In her studies of women political leaders in Westminster democracies, Trimble (2017) demonstrated that the news media regularly and extensively depict women leaders as lacking requisite competence, strength, experience and qualifications. In Ardern's case, a notable moment occurred early in the campaign, when a breakfast host asked whether she would consider having a baby while leader. Although this was greeted with domestic and international outrage, a focus on motherhood is a common feature of media coverage of women leaders (Thomas & Bittner, 2018; Trimble et al., 2019).

The contrast between Ardern and Prime Minister Bill English was distinctive in several key ways. English had his own appeal—a wry sense of humour and a straightforward style. He had considerable experience, having guided New Zealand's economy safely through the global financial crisis (as finance minister) and overseen a period of solid economic growth. While his 2002 attempt to win an election as party leader had failed dismally, and his personality and popularity as leader was not as strong as his predecessor John Key, most expected National to win comfortably under his leadership (Vowles, Coffé & Curtin, 2017).

However, Ardern's comparative youth, her sudden elevation to the leadership and her rhetoric of positivity prompted heightened media interest in a way that edged in the direction of mania. Over the 53-day campaign Ardern, featured in 273 *New Zealand Herald* articles, 54 of which were published in the first week.[2] One commentator noted that:

---

2   Jennifer thanks Victoria Woodman, Bethan Owens and Linda Trimble for their assistance and insights in collating this material.

> A woman campaigning for high office serves her gender much better
> if everything she says and does carries the unspoken assumption
> that it is perfectly natural for a woman to be in contention, which
> it is. It did not seem quite so natural for a 37-year-old woman to
> be stepping into contention this week but that was on account of
> her age, not her gender. (Roughan, 2017)

However, in answer to the question 'is Jacinda Ardern old enough to be
Prime Minister?', 79 per cent of respondents to a Newshub-Reid Research
Poll (Gower, 2017a) responded 'yes'; only 17 per cent and 4 per cent
answered 'no' and 'don't know', respectively.

Ardern's first press conference was labelled 'a command performance that
stunned most of those watching, and especially those who have believed
she was not a woman of substance' (Young, 2017). Another wrote, 'it is
hard to remember the last time the press pack was so palpably smitten'
(Manhire, 2017). She was described as an 'emergency leader' (Manhire,
2017), although 'those expecting her to be the party's salvation [Joan
of Arc] and deliver them the Government benches in eight weeks have
set their expectations too high' (O'Sullivan, 2017). In a reference to the
former leader Andrew Little, the latter writer hoped Ardern would not be
'"Angry Andy" on steroids' (O'Sullivan, 2017).

Ardern proved herself to be anything but angry. Moreover, as we argue
here, she was able to craft her political rhetoric to engage with people's
emotions in a way that ran counter to the exclusionary populist approaches
of leaders elsewhere. The connection between politics and emotions is
not new; however, it has garnered considerable scholarly interest in recent
years (Fording & Schram, 2017; Johnson, 2020; Valentino, Oceno &
Wayne, 2018). Most accept that Trump's populist provocations during
the 2016 presidential election campaign took emotionality to a new
level, with his aggressive anti-immigrant stance and his appeals to
'American' workers whose interests, he argued, were served best through
protectionism (Weber, 2018). Much like populist-right leaders in Europe,
Trump successfully tapped into the insecurities, fears and anger of a large
group of voters. His was an implicit appeal to white male workers, who
perceived themselves as forgotten during Obama's presidency and likely to
continue to be so if Hillary Clinton won.

However, as Carol Johnson reminds us, 'emotion is regularly utilised by male and female politicians of all political persuasions' (2013, p. 24). For example, Hillary Clinton adopted Obama's discourse of kindness in her campaign for the presidency. 'Love and kindness' was the title of one high-profile advertisement, released in April 2016, with a modified version uploaded onto Clinton's official YouTube channel just before election day (Clinton, 2016). These advertisements featured numerous close-ups of Clinton with African Americans and women; further, in the voice overs, Clinton called for the audience to 'support each other, be kind to each other, lift each other up' (2016). Weber has argued that this messaging represents a call to voters to become more compassionate towards African Americans and women, reinforcing that it is these two groups who need 'to be supported in their struggle for equal opportunities and social justice' through a collective outpouring of compassion (2018, p. 58).

Weber (2018) and Hochschild (2016) have argued that naming some groups as more worthy of compassion and kindness risked causing resentment among those who themselves felt excluded by partisan demands for social justice and redistribution, at a cost to their values and livelihoods. Weber concluded that, like Trump, Clinton and her campaign team sought to create 'a specific emotional atmosphere' that promoted feelings of kindness; however, this enabled Trump's campaign rhetoric to gain further resonance among those who felt alienated by Clinton's message. As such, both campaigns presented elements of exclusion of 'the other' (Weber, 2018, p. 59).

Exclusionary populist rhetoric may be a natural fit for political leaders advocating for the 'silent majority'. However, the point of this brief vignette is to illustrate that the articulation of an inclusive campaign message, based on kindness, may prove divisive if done in such a way that demands compassion for marginalised groups from those who themselves feel alienated. The use of 'kindness' has produced reactions on both the right and the left, including claims that the use of the term 'kindness' represents a 'wishy-washy' politics with little substance and a new form of virtue signalling (Landesman, 2018). However, in the United States, some concern also exists among Republicans regarding the way 'the notion of a caring left and a mean-spirited right might cause many voters to reflexively oppose conservative candidates on the ground that they are less decent than their liberal opponents' (Horowitz et al., n.d., p. 4).

In the case of the 2017 New Zealand election, National's campaign did not come across as mean-spirited—beneficiaries were not a target, as they had been in 2011 (Curtin, 2014). Rather, the emphasis was on National's record in government and Bill English's credentials as a safe and decent leader. By contrast, Jacinda Ardern's campaign message, from the outset, appeared designed to evoke an emotional response. In her speech at Labour's campaign launch in Auckland Town Hall, surrounded by Labour faithfuls, including Helen Clark, Ardern emphasised that, for her, politics was connected to feelings of empathy, one result of her childhood observation of poverty, unemployment and hardship: 'understanding the issues people in our communities face, their experiences, and never being satisfied that things ... can't be changed or made better. That is why I chose politics. That is why I am here' (Ardern, 2017a). She spoke of focusing on love and hope, rather than grief and loss, and the need to build a 'confident and caring nation that includes each and every person, in each and every town and region' (Ardern, 2017a). She wanted to enable people to feel 'secure' in a time when they have been feeling increasingly insecure (Ardern, 2017a).

Labour subsequently released a 90-second video that was not unlike Clinton's 'Love and Kindness' campaign video. It included images of teachers and children at school, couples cooking in kitchens, business owners delivering food and haircuts, workers on building sites, offices and farms, in addition to Labour supporters and caucus members at the campaign launch. A range of different ethnicities and genders are represented in each of the shots and Ardern herself provides the voice over. She speaks of this as:

> Being an opportunity we don't want to miss, an opportunity to build a better, fairer New Zealand ... to give everyone a voice ... They will dismiss our optimism. They will say that kindness will stand in the way of progress ... but we can do better. (New Zealand Labour Party, 2017)

In contrast to the Clinton video, the voters targeted by Ardern in her emotional appeals were not specific groups in society but a broad section of the New Zealand community. Her message of hope was picked up in memes and photos across social media; it also reflected a desire of some in the Labour Party to move away from negative campaigning. Ardern's 'relentless positivity' approach was supplemented with a commitment to the needs of younger generations and she appeared able to make her age a political asset. For instance, she articulated climate change as her generation's 'nuclear-free moment' and labelled herself as 'youth-adjacent'. Her vision was delivered through media that reached both older and younger generations (Television, Facebook, YouTube and Instagram).

In the ways outlined above, Ardern constituted a fresh, new, but also untested leader. So, how did voters respond? Drawing on our analyses of the 2017 NZES, we find that, on an emotional level, most respondents expressed positive emotions regarding Jacinda Ardern becoming the Labour leader (see Table 6.1). The most common responses were 'happy' (29.9 per cent) and 'hopeful' (27.7 per cent), followed by 20.9 per cent who felt 'uneasy'. Women were significantly more 'hopeful' and 'proud' than men; more men than women felt 'disgusted', although this represented only 2.1 per cent of the sample.

Table 6.1: Emotional responses to Jacinda Ardern becoming party leader (%)

Emotion	Women	Men	Gender difference	Overall sample
Happy	28.9	30.9	–2.0	29.9
Hopeful	29.3	26.1	3.2*	27.7
Uneasy	22.1	19.7	2.4	20.9
Confident	11.3	11.1	0.2	11.2
Proud	11.9	8.6	3.3**	10.3
Afraid	6.7	7.2	–0.5	7.0
Disgusted	1.4	2.9	–1.5**	2.1
Angry	2.4	1.8	0.6	2.1

Note: We tested for statistically significant gender differences with a series of Chi-square tests: * p < .05; ** p < .01. Respondents were asked about their emotional responses to the statement 'Jacinda Ardern becoming Labour party leader'. Respondents were able to tick boxes for multiple emotion words.
Source: New Zealand Election Study (2017).

When we split the sample into Labour and National Voters (see Table 6.2), we find that Labour-voting men were significantly more likely than Labour-voting women to feel 'uneasy' and 'afraid' of Ardern becoming leader, while Labour-voting women expressed much higher levels of pride, hope and happiness than their male counterparts. Unsurprisingly, those who voted National were less positive regarding Ardern; approximately 40 per cent of men and women felt 'uneasy', although twice as many National-voting men than women felt 'happy' regarding Ardern.

Table 6.2: Emotional responses to Jacinda Ardern by party and gender (%)

Emotion	Labour women	Labour men	Gender difference	National women	National men	Gender difference
Angry	0.0	2.7	–2.7**	5.6	3.9	1.7
Disgusted	0.4	1.4	–1.0*	2.8	6.4	–3.6**
Afraid	0.5	7.3	–6.8**	13.2	12.0	1.2
Uneasy	1.8	24.2	–22.4**	41.2	37.9	3.3
Confident	21.5	10.8	10.7**	4.6	4.2	0.4
Proud	22.4	10.4	12.0**	2.6	1.7	0.9
Hopeful	45.7	25.5	20.2**	16.2	16.0	0.2
Happy	50.2	27.4	22.8**	10.6	20.2	–9.6**

Note: We tested for statistically significant gender differences with a series of Chi-square tests: * p < .05; ** p < .01. Respondents were able to tick boxes for multiple emotion words.
Source: New Zealand Election Study (2017).

Figure 6.1 reveals that, on average, both men and women found Ardern more likeable than English, however, women liked Ardern more, on average, than did men. This reflects the experience of Helen Clark, whereby women rated Clark as more likeable throughout her term as prime minister and, in 2008, found her more likeable than John Key. The reverse was the case for men in 2008 (Curtin, 2014).

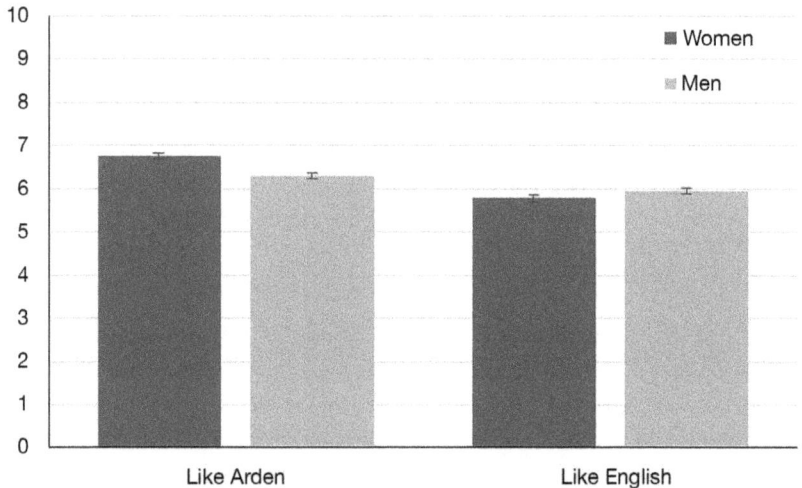

Figure 6.1: Likeability of Jacinda Ardern and Bill English.
Source: New Zealand Election Study (2017).

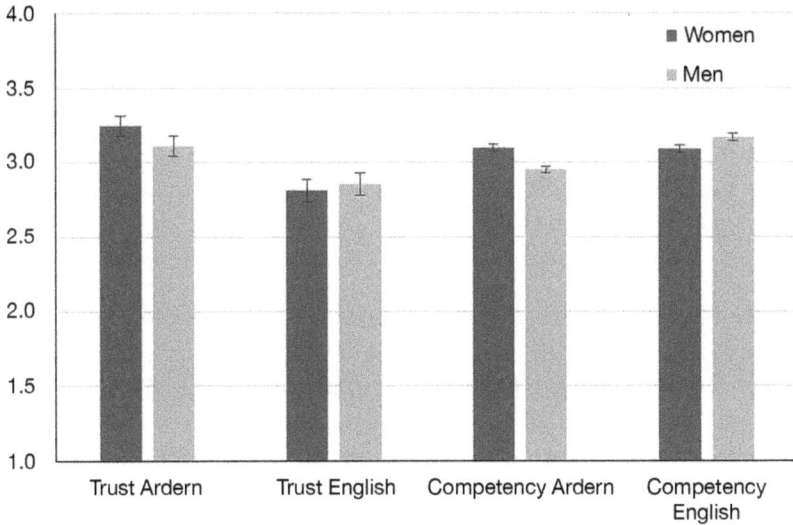

Figure 6.2: Gender and attitudes to leadership qualities.
Source: New Zealand Election Study (2017).

Given the populism literature argues that anti-elitism and distrust feed the rise of populist leaders, we also examined how respondents rated Ardern and English on how well the qualities of 'trust' and 'competency'. If strong populist sentiment was present among voters, we might expect to see low levels of support for the major party leaders and, potentially, less support for Ardern—in that populists might associate her with the progressive left, feminism and the millennial generation. Participants were asked to rank Ardern and English on trust and competency statements across a four-point scale from 'not at all well' to 'very well' (see Figure 6.2). Although English fared lower overall on trust than Ardern, his score was still well above the scale mid-point. On average, women saw Ardern as slightly more trustworthy than their male counterparts (an average of 3.3 compared to 3.1; $p < .001$). A similar, albeit smaller, gender gap is evident with respect to competency (an average of 3.1 for women and 3.0 for men; $p < .001$). By contrast, there was no significant gender difference in ratings of English's trustworthiness; men (an average of 3.2) viewed English as more competent than did women (3.1; $p = .013$).

Generational diversity also forms part of the populist story. Norris and Inglehart (2019) argued that traditional values, social norms and behaviours that were once mainstream are slowly becoming less politically relevant. Instead, new generations, who are more socially liberal and post-materialist in orientation, are entering the electorate and challenging the dearly held beliefs of earlier generations. Some older voters may find greater gender equality, tolerant sexual norms and cultural diversity to be unfamiliar; these may even appear threatening to their way of life (Norris & Inglehart, 2019, pp. 34–35). As such, we might expect to see generational gender differences in responses to Jacinda Ardern as a political leader, given that she represents generation X and, early in her campaign, openly identified herself as a feminist social democrat.

Figure 6.3 confirms this assertion, indicating that, among women voters, Ardern's likeability ratings are higher among the younger generations, with interwar women less likely than their male counterparts to rate Ardern as likeable. By contrast, Bill English, whose more traditional values are likely to appeal to older voters, is rated neutral on likeability (5) by younger generations of women. However, in terms of trust and competence, we found little difference in male and female responses to Ardern across the generations.

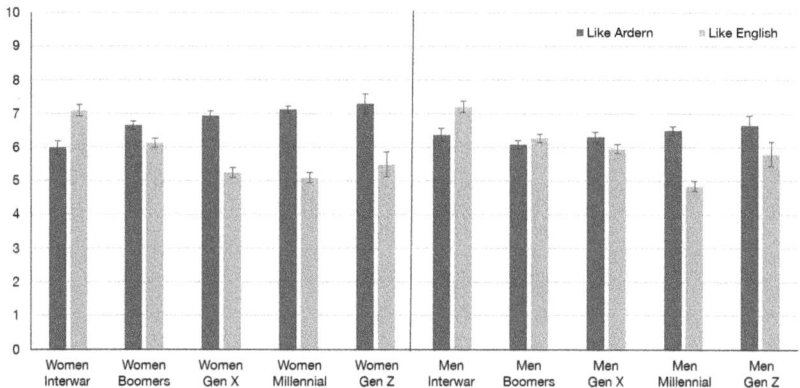

Figure 6.3: Likeability for Ardern and English by gender and generation.
Source: New Zealand Election Study (2017).

To what extent, then, did Ardern's campaign message of kindness and inclusivity appeal to populist and authoritarian voters, irrespective of generation? At first glance, we find a correlation between 'liking' Ardern and populist attitudes, although the relationship is relatively small (r = 0.06). By contrast, there is a stronger negative correlation between 'liking' Ardern and authoritarianism (r = 0.23).

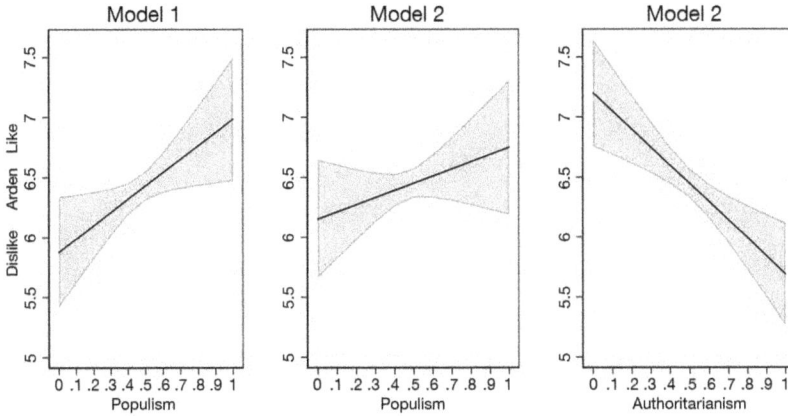

Figure 6.4: Populist and authoritarian attitudes in relation to the likeability of Jacinda Ardern.[3]

Source: New Zealand Election Study (2017).

Figure 6.4 demonstrates this with simple regressions of authoritarianism and populism together against the likeability of Ardern (details are given in Table A6.1). Model 1, depicted in the first panel, represents the effects of populism and authoritarianism controlling for each other, plus gender, political efficacy and left–right position (see also Figure 6.5). Ardern's appeal is, indeed, stronger among populists; she also appeals more to the left and to those who demonstrate higher levels of political efficacy. These 'likeability' responses may speak to the optimism of Ardern's campaign and a belief that change is possible under her leadership.

Model 2 (panel 2) investigates whether the effects of populism and authoritarianism can be reduced by the addition of other variables. For this purpose, we controlled for whether a participant was of Māori ethnicity, their income level, whether they lived in a household with a union member and whether they lived in a rural area, because we know that these variables relate to higher levels of populism. When we add these controls, we find the effects of populism on Ardern's likeability levels are halved and no longer significant. Nor are age, occupation, asset ownership and beneficiary status significant. By contrast, as demonstrated in Model 2 (panel 3), authoritarians are highly unlikely to find Ardern likeable— this result holds when the control variables are included.

---

3   We thank Jack Vowles for his assistance with this part of the analysis.

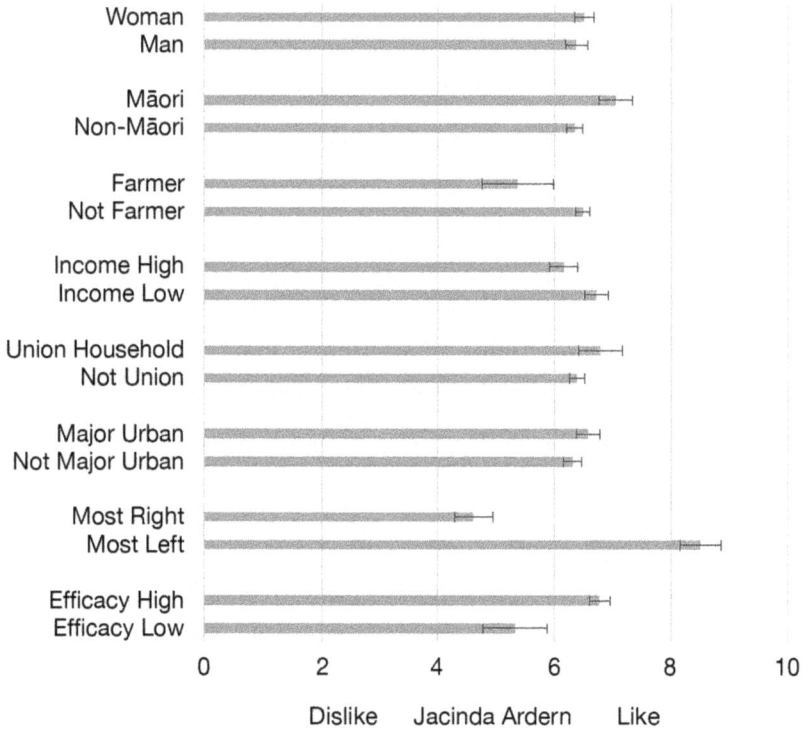

Figure 6.5: Average scores for the likeability of Ardern by demographics.
Source: New Zealand Election Study (2017).

Nevertheless, we observe a stark gender gap in responses to the question regarding who voters most wanted to be prime minister. Table 6.3 reveals that, while women were evenly split between Ardern and English, we see a 10 percentage-point difference between men, who preferred English over Ardern. This gap resembles the one found with respect to vote choice (discussed later in this chapter).

Table 6.3: Preferred prime minister by gender

Gender	Jacinda Ardern	Bill English	Other
Women	42.8	41.7	15.6
Men	37.1	47.1	15.9

Source: New Zealand Election Study (2017).

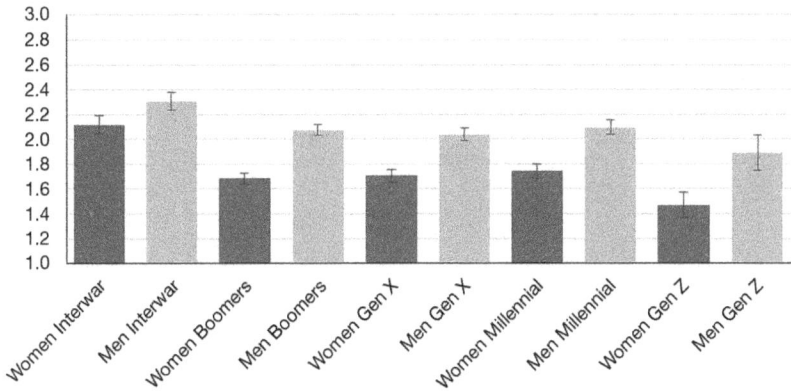

Figure 6.6: Average scores by gender and generation for 'On the whole, men make better political leaders than women do'.
Source: New Zealand Election Study (2017).

To further investigate voters' preferences on gender and leadership, we included a question concerning whether men make better political leaders than women. Answers were indicated on a 1 (strongly disagree) to 5 (strongly agree) scale, with 3 being neutral. Overall, there was a low average level of agreement with this statement; however, we found a statistically significant gender difference (p < .001), where the average scores for men and women were 2.1 and 1.8, respectively. When we broke this down further by generation, interwar-generation women and men were more likely than younger-generation women to only partly disagree with this statement. More generally, women of all generations were more likely than their male counterparts to strongly disagree (see Figure 6.6; note that the *y* axis only displays values up to 3, neutral).

That voters of all ages do not strongly agree that men make better leaders is unsurprising, given that women prime ministers are no longer a novelty in New Zealand politics. Besides Labour prime ministers Clark and Ardern, New Zealand's first female prime minister was National Party leader Jenny Shipley (1997); National also appointed Paula Bennett to the position of deputy prime minister when Bill English took over from John Key. Further, both the Greens and the Māori Party appoint male and female co-leaders—this is required by their constitutions.

However, presumably due to her age, Ardern was questioned almost immediately upon becoming leader regarding her views on having a family (Ainge Roy, 2017). Most notably, Ardern was challenged by former NZ cricketer, sports reporter and self-identified National supporter, Mark

Richardson, on national television regarding her motherhood intentions (McConnell, 2017). Richardson added that 'if you are the employer of a company you need to know that type of thing from the woman you are employing … the question is, is it OK for a PM to take maternity leave while in office?' Ardern provided a fiery response, with her finger pointed at Richardson, stating:

> It is totally unacceptable in 2017 to say that women should have to answer that question in the workplace, it is unacceptable … It is a woman's decision about when they choose to have children and it should not predetermine whether or not they are given a job. (Bracewell-Worrall, 2017)

This exchange provoked an outpouring of support from women on social media in New Zealand and in mainstream media across the world (Ainge Roy, 2017).

When we compare the media reaction with NZES responses to the statement 'society would be better off if more women stayed home with their children', we found that, unsurprisingly, support for this statement has decreased over time (see Figure 6.7). The gender difference in endorsement has also closed—it was statistically significant in 1999 (p = .011) and 2002 (p = .003), but not in 2017 (p = .864) (see Figure 6.8). Moreover, there exist clear generational differences in agreement in this statement—generation appears to be more important than gender.

Thus, we could infer that Ardern was only likely to provoke a cultural populist backlash if her leadership style and campaign message focused on post-materialist and socially progressive issues, at the expense of the material and moral concerns of more conservative, older voters. In fact, it appears that, despite her claims that climate change was her generation's 'nuclear-free moment' and championing a woman's right to choose (further details on this point are provided below), her most vocal opponents turned out to be Labour's traditional foes: the farming lobby.[4] Indeed, a group of farmers staged a high-profile protest against Labour's proposed water tax, which featured a placard calling Ardern a 'pretty communist' (Wilson, 2017).

---

4   Figure 6.5 shows that farmers are less likely than non-farmers to find Ardern likeable, although the average is close to 5, which represents a neutral rating.

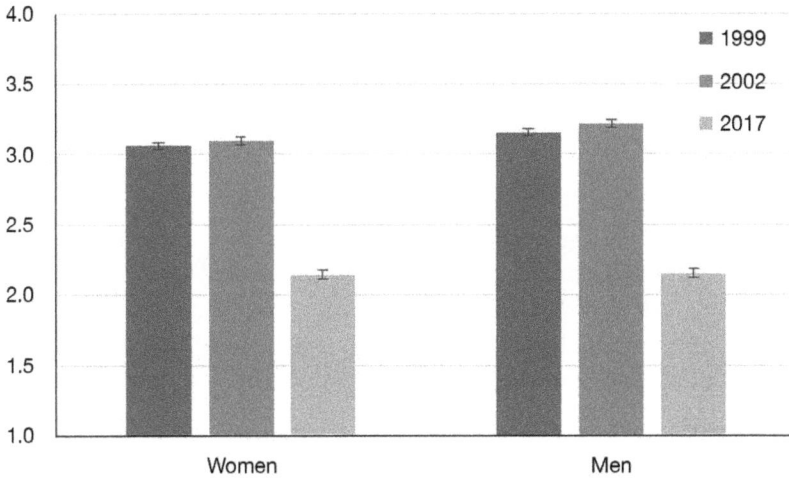

Figure 6.7: Average scores by gender to the statement 'Society would be better off if women stayed home with their children' (over time).

Note: This is a five-point scale (1 is 'strongly disagree', 3 is 'neutral' and 5 is 'strongly agree').

Source: New Zealand Election Study (2017).

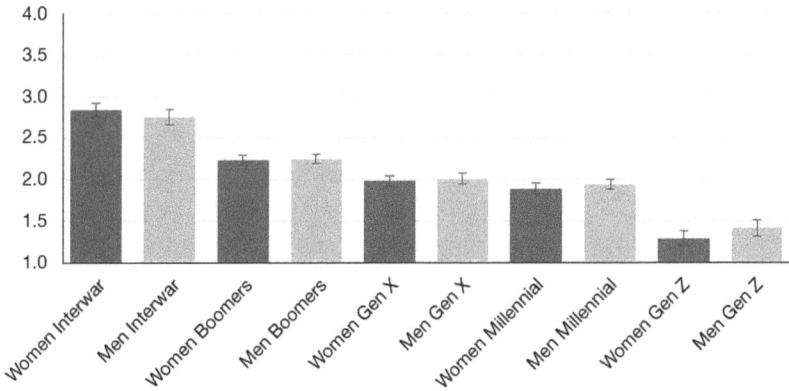

Figure 6.8: Average scores by gender and generation to the statement 'Society would be better off if women stayed home with their children'.

Note: This is a five-point scale (1 is the lowest possible score, 3 is neutral and 5 is the highest possible score). However, our y axis only goes up to 4; the interwar generation is fairly neutral.

Source: New Zealand Election Study (2017).

A Re-Emerging Gender Gap?

Most of the studies that investigate gender gaps in populist vote choice focus on radical right parties in Europe, where such parties receive a considerable minority of the vote and win seats in either national or European elections, assisted in part by proportional representation. These analyses show that, generally, men are more likely to vote for radical right parties, although there is considerable cross-national variation in both trends and explanations, including socio-economic characteristics and the party's status as a political outsider (Immerzeel, Coffé & van der Lippe, 2015; Spierings & Zaslove, 2015).

New Zealand First is considered by international scholars to be the closest New Zealand has to a radical right populist party (Moffitt, 2017; Norris & Inglehart, 2019). However, as explained in Chapter 2, this is a dubious categorisation for numerous reasons. Moreover, the party is perennially at risk of not winning the 5 per cent of the party vote needed to enter parliament and it is difficult to categorise the party or its leader as a political 'outsider', given Winston Peters' long parliamentary career. Nevertheless, we know from previous NZES analyses that, in 2011, the only statistically significant gender difference in party vote was for New Zealand First, with women being less likely than men to vote for Winston Peters' party (Coffé, 2013). In 2014, we found a marginally significant male bias for New Zealand First when controlling for social and demographic factors (Vowles et al., 2017, p. 196). On the same basis, Chapter 2 reports the continuation of this male bias towards New Zealand First.

There is little evidence of a male backlash, given that Labour's vote increased in 2017 among both men and women, with women being a little more likely to move to Labour, other factors held equal. Using the raw data, and focusing just on the two major parties, what do we find in terms of gender differences in relation to vote choice? New Zealand women had once been more conservative than men; however, this trend began to change from 1993 onwards. Between 1999 and 2008, under the leadership of Helen Clark, a significant and sustained gender gap appeared. However, many women voters returned to National under John Key's leadership and Labour's male leaders seemed unable to reverse this decline. From this point forth, the party steadily lost its share of the vote, with both women and men deserting Labour between 2011 and 2014

(Curtin, 2017). When Ardern became Labour leader, some speculated that she would be able to win back the women's vote. Ten days after her first press conference as Labour leader, a Newshub-Reid Research Poll showed Labour's support had increased from 25 per cent to 33 per cent, with almost two-thirds of that vote (63 per cent) coming from women (Gower, 2017b). Table 6.4 confirms the re-emergence of a significant gender gap among Labour voters in 2017. Men provided a considerable share of Labour's new votes (up six points); however, women's support was up by 11 points.

Table 6.4: The gender gap in party vote (National/Labour parties; 1996–2017)

Year	National			Labour		
	Women	Men	Gap	Women	Men	Gap
1996***	33	35	–2	32	24	8
1999***	31	30	1	43	34	9
2002 ns	19	18	1	44	39	5
2005***	32	38	–6	41	33	7
2008**	36	40	–4	37	30	7
2011 ns	41	40	1	29	25	4
2014 ns	34	37	–3	21	18	3
2017**	35	33	–2	33	24	9

Note: Significance on basis of 2x2 tables (National and Labour voters only).

*** p < .001, ** p < .05, * p < .10, ns not significant.

Source: Data for 1963–1999 adapted from J. Vowles (2002, p. 94); data for 2002–2011 from Curtin (2014, p. 134; see also Coffé, 2013); data for 2014 from Vowles, Coffé and Curtin (2017, p.195); and data for 2017 from New Zealand Election Study (2017).

We see that women were significantly more likely to give their party vote to Labour (33 per cent) than were men (24 per cent). However, if we turn the attention of our analysis beyond the two main parties, we find that Labour's increased share of the women's vote does not appear to have come at the expense of National but rather from a decrease in women's support for the Greens. In Figure 6.9, the left columns represent the party vote in 2017 and the right columns the party vote in 2014, split by gender. Here we see that the statistically significant gender gap for the Greens that was evident in 2014 had evaporated by 2017. By contrast, male voters' support for National decreased by four points while their support for Labour increased by six points.

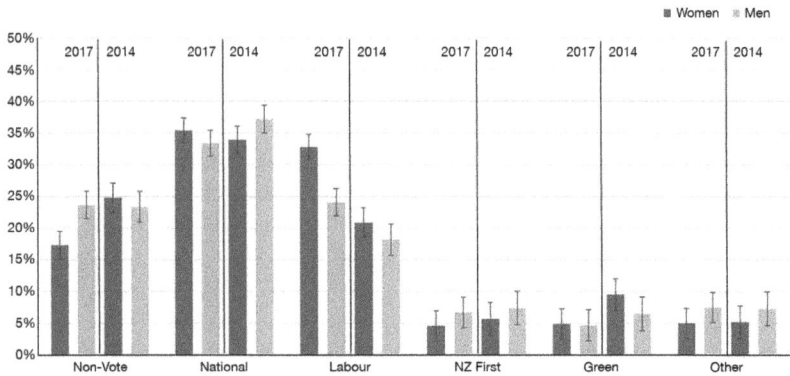

Figure 6.9: Gender gap, voters and non-voters (2014–2017).
Source: New Zealand Election Study (2014, 2017).

Some commentators claimed that a focus on women was likely to marginalise Labour's traditional working-class base; however, historically, the women's vote for Labour does not appear to have come at the expense of this group (Curtin, 2017). When Helen Clark was elected in 1999, there existed a 12-point gap between those in households where the principal income earner was in a manual or manual/service occupation, compared to those in a non-manual or middle-class household (see Chapter 2). In 2002, Labour increased its share of the middle-class vote but lost some of its working-class support to non-voting (Vowles, 2014, p. 40). Over the elections after Clark's government lost power in 2008, Labour's support became increasingly dependent on its traditional working-class base as its overall vote declined. However, working-class support was also in decline, most evident in 2011. By contrast, in 2017, middle-class and working-class vote shares for Labour were almost identical.

It is worth remembering that both class and gender cleavages may feed a return of voters to Labour. Large numbers of women are in low-paid jobs, such as call centre operators, carers, clerical and manual workers (Stats New Zealand, 2019). Women earn less, are more likely to take breaks to care for family and to work part time; further, they leave the labour market with fewer assets and less superannuation (Curtin, 2017; Huang & Curtin, 2019; Ministry for Women, 2019). Unsurprisingly, campaigns for pay equity increased in visibility and intensity leading up to the 2017 election.

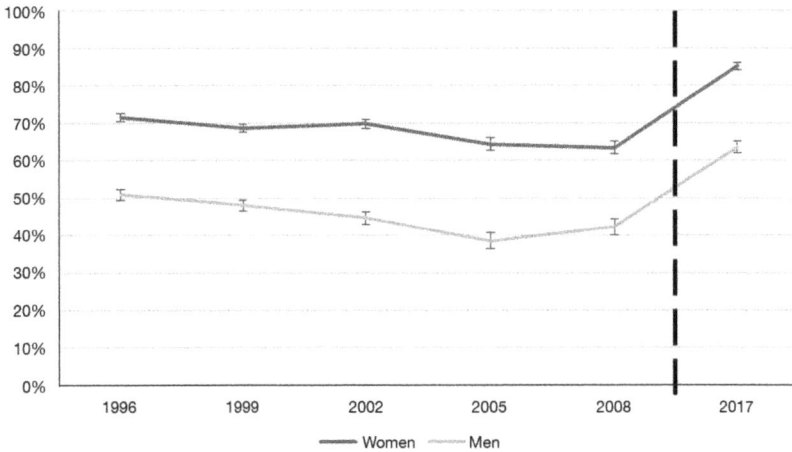

Figure 6.10: Agree or strongly agree that 'The law should be strengthened to reduce pay differences between women and men' (%).

Note: This was assessed on a 1 to 5 agreement scale. This question was not run in the nine years between 2008 and 2017—we should assume that there has been an incremental increase in support for this statement over that nine-year period.

Source: New Zealand Election Study (2017).

In February 2017, the New Zealand Council of Trade Unions (NZCTU) released the 'Treat her right' musical video, in which actor Miriama McDowell played an 'everywoman': cleaner, childcare worker and aged care worker, conveying the message that 'it's time to vote for political parties that support equal pay' (Idealog, 2017). This followed a hard-fought, five-year equal-pay campaign, led by aged-care worker Kristine Bartlett, with the Service and Food Workers Union, against Terranova. The case began in the Employment Court in 2012 and went all the way to the Supreme Court, with a final ruling that gender bias was the cause of Bartlett's low wages. The gender pay gap has hovered near 9 per cent for the past 10 years; however, this figure masks the disparities experienced by different groups of women. For example, the gender pay gap for Pacific women in the public service was 21 per cent in 2017 (Human Rights Commission, 2018).

Jacinda Ardern had made her support for pay equity known well before the election, participating, along with Julie Anne Genter, in the making of the NZCTU video. Ardern also attended a rally in central Auckland and stated that Labour 'will not rest until we have pay equity in New Zealand' (McCann, 2017; Tan, 2017). Figure 6.10 indicates increasing support from both men and women for the gender pay gap to be addressed through legislation.

Another significant gender gap is evidenced by the fact that women were more likely than men to vote in 2017, whereas there was no significant gap in the non-vote in 2014. In fact, women's share of the non-vote decreased by 7.5 points in 2017. Over the past 10 years, there has been increasing interest in the extent to which high-profile women leaders motivate women's political interest, engagement and propensity to turn out. This is referred to as the symbolic effects of women's political leadership. However, although we might think that women as leaders would inspire women voters, some have argued this is not necessarily the case. Women leaders may choose to 'mask' their feminism and avoid advocating for women, because they feel obliged to present themselves as 'masculine' to demonstrate competence and to combat the negative and trivialising media coverage often meted out to women candidates (Curtin, 2008; Duerst-Lahti, 2006; Trimble, 2017; Trimble et al., 2019). Some cross-national evidence suggests support for this conclusion—that is, that women leaders do not necessarily result in increased political engagement among women (Carreras, 2017). However, we appear to find evidence to the contrary. In addition to the decrease in the number of women non-voters, we observed an increase in the average level of political interest among both women and men, compared to 2014. Further, the gender gap in political interest reduced from 0.2 in 2014 to 0.1 in 2017 (see Figure 6.11).

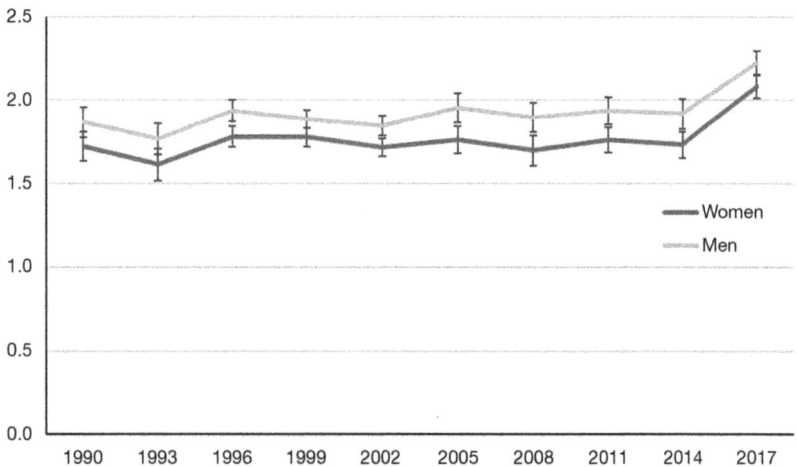

Figure 6.11: Interest in politics by gender.
Source: New Zealand Election Study (2017).

This is, perhaps, an unsurprising finding. As we have already demonstrated, Ardern did not adopt a masculine style, ranked relatively high in terms of competence; further, the media coverage she received was not wholly trivialising. Trimble et al. (2019) found that women leaders who are the 'first' of their kind receive more personalised coverage than women who have had female predecessors. However, Ardern is comparatively young, resulting in her retaining a degree of novelty, and she chose to champion various women's issues. One interpretation of this result is that new generations of voters may become more interested when politics is less 'masculine' and when the media refrain from deploying stereotypical gender tropes.

Populism, Feminism and Cultural Backlash

Media coverage of the 2017 New Zealand election campaign and its result shone the spotlight on Jacinda Ardern, her role in growing Labour's vote share and in her coalition negotiations with New Zealand First leader Winston Peters. However, as we argue in Chapter 1, there are two key aspects to the populism question: leaders and voter opinion both matter. In the remainder of this chapter, we turn our analysis to the latter, exploring gender gaps that appear on measures that might equate to a cultural backlash (Norris & Inglehart 2019). Even if nascent, such a backlash may result in certain populations finding their voice in reaction to the sudden rise, and popularity of, a young, feminist and progressive Labour leader.

We selected several questions from the NZES that we believe might capture voters' views on 'feminist', 'postmaterialist' and 'identity politics' issues. We begin with abortion because, unlike many of her predecessors, Jacinda Ardern took an explicit stand on this conscience issue during the 2017 election campaign, supporting the need to remove abortion from the *Crimes Act*. Many women's organisations had been advocating that a change was long overdue; further, values surveys suggested New Zealanders' attitudes towards the issue are now more accepting of abortion, regardless of the reason (Huang cited in Martin, 2019).

Historically, some Labour leaders had been equivocal on the issue, in part because it was seen to be a conscience issue and also because some legal experts were concerned that disrupting the status quo might result in a campaign that led to increased restriction rather than liberalisation (McCulloch, 2013). However, the NZES data reveal the occurrence of a shift over time, with fewer people believing that abortion is always wrong. Close to 65 per cent of respondents disagreed with this statement in 2017, compared to 60 per cent in 2014 and 54 per cent in 2008 (see Figure 6.12). When we disaggregated this by generation, we found no gender differences among the interwar generation (most opposed) and generation Z (least opposed) (see Figure 6.13).[5]

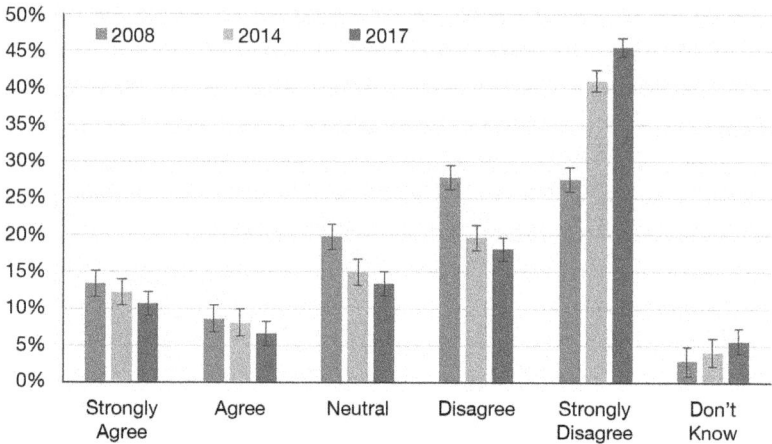

Figure 6.12: Views on the statement 'Abortion is always wrong' across years.

Source: New Zealand Election Study (2017).

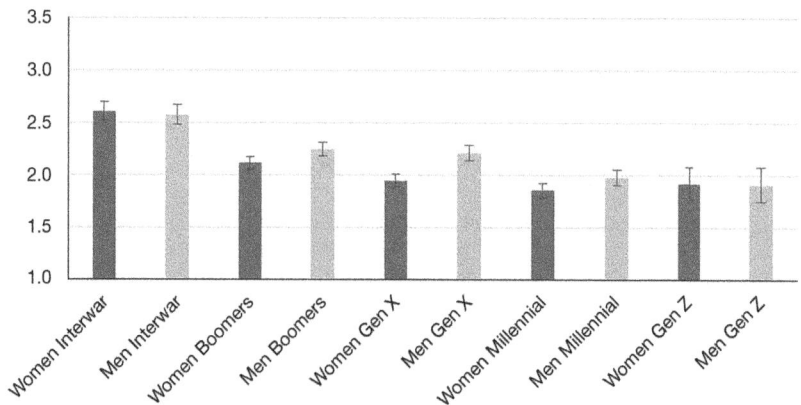

Figure 6.13: Gender-generational differences on abortion.

Source: New Zealand Election Study (2008, 2014, 2017).

5   Agreement was rated on a scale from 1 to 5; however, the *y* axis presents only up to 3.5 because there was a low overall level of agreement with this statement.

We also observed some gender differences in attitudes towards a range of other issues that we believe may capture the idea that some 'identity' groups are privileged at the expense of others (see Table 6.5). We also included a question on climate change and one on welfare benefits (the latter is our best-fit proxy for 'kindness').

Table 6.5: Social, cultural and environmental attitudes by gender

Issue	% Agreeing		
	Women	Men	Gap
Reference to the Treaty of Waitangi should be removed from the law	33.3	40.2	–6.9
Māori should have more say in all government decisions	23.9	16.5	7.4
To act against climate change policies are needed to reduce carbon emissions	78.7	67.8	10.9
Many people who get welfare benefits don't really deserve any help	31.8	38.5	–6.7
Nothing needs to be done to get more women into parliament: it will happen naturally	33.1	45.3	–12.2

Source: New Zealand Election Study (2017).

Across each of these attitudinal variables, we observed that women are more likely than men to be socially progressive. This fits with what we already know about gender, populism and authoritarianism in New Zealand. Specifically, our analyses above indicate that, while women scored slightly higher on populism, they scored significantly lower than men on the authoritarianism scale.

We also asked respondents a range of questions regarding whether there should be more women in parliament and, if so, what mechanisms would best facilitate gender equality in politics. Women's parliamentary representation increased to a new high of 39 per cent after the 2017 election and reached 41 per cent in 2019. This outcome is the result of a new gender target introduced by Labour following the 2014 election and an increase in the number of National women candidates on the party list (Electoral Commission, 2014, 2017).

This increase, along with high-profile women in leadership positions of both Labour and National (in addition to Ardern, Paula Bennett had become deputy prime minister of the National government in December 2016), contrasted with the 2014 election, where the leaders and deputies of the major parties were all men. As such, this increase may have influenced respondents' views to questions regarding whether any additional measures to increase women's representation were required. For example, gender quotas and voluntary party targets had limited support from women and men. Men were more likely than women to think that equality of representation would happen naturally (45 per cent compared to 33 per cent), while women were more likely than men to say that more should be done to encourage women to enter politics (27 per cent compared to 19 per cent). We also know that authoritarianism is generally associated with more traditional attitudes to gender roles (see Chapter 3). Currently, it remains to be seen whether authoritarian tendencies among some male voters convert into something more akin to a cultural backlash against women's presence in politics, given that Prime Minister Ardern became a mother in office and returned to work following only six weeks of maternity leave.

Conclusion

The rhetoric of kindness in politics is not unique to the leadership of Jacinda Ardern. In Australia, Kevin Rudd called on politicians 'to be a little kinder and a little gentler with each other' (Jones, 2013) and, in the United States, Obama spoke of the way kindness informed his political beliefs: 'When I think about what I'm fighting for, what gets me up every single day, that captures it just about as much as anything' (Obama, 2013). In 2015, as the new leader of the British Labour Party, Jeremy Corbyn told his party's conference delegates that he intended to promote a '"kinder, more inclusive" form of political debate that is led from the "bottom up, not top down"' (Wright & Morris, 2015).

The continuing electoral success of radical right parties elsewhere suggests that it would be wrong to assume that discourses of compassion and hope will deter or neutralise the divisive language of exclusionary authoritarian populism. Our analysis of Ardern's campaign also indicates the prematurity of such a conclusion. We found that her rhetoric of optimism and kindness appealed to those whose efficacy and attitudes reflected a pluralist variant of populism, common to a range of voters in New Zealand. However, authoritarian-leaning voters were impervious to such messaging, irrespective of their position on the left–right spectrum.

Nevertheless, since becoming prime minister, Ardern has continued to frame her political position, and her government's policies, as being informed by a commitment to kindness, both within New Zealand and on the international stage. In her Speech from the Throne in November 2017, Ardern said her government was one that wanted 'to foster a kinder, more caring society.[6] This will involve government leading the way and facing up to its responsibilities and the legacies from the past' (Ardern, 2017b). After her first 100 days in office, she spoke of looking forward 'to tomorrow and the next few hundred days after that … as we work to leave a legacy of a stronger, fairer, kinder New Zealand' (Ardern, 2018a). At her first prime ministerial visit to the Treaty Grounds on Waitangi Day, she referred to:

> What we value … collectively … the importance of manaakitanga, of hospitality, of generosity, of caring for one another. And that it is possible to have a government that does that too. (Ardern, 2018b)

Finally, at the United Nations General Assembly, in a speech that covered issues of foreign policy and climate change, Ardern stated that:

> It is time to step back from the chaos and ask what we want. It is in that space that we'll find simplicity. The simplicity of peace, of prosperity, of fairness. If I could distil it down into one concept that we are pursuing in New Zealand it is simple and it is this. Kindness. (Ardern, 2018c)

Therefore, in one sense, Ardern's words of compassion and inclusion following the Christchurch massacre were consistent with her previous articulations of who comprised the people of New Zealand (Ardern, 2019).

Questions remain as to whether this type of political communication, when delivered by a relatively young woman leader, will appeal on an emotional level to voters across the political and demographic spectrum (Johnson, 2020). The gender and generational gaps in vote choice and attitudes to 'feminist' issues identified in this chapter suggest that intergenerational differences may become more prevalent over time; younger voters' responses suggest that a more progressive politics may emerge to challenge traditional voters. However, if Ardern's government is not able to translate the rhetoric

---

6   In New Zealand, the Speech from the Throne is the first formal opportunity for a government to outline its legislative intentions. It is drafted by the prime minister in consultation with officials and read by the governor-general, as the Monarch's representative, on the second sitting day of a parliamentary term.

of kindness into policies that deliver material wellbeing, both economic and social, in a way that is demographically and culturally inclusive, a more exclusionary version of populism may yet emerge in New Zealand.

References

Abi-Hassan, S. (2017). Populism and gender. In C. R. Kaltwasser, P. Taggart, P. O. Espejo & P. Ostiguy (Eds), *The Oxford handbook of populism* (pp. 426–447). Oxford, United Kingdom: Oxford University Press. doi.org/10.1093/oxfordhb/9780198803560.013.16

Ainge Roy, E. (2017). 'Unacceptable': New Zealand's Labour leader asked about baby plans seven hours into the job. *The Guardian*. Retrieved from www.theguardian.com/world/2017/aug/02/unacceptable-new-zealands-labour-leader-asked-about-baby-plans-six-hours-into-job

Ardern, J. (2017a). *Jacinda's speech to campaign launch*. Retrieved from www.labour.org.nz/jacindas_speech_to_campaign_launch

Ardern, J. (2017b). Speech from the Throne. *Beehive*. Retrieved from www.beehive.govt.nz/speech/speech-throne-2017

Ardern, J. (2018a). Speech: Ardern: The 100-day plan and beyond. *Scoop*. Retrieved from www.scoop.co.nz/stories/PA1801/S00122/speech-ardern-the-100-day-plan-and-beyond.htm

Ardern, J. (2018b). Full speech. Jacinda Ardern addresses crowd from Waitangi's upper marae. *TVNZ News*. Retrieved from www.tvnz.co.nz/one-news/new-zealand/full-speech-jacinda-ardern-addresses-crowd-waitangis-upper-marae

Ardern, J. (2018c). Watch: Jacinda Ardern's full speech to the UN General Assembly. *Newshub*. Retrieved from www.newshub.co.nz/home/politics/2018/09/jacinda-ardern-s-full-speech-to-the-un-general-assembly.html

Ardern, J. (2019). Jacinda Ardern statement on mass shooting. *Scoop*. Retrieved from www.scoop.co.nz/stories/PA1903/S00114/jacinda-ardern-statement-on-mass-shooting.htm

Betz, H.-G. & Meret, S. (2011). Right-wing populist parties and the working class vote: What have you done for us lately? In J. Rydgren (Ed.), *Class politics and the radical right* (pp. 107–121). London, United Kingdom; New York: Routledge.

Bracewell-Worrall, A. (2017). Jacinda Ardern: It is 'totally unacceptable' to ask women about baby plans. *Newshub*. Retrieved from www.newshub.co.nz/home/election/2017/08/jacinda-ardern-it-is-totally-unacceptable-to-ask-women-about-baby-plans.html

Carreras, M. (2017). High-profile female executive candidates and the political engagement of women: A multilevel analysis. *Political Research Quarterly, 70*(1), 172–183. doi.org/10.1177/1065912916680034

Clinton, H. (2016). Love and kindness. Hillary Clinton. *YouTube*. Retrieved from www.youtube.com/watch?v=GHp69F7vrLU

Coffé, H. (2013). Gender and party choice at the 2011 New Zealand general election. *Political Science, 65*(1), 25–45. doi.org/10.1177/0032318713485346

Curtin, J. (2008). Women, political leadership and substantive representation: The case of New Zealand. *Parliamentary Affairs 61*(3), 490–504. doi.org/10.1093/pa/gsn014

Curtin, J. (2014). From presence to absence? Where were the women in 2011? In J. Vowles (Ed.), *The new electoral politics in New Zealand: The significance of the 2011 election* (pp. 125–140). Wellington, New Zealand: Institute for Governance and Policy Studies.

Curtin, J. (2017). Jacinda Ardern's rise goes above identity politics. *Newsroom*. Retrieved from www.newsroom.co.nz/@ideasroom/2017/08/04/41221/jacinda-arderns-rise-goes-above-identity-politics

Curtin, J. (2018, 10 April). *How Prime Minister Jacinda Ardern is reshaping political leadership in New Zealand* (Paper presentation). Center for Australian, New Zealand and Pacific Studies, Georgetown University, Washington DC.

Duerst-Lahti, G. (2006). Presidential elections: Gendered space and the case of 2004. In S. J. Carroll & R. L. Fox (Eds.), *Gender and elections: Shaping the future of American politics* (pp. 12–42). New York: Cambridge University Press. doi.org/10.1017/cbo9780511807282.002

Electoral Commission. (2014). *2014 general election overview*. Retrieved from www.elections.nz/democracy-in-nz/historical-events/2014-general-election/

Electoral Commission. (2017). *2017 general election overview*. Retrieved from www.elections.nz/democracy-in-nz/historical-events/2017-general-election/

Fording, R. C. & Schram, S. F. (2017). The cognitive and emotional sources of Trump support: The case of low-information voters. *New Political Science, 39*(4), 670–686. doi.org/10.1080/07393148.2017.1378295

Gower, P. (2017a). Newshub poll. Jacinda Ardern preferred as PM over Andrew Little. *Newshub*. Retrieved from www.newshub.co.nz/home/politics/2017/03/newshub-poll-jacinda-ardern-preferred-as-pm-over-andrew-little.html

Gower, P. (2017b). Newshub poll: Women key driver behind Jacinda Ardern's surge. *Newshub*. Retrieved from www.newshub.co.nz/home/election/2017/08/newshub-poll-women-key-driver-behind-jacinda-ardern-s-surge.html

Hochschild, A. R. (2016). *Strangers in their own land: Anger and mourning on the American right*. London, United Kingdom: The New Press. doi.org/10.18261/ issn.2535-2512-2017-05-05

Horizon Poll. (2011). Public back Shearer over Cunliffe for Labour leadership. *Horizon Poll*. Retrieved from www.horizonpoll.co.nz/page/195/public-back-

Horowitz, M., O'Sullivan, J., Charen, M., Chavez, L., Crouse, J., Farris, M., … Shays, C. (n.d.) *Challenging the caricature: A record-based strategy for long term conservative majoritie*s. Retrieved from nebula.wsimg.com/938dda95d 96397d4587d736dd3fcea3e?AccessKeyId=9BECAAD60CA7EAF6F4E9

Huang, Y. & Curtin, J. (2019). *A review of gender differences in retirement income*. Research report prepared for the Commission for Financial Capability's Review of Retirement Income Policy, July. Auckland, New Zealand: Public Policy Institute. doi.org/10.17608/k6.auckland.9699443

Human Rights Commission. (2018). Pacific women paid lowest in New Zealand's Public Service. *Scoop*. Retrieved from www.scoop.co.nz/stories/PO1812/ S00200/pacific-women-paid-lowest-in-new-zealands-public-service.htm

Idealog. (2017). Treat her right: Kiwi women get their groove on to fight for equal rights. *Idealog*. Retrieved from www.idealog.co.nz/venture/2017/02/ treat-her-right-kiwi-women-get-their-groove-fight-equal-rights

Immerzeel, T., Coffé, H. & van der Lippe, T. (2015). Explaining the gender gap in radical right voting: A cross-national investigation in 12 Western European countries. *Comparative European Politics, 13*(2), 263–286. doi.org/10.1057/ cep.2013.20

Johnson, C. (2013). From Obama to Abbott: Gender identity and the politics of emotion. *Australian Feminist Studies, 28*(75), 14–29. doi.org/10.1080/0816 4649.2012.759311

Johnson, C. (2020). Gender, emotion and political discourse: Masculinity, femininity and populism. In O. Feldman (Ed.), *The rhetoric of political leadership: Logic and emotion in public discourse* (pp. 16–33). Cheltenham, United Kingdom: Edward Elgar.

Jones, D. M. (2013). A political melodrama: We do really need to talk about Kevin. *The Spectator*. Retrieved from www.spectator.co.uk/2013/08/a-political-melodrama/

Keall, C. (2017). Mainstream media gripped by Jacinda-mania. *National Business Review*. Retrieved from www.nbr.co.nz/opinion/no-open-mainstream-media-gripped-jacinda-mania

Landesman, C. (2018). Let's get real. Kindness is not going to save you—or the world. *The Spectator*. Retrieved from www.spectator.co.uk/2018/06/lets-get-real-kindness-is-not-going-to-save-you-or-the-world/

Litt, P. (2008). 'Trudeaumania': Participatory democracy in the mass-mediated nation. *Canadian Historical Review, 1*, 27–53. doi.org/10.3138/chr.89.1.27

Malik, N. (2019). With respect: How Jacinda Ardern showed the world what a leader should be. *The Guardian*. Retrieved from www.theguardian.com/world/2019/mar/28/with-respect-how-jacinda-ardern-showed-the-world-what-a-leader-should-be

Manhire, T. (2017). Ardern-up! Strategies for Jacinda effect. *New Zealand Herald*. Retrieved from www.nzherald.co.nz/nz/news/article.cfm?c_id=1&objectid=11898680

Martin, H. (2019). Legalised abortion generally supported by New Zealanders. *Stuff*. Retrieved from www.stuff.co.nz/national/health/113583741/legalised-abortion-generally-supported-by-new-zealanders--auckland-university-survey

McCann, M. (2017). Labour will not rest until women have pay equity—Jacinda Ardern. *Newshub*. Retrieved from www.newshub.co.nz/home/election/2017/08/labour-will-not-rest-until-women-have-pay-equity-jacinda-ardern.html

McConnell, G. (2017). Mark Richardson declares himself a National supporter, does that matter? *Stuff*. Retrieved from www.stuff.co.nz/entertainment/tv-radio/96705816/mark-richardson-declares-himself-as-a-national-supporter-does-that-matter

McCulloch, A. (2013). *Fighting to choose: The abortion rights struggle in New Zealand*. Wellington, New Zealand: Victoria University Press.

Meret, S. (2015). Charismatic female leadership and gender: Pia Kjærsgaard and the Danish People's Party. *Patterns of Prejudice, 49*(1–2), 81–102. doi.org/10.1080/0031322x.2015.1023657

Ministry for Women. (2019). *Gender pay gap*. Retrieved from www.women.govt.nz/work-skills/income/gender-pay-gap

Moffit, B. (2017). Populism in Australia and New Zealand. In C. R. Kaltwasser, P. Taggart, P. O. Espejo & P. Ostiguy (Eds.), *The Oxford handbook of populism* (pp. 121–139). Oxford, United Kingdom: Oxford University Press. doi.org/10.1093/oxfordhb/9780198803560.013.5

Nagel, J. (1993). Populism, heresthetics and political stability: Richard Seddon and the art of majority rule. *British Journal of Political Science, 23*(2), 139–174. doi.org/10.1017/s0007123400009716

New Zealand Election Study. (2008). *New Zealand Election Study* [dataset]. Retrieved from www.nzes.org/exec/show/data

New Zealand Election Study. (2014). *New Zealand Election Study* [dataset]. Retrieved from www.nzes.org/exec/show/data

New Zealand Election Study. (2017). *New Zealand Election Study* [dataset]. Retrieved from www.nzes.org/exec/show/data

New Zealand Labour Party. (2017). Let's do this TV ad. *YouTube*. Retrieved from www.youtube.com/watch?v=E_kycR6u0Tg

Norris, P. & Inglehart, R. (2019). *Cultural backlash: Trump, Brexit and authoritarian populism*. Cambridge, United Kingdom: Cambridge University Press. doi.org/10.1017/9781108595841

Obama, B. (2013). Kindness covers all my beliefs. *West Wing Week*. Retrieved from www.obamawhitehouse.archives.gov/photos-and-video/video/2013/11/27/west-wing-week-112913-or-kindness-covers-all-my-political-beliefs

O'Sullivan, F. (2017). Can Ardern pull bunny out of new hat? *New Zealand Herald*. Retrieved from www.nzherald.co.nz/business/news/article.cfm?c_id=3&objectid=11897794

Roughan, J. (2017). Game on, but Jacinda Ardern should be careful with the women's card. *New Zealand Herald*. Retrieved from www.nzherald.co.nz/nz/news/article.cfm?c_id=1&objectid=11898826

Ryan, M. K. & S. Haslam, A. (2005). The glass cliff: Evidence that women are over-represented in precarious leadership positions. *British Journal of Management, 16*(2), 81–90. doi.org/10.1111/j.1467-8551.2005.00433.x

Sawer, M. & Hindess, B. (2004). *Us and them: Anti-elitism in Australia*. Perth, Australia: API Network.

Spierings, N. & Zaslove, A. (2015). Gendering the vote for populist radical-right parties. *Patterns of Prejudice, 49*(1–2), 135–162. doi.org/10.1080/0031322X.2015.1024404

Spierings, N., Zaslove, A., Mügge, L. M. & de Lange, S. L. (2015). Gender and populist radical-right politics: An introduction. *Patterns of Prejudice, 49*(1–2), 1–15. doi.org/10.1080/0031322X.2015.1023642

Stats New Zealand. (2017). *Gender pay gap unchanged since 2017*. Retrieved from www.stats.govt.nz/news/gender-pay-gap-unchanged-since-2017

Tan, L. (2017). Ardern: Labour will not rest until there is pay equity. *New Zealand Herald*. Retrieved from www.nzherald.co.nz/nz/news/article.cfm?c_id=1&objectid=11902857

Thomas, M. & Bittner, A. (2018). *Mothers and others. The role of parenthood in politics*. Vancouver, Canada: University of British Columbia Press.

Trimble, L. (2017). *Ms Prime Minister: Gender, media and leadership*. Toronto, Canada: University of Toronto Press. doi.org/10.1017/s0008423918001087

Trimble, L., Curtin, J., Wagner, A., Auer, M. & Woodman, V. K. G. (2019). Gender novelty and personalised news coverage in Australia and Canada. *International Political Science Review* [Advance online publication]. doi.org/10.1177/0192512119876083

Valentino, N. A., Wayne, C. & Oceno, M. (2018). Mobilising sexism: The interaction of emotion and gender attitudes in the 2016 US presidential election. *Public Opinion Quarterly, 82*(S1), 213–235. doi.org/10.1093/poq/nfy003

Vowles, J. (2014). Putting the 2011 election in its place. In J. Vowles (Ed.), *The new electoral politics in New Zealand: The significance of the 2011 election* (pp. 27–52). Wellington, New Zealand: Institute for Governance and Policy Studies.

Vowles, J., Coffé, H. & Curtin, J. (2017). *A bark but no bite: Inequality and the 2014 New Zealand general election*. Canberra, Australia: ANU Press. doi.org/10.22459/BBNB.08.2017

Weber, A-K. (2018). The pitfalls of 'love and kindness': On the challenges to compassion/pity as a political emotion. *Politics and Governance, 6*(4), 53–61. doi.org/10.17645/pag.v6i4.1393

Wilson, S. (2017). Tinkerbell, the pretty communist and other things the dairy farmers said. *The Spinoff*. Retrieved from www.thespinoff.co.nz/politics/19-09-2017/tinkerbell-the-pretty-communist-and-other-things-the-dairy-farmers-said/

Wright, O. & Morris, N. (2015). Jeremy Corbyn to pledge to put kindness back into British Politics in Labour Party Conference speech. *The Independent*. Retrieved from www.independent.co.uk/news/uk/politics/jeremy-corbyn-to-pledge-to-put-kindness-back-into-british-politics-in-labour-party-conference-speech-a6670951.html

Wright, R. (2016). *Trudeaumania: The rise to power of Pierre Elliott Trudeau* (1st ed.). Toronto, Ontario, Canada: Harper Collins.

Young, A. (2017). Ardern does not need to be Labour's Joan of Arc. *New Zealand Herald*. Retrieved from www.nzherald.co.nz/nz/news/article.cfm?c_id=1&objectid=11897774

Appendix

Table A6.1: Social and demographic correlates of likeability of Ardern

Variables	(1)	(2)
	Dislike Ardern	Like Ardern
Female (Male)	0.155	0.137
	(0.135)	(0.133)
Authoritarianism	−1.636***	−1.510***
	(0.453)	(0.431)
Populism	1.109**	0.597
	(0.486)	(0.527)
Efficacy	1.706***	1.447***
	(0.320)	(0.341)
Right-left position	−0.411***	−0.390***
	(0.033)	(0.032)
Māori (non-Māori)		0.692***
		(0.167)
Farmer		−1.117***
		(0.317)
Household income		−0.142***
		(0.047)
Union household		0.406**
		(0.194)
Major urban		0.264**
		(0.128)
Constant	7.462***	7.935***
	(0.406)	(0.431)
Observations	3,449.000	3,344.000
R-squared	0.184	0.211

Note: Robust standard errors in parentheses.

*** $p < 0.01$, ** $p < 0.05$, * $p < 0.1$.

Source: New Zealand Election Study (2017).

7

MĀORI AND THE 2017 GENERAL ELECTION— PARTY, PARTICIPATION AND POPULISM

Lara Greaves and Janine Hayward

Introduction

Aotearoa New Zealand is not easily placed within the contours of current populist theory (as discussed in Chapter 1). Māori politics, and particularly the Māori electorates, are distinctive features of New Zealand that disrupt conventional assumptions regarding populism. The Māori electorates are also a focus of opposition for those who refuse to acknowledge the status of Māori as tangata whenua (indigenous peoples). This chapter investigates how populism among Māori and non-Māori shape attitudes to the Māori electorates.

First, this chapter discusses the politics of the Māori electorates in 2017. The 2017 general election had significant consequences for Māori, because the Māori Party failed to win any seats. It had been represented in parliament since 2004 and had been a support partner of the National Party–led Government since 2008. Meanwhile, more Māori were elected to parliament than ever before and Māori voter turnout increased. This chapter uses New Zealand Election Study (NZES) data to ask two questions regarding the 2017 general election in relation to Māori. First, was the decline of the Māori Party predictable? Second, did Māori voter turnout provide a reliable indication of Māori political participation overall? We begin this chapter with a discussion of what we mean by 'Māori', the historical origins of the Māori electorates and the emergence of the Māori Party in 2004.

In exploring the NZES data, we split the Māori participants into three categories, based on their self-identified ethnicity and their Māori descent indicator (from the electoral roll). These categories allow us to provide a picture of the Māori electorates and to examine the preferences of Māori voters on the general roll. The categories are: Māori on the Māori electoral roll (7 per cent with NZES standard sample weights applied; n = 243; unweighted n = 610); Māori on the general roll (6.7 per cent; n = 230, unweighted n = 179) and non-Māori on the general roll (86.3 per cent, n = 2,973, unweighted n = 2,675).

However, Māori identity is complex—the decision to identify as Māori may change over time as people learn more about their ancestry and as social norms change (Carter, Hayward, Blakely & Shaw, 2009). Participants' responses to questions of identity in the NZES created some unexpected results. The 'Māori on the Māori roll' category includes all those participants who said they have Māori ancestry—as required by the *Electoral Act 1993*—and who enrolled on the Māori electoral roll. The 'Māori on the general roll' category includes all those who said they were of Māori descent and Māori ethnicity and who enrolled on the general roll.[1] 'Non-Māori on the general roll' includes all participants who did not indicate Māori ethnicity or Māori descent.

The Māori electoral roll requires some introduction. In 1867, the government created four Māori electorates under the *Māori Representation Act*, as a temporary measure to enfranchise Māori males who were not able to vote due to the property requirement (most Māori owned land collectively). Motivations for establishing the Māori electorates are the subject of debate, ranging from humanitarian concerns for Māori rights to representation to a desire to undermine Māori rangatiratanga (sovereignty/authority) and

---

1   In 2017, 3.1 per cent of participants who chose 'Māori' as one of their ethnic group affiliations did not indicate that they have Māori ancestry when enrolling to vote. In other words, they identified as Māori for the survey but have not identified themselves as being of Māori descent for electoral purposes. A very small group of survey participants (1.6 per cent; n = 39) said they were of Māori ancestry but did not identify their ethnicity as Māori: they are included in the 'non-Māori on the general roll' group. Of these, 26 did not answer the ethnicity question, 12 identified as European and one as Pasifika.

ring-fence and marginalise Māori electoral power (Geddis, 2006; Irons Magallanes, 2005; Miller, 2015; Parliamentary Library, 2003). Until 1967, non-Māori were not allowed to stand for election in the Māori electorates and, until 1975, 'full-blooded' and 'half-caste' Māori had to enrol in the Māori electorates (Geddis, 2006). The number of general electorates increased as the population in those electorates grew. However, the number of Māori electorates (four) remained fixed until 1996. By 1996, there were more than twice the number of electors in the Māori electorates than in the general electorates (Durie, 1998).

A major change to the Māori electoral roll occurred when New Zealand changed its electoral system in 1993 and, at the same time, the number of Māori electorates became dependent on the number of Māori on the electoral roll, rather than the electorates being fixed at four. Every five years—for a period of four months—the Māori Electoral Option (MEO) allows persons of Māori descent to decide whether they wish to be enrolled on the Māori or the general roll (Geddis, 2006). Following the MEO in 2013, prior to the 2017 election, 55 per cent of voters of Māori descent were on the Māori roll and there were seven Māori electorates (Electoral Commission, 2013).

Over the years, several minor parties have been set up as 'Māori' parties, including Mana Motuhake (1979), which merged with Alliance in 1991; Mana Māori Movement (1993); and smaller parties such as Mana Wāhine Te Ira Tāngata (1998), Te Tāwharau (1996), Piri Wiri Tua (1999) and the MANA Movement (2011), formed by Hone Harawira following his departure from the Māori Party. The Māori Party has been the most successful of these. It was created in 2004 after Labour Party member of parliament (MP) Tariana Turia resigned from her seat in parliament and her ministerial portfolios over the controversial *Foreshore and Seabed Act* (Godfery, 2015). Her resignation caused a by-election in the Te Tai Hauāuru seat, which Turia reclaimed under the Māori Party banner. The Māori Party is a kaupapa and tikanga (customs) Māori-based party that its founders claimed would be 'neither left nor right, but Māori' (Godfery, 2017a). The party describes its core values as manaakitanga (the importance of the mana of people), rangatiratanga (humility, leadership, diplomacy and knowledge of benefit), whanaungatanga (social organisation of whānau, hapū and iwi and reciprocal obligations), kotahitanga (unity, purpose and direction) and wairuatanga (spirituality) (Māori Party, 2017). Through its success in the Māori electorates, the Māori Party was in parliament from 2004 to 2017, although the party never crossed the 5 per cent party vote threshold. Its highest party vote share was 2.4 per cent in 2008; from this time until 2017, it offered support to the National-led coalition government.

The Māori Party and the 2017 Election

The 2017 general election initially appeared uneventful, although some speculated that the Māori Party would hold the balance of power (Godfery, 2017b; Mills, 2018; Tarrant, 2017). When campaigning began in earnest in July 2017, the election seemed a foregone conclusion, with National Party leader Bill English up against Labour Party leader Andrew Little. However, the campaign took a surprising turn just two months from election day when Green Party co-leader Metiria Turei (Ngāti Kahungunu) admitted to benefit fraud during the 1990s. Her admission highlighted the challenges of living on benefits and led to a surge in the polls for the Green Party from 11 to 15 per cent by the end of July (22–27 July, One News Colmar Brunton poll; Curia, 2017a; also see Chapter 2, Figure 2.1). At the same time, Labour Party support dropped from 27 per cent to an historic low of 24 per cent (22–27 July, One News Colmar Brunton poll; Curia, 2017a; 20–28 July, Newshub Reid Research; Gower & Barraclough, 2017). In response to the poll results, Labour Party leader Andrew Little stood down and Jacinda Ardern became Labour Party leader, with Kelvin Davis (the Ngāpuhi MP from the Te Tai Tokerau Māori electorate) as deputy leader. As the new leadership team rolled out its election campaign strategy, Labour Party polling increased to 33 per cent over the first week and rose to 44 per cent (9–13 September, One News Colmar Brunton Poll; Curia, 2017b) before settling at 37 per cent on election night (Electoral Commission, 2017). Meanwhile, Turei had resigned as Green Party co-leader in August (Davidson, 2017); Green Party support then continued to drop to a final low point of 4.9 per cent in the polls shortly before the election, putting them at risk of failing to achieve the 5 per cent threshold (6–11 September, Newshub Reid Research; Newshub, 2017).

For voters in the Māori electorates, the battle lines were drawn well before the campaign period started and the Labour leadership changed. In February 2017, the MANA and Māori parties announced an agreement not to stand candidates against each other in key electorates. Consequently, Māori and MANA party candidates were not competing against one another for the electorate vote, to give both parties a better chance at returning to parliament (Bargh, 2017). Godfery (2018) has argued that this agreement between MANA and the Māori Party was a flawed strategy from the outset, because voters in those electorates had no good reason to back candidates from parties they did not support. However, in contrast to Godfery's assertion, the 2017 NZES results show that support for both parties is moderately positively correlated for those on the Māori roll ($r = .63$). The 2014 results indicate that this is a sensible strategy. In 2014, Hone Harawira from MANA lost Te Tai Tokerau by 743 votes to Kelvin Davis (Labour; see Table 7.1), while the Māori Party candidate, Te Hira Paenga picked up 2,579 votes. Although the combined vote of Māori and MANA outpolled Labour across Māori electorates in 2014 (Vowles, Coffé & Curtin, 2017), a repeat of the close race was far from certain. Harawira had partnered with internet millionaire Kim Dotcom to contest the 2014 election under the 'Internet-MANA party' banner; therefore, his loss in Te Tai Tokerau meant that MANA had no parliamentary representation between 2014 and 2017. As shown in Figure 7.1, MANA's support in the Māori electorates did not rebound in the 2017 election; instead, it suffered a sharp decline.

A further boost for the Māori Party occurred in March 2017, when the Māori King turned his back on an established alliance with Labour and endorsed the Māori Party candidate over his own cousin and Labour MP Nanaia Mahuta. He defended this position, saying that he was disappointed the Labour Party would not consider the Māori Party as a coalition partner if Labour won the upcoming election (Forbes, 2017). In response, the Labour Party warned that Labour's Māori MPs would beat the Māori Party MPs in all the Māori electorates and that this would 'send a message to the King' (Moir, 2017). Labour raised the stakes further still when they stood most of their candidates in the Māori electorates, rather than on the party list; therefore, voters in those electorates had to vote for the Labour candidate if they wanted that candidate elected to parliament (Radio New Zealand, 2017).

Leading up to the election, polling had indicated that the Māori Party would win one or more of the Māori seats (Bracewell-Worrall, 2017). However, very few publicly released polls were conducted in these electorates, due to rising costs and dropping response rates (Tahana, 2018). The election delivered 29 MPs of Māori descent from each of the political parties in parliament, including seven Labour MPs from the Māori electorates; however, no MPs from the Māori Party won a seat and the party only received 1.2 per cent of the party vote (Koti, 2017).

The party had hoped that Te Ururoa Flavell would hold his seat of Waiariki (encompassing the broader Bay of Plenty area) and bring Marama Fox back into parliament with him on the basis of the party vote. However, Flavell lost by 1,719 votes to popular television personality Tamati Coffey (Labour Party). Therefore, the Māori Party was out of parliament. This result was largely unanticipated by both commentators and polls (Godfery, 2017b; Mills, 2018; Tarrant, 2017). Māori Party co-leaders Fox and Flavell could not hide their shock and dismay on election night; Fox accused Māori voters of having 'gone back like a beaten wife to the abuser' (Māori Television, 2017).

Could this result have been predicted? When seen in historical context, 2017 marked an additional point of decline for the Māori Party, whose support had faltered since the 2008 election. Table 7.1 shows the winners of the Māori electorates since 2002 (and their closest opponents). Prior to 2002, Labour held all seven electorates with large margins (from 23.6 per cent to 72.2 per cent of the vote). In 2005, former Labour MP Tariana Turia retained her seat for the Māori party with a 29.5 per cent margin over the new Labour candidate. The Māori Party gained 2.1 per cent of the party vote overall (with 27.7 per cent of the party vote in the Māori electorates) and won three further seats in parliament. In 2008, the Māori Party retained the same seats with larger margins of victory over the Labour candidates and slightly increased their party vote share to 2.4 per cent (28.4 per cent in the Māori electorates), which increased their caucus by one MP to five seats in total.

In 2008, the Māori Party entered into a coalition agreement with the National Party. Māori voters have traditionally shown low levels of support for National (Greaves, Robertson et al. 2017; Sullivan, von Randow & Matiu, 2014; Vowles et al., 2017). Table 7.1 and Figure 7.1 show that support for the Māori Party in the Māori electorates dropped sharply—to 15.6 per cent in 2011. Both co-leaders Sharples and Turia retired before the 2014 election, at which point support for the Māori Party declined further—to 14 per cent.

Although the Māori Party's failure to win any seats in 2017 was surprising for some, the data show that voters had been moving away from the Māori Party since 2011. The Vote Compass Post-Election Sample data show the flow of party votes between the 2014 and 2017 elections (see Chapter 2, Table 2.2 for more details). This reveals to whom Māori Party voters (in 2014) gave their party vote in 2017 and whether the party vote moved from the Māori Party in 2014 to Labour in 2017, as implied by Figure 7.1.

Table 7.1: The proportion of the vote gained by candidates in the Māori electorates by party across election

	Te Tai Tokerau		Tāmaki Makaurau		Hauraki Waikato (was Tainui)		Waiariki		Te Tai Hauāuru		Ikaroa-Rāwhiti		Te Tai Tonga	
2002	Samuels (L)	50.4	Tamihere (L)	73.3	Mahuta (L)	48.9	Ririnui (L)	61.9	Turia (L)	71.4	Horomia (L)	78.1	Okeroa (L)	63.2
	Mangu (IND)	16.2	Turei (G)	12.8	Jackson (ALL)	25.3	Vercoe (MMM)	17.5	Mair (MMM)	9.6	Philip-Barbara (MMM)	5.8	Karaitiana (N)	11.1
Margin		34.2		60.5		23.6		44.4		61.8		72.2		52.1
2005	Harawira (M)	52.4	Sharples (M)	52.4	Mahuta (L)	52.7	Flavell (M)	54.6	Turia (M)	63.0	Horomia (L)	53.7	Okeroa (L)	47.2
	Samuels (L)	33.4	Tamihere (L)	41.2	Greensill (M)	42.3	Ririnui (L)	39.5	Mason (L)	33.5	Poananga (M)	42.8	Ohia (M)	34.1
Margin		19.0		11.1		10.3		15.1		29.5		10.9		13.1
2008	Harawira (M)	62.0	Sharples (M)	66.0	Mahuta (L)	52.5	Flavell (M)	68.6	Turia (M)	70.6	Horomia (L)	51.5	Katene (M)	47.3
	Davis (L)	29.4	Wall (L)	27.3	Greensill (M)	47.5	Ririnui (L)	31.8	Mason (L)	29.4	Fox (M)	43.0	Okeroa (L)	41.8
Margin		32.5		38.6		5.0		36.8		41.2		8.5		5.5
2011	Harawira (MMM)	43.3	Sharples (M)	40.4	Mahuta (L)	58.4	Flavell (M)	43.0	Turia (M)	48.3	Horomia (L)	60.7	Tirakatene (L)	40.6
	Davis (L)	37.1	Jones (L)	35.1	Greensill (M)	22.8	Sykes (MANA)	32.5	Peke-Mason (L)	29.8	Raihania (M)	23.1	Katene (M)	31.8
Margin		6.2		5.3		35.5		10.6		18.4		37.6		8.8

	Te Tai Tokerau		Tāmaki Makaurau		Hauraki Waikato (was Tainui)		Waiariki		Te Tai Hauāuru		Ikaroa-Rāwhiti		Te Tai Tonga	
2014	Davis (L)	44.7	Henare (L)	38.3	Mahuta (L)	61.6	Flavell (M)	45.6	Rurawhe (L)	41.3	Whaitiri (L)	46.3	Tirakatene (L)	42.9
	Harawira (MMM)	41.3	McLean (M)	30.8	Susan Cullen (M)	22.7	Waititi (L)	27.3	McKenzie (M)	33.4	Nikora (MANA)	24.1	Button (M)	24.9
Margin		3.4		7.4		38.9		18.2		7.9		22.2		18.1
2017	Davis (L)	54.0	Henare (L)	48.8	Mahuta (L)	71.6	Coffey (L)	53.7	Rurawhe (L)	45.0	Whaitiri (L)	55.1	Tirakatene (L)	45.9
	Harawira (MMM)	33.5	Taurima (M)	29.0	Papa (M)	28.4	Flavell (M)	46.3	Tamati (M)	40.2	Fox (M)	36.2	Turei (G)	25.3
Margin		20.5		19.8		43.1		7.5		4.8		18.9		20.6

Note: L = Labour; M = Māori; N = National; G = Green; IND = Independent candidate; MMM = Mana Māori Movement; ALL = Alliance.

Source: Electoral Commission (2017).

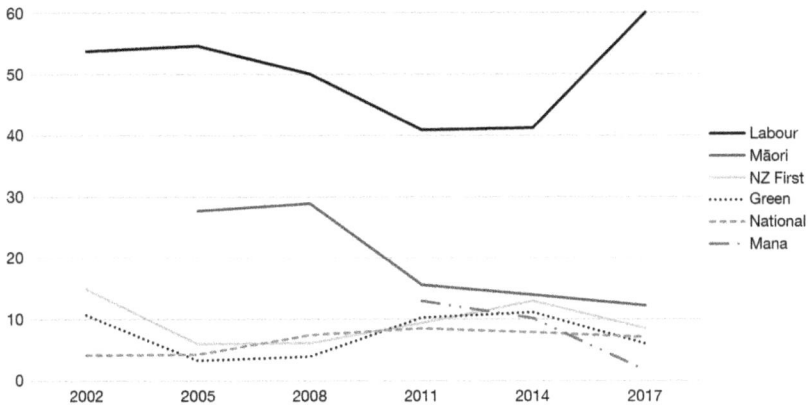

Figure 7.1: The proportion of the party vote in the Māori electorates by party across elections.

Source: Electoral Commission (2017).

Although these response categories are small, the table illustrates that Māori Party voters in 2014 who changed their vote in 2017 were most likely to vote for Labour, or National or not to vote. MANA party voters tended to shift their 2014 Internet-MANA Party vote to Labour in 2017, to the Greens or did not vote.

How can this shift from the Māori Party to Labour be understood? We can examine support for each party through two measures. First, NZES participants were asked to rate how much they liked each party on a scale from 0 (strongly dislike) to 10 (strongly like), where a score of 5 is 'neutral'. The results are displayed in Figure 7.2. The Labour Party scored best among Māori voters on both electoral rolls (an average score of 7.4 for Māori on the Māori roll and 6.5 for Māori on the general roll), with regard to how much voters liked the party and how few voters would never vote for the party. In fact, Labour had the highest overall average likeability across all voters with a score of 5.9.

Second, participants were asked to select which parties they would never vote for—a clear indicator of dislike. While National maintained its party vote among Māori voters from 2014 to 2017, Māori voters supported National at lower rates than did non-Māori. Māori on the Māori roll tended to dislike National (with an average rating of 3.3) compared to non-Māori who were more neutral or tended to like National (with an average rating of 6.1). Additionally, half of Māori on the Māori roll said that they would never vote for National, compared with 36 per cent of Māori on the general roll and 18.3 per cent of non-Māori.

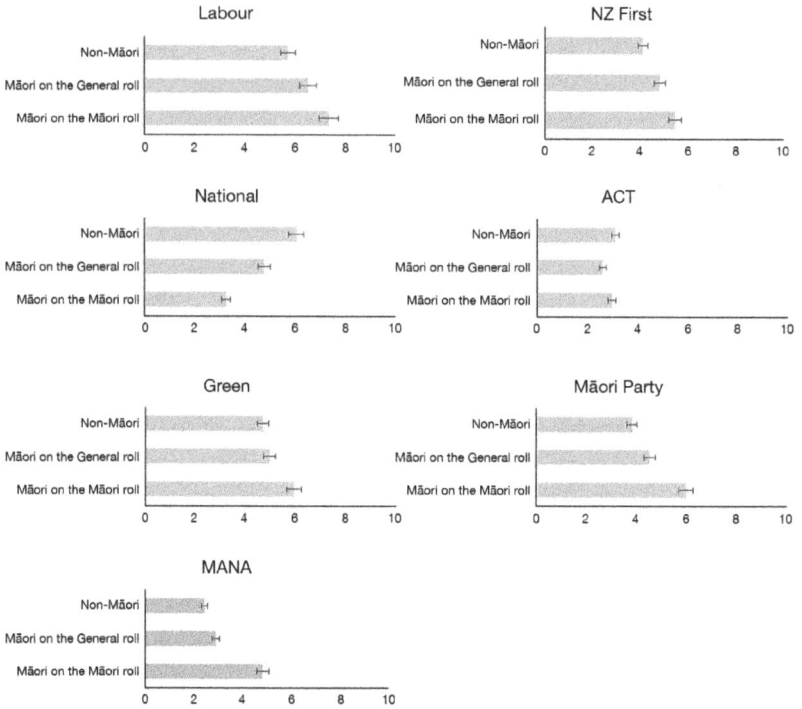

Figure 7.2: Mean likeability ratings by party in 2017 (from 0 [strongly dislike] to 10 [strongly like]) across Non-Māori, Māori on the general roll and Māori on the Māori roll.

Source: New Zealand Election Study (2017).

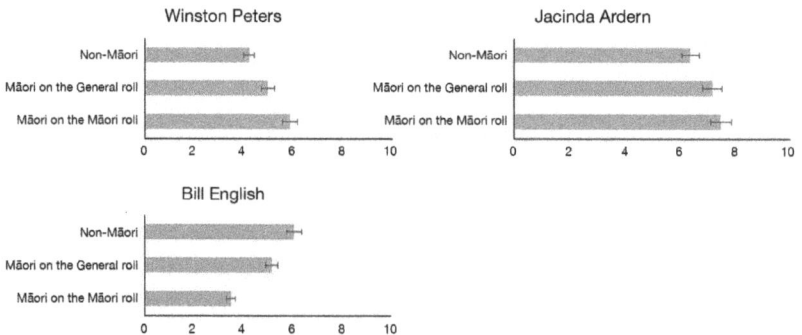

Figure 7.3: Mean likeability ratings for party leaders (0 [strongly dislike] to 10 [strongly like]).

Source: New Zealand Election Study (2017).

The popularity of Labour leader Jacinda Ardern may also explain the shift of Māori voters from the Māori Party towards Labour. Figure 7.3 shows exceptionally high likeability for Ardern, with an average score of 7.5 out of 10 for Māori on the Māori roll and 7.2 for Māori on the general roll (see Chapter 6 for further details of Ardern's likeability). We do not have data on the likeability of Kelvin Davis; however, it is possible that having a Māori deputy leader has positively affected Ardern's likeability among Māori.

Certainly, early media representations of Ardern and Davis in the leadership suggested that they would, together, be Labour's 'saviours' (Robins, 2017). However, to put these numbers in perspective, we ran the same analyses for all party leaders across the 2017, 2014 and 2011 NZES datasets, split by Māori descent and roll type. Ardern's likeability rating was higher than any leader during this period; the next highest rating was an average of 6.4 for non-Māori liking John Key in 2014. Therefore, it seems clear that the Māori Party's ongoing association with the National Party has cost it its remaining seats in 2017 (Godfery, 2018, p. 395). As Labour's popularity increased in 2017, Māori moved their support back to Labour.

Māori Voter Turnout and Political Participation

Māori have lower voter turnout than non-Māori—the lowest overall turnout in the Māori electorates (Sullivan et al., 2014; Vowles et al., 2017). In 2017, 79 per cent of all enrolled voters turned out to vote in the election (Electoral Commission, 2017). Overall, for voters of Māori descent (on both rolls), turnout was 71.1 per cent; it was 80.4 per cent for non-Māori. Māori voter turnout increased in 2017 in the younger age groups. In 2014, overall turnout for those of Māori descent was 67.6 per cent (compared with 78.3 per cent for non-Māori). In 2014, turnout for those in the 18–24 age bracket was 55 per cent, which increased to 62 per cent in 2017, whereas turnout for the 25–29 age bracket was 56 per cent in 2014 and 62 per cent in 2017.

Why did Māori voter turnout (and overall turnout) increase in the 2017 election? The closeness of a race has been shown to motivate voter turnout—in a close race, voting seems to be less burdensome, in a trade-off where one's individual vote may make a difference to the final outcome (Blais, 2000; Geys, 2006; Vowles, 2010). Although this was not reflected in the polls, the Māori electorates were perceived to be close; some commentators even predicted that the Māori Party could hold the balance of power (Godfery, 2017b; Mills, 2018). However, the highest increase in turnout between 2014 and 2017 across the Māori electorates was in Te Tai Tonga (5.6 per cent; see the right column in Table 7.2), followed by Waiariki (4.2 per cent), which, along with Te Tai Hauāuru, was one of two Māori electorates with winning margins under 10 per cent in 2016. The lowest increases were in Tamaki Makaurau (0.8 per cent) and Te Tai Tokerau (2.9 per cent) (Electoral Commission, 2017). Therefore, these increases in turnout could not be explained by the closeness of the race; however, perhaps other differences across electorates—such as age or economic deprivation and between-iwi differences—underlay these shifts. This is consistent with the findings of Vowles (2015), who showed that the closeness of the national-level race, rather than the closeness of the race in an individual Māori electorate, is more important in motivating Māori turnout.

Table 7.2: Turnout by electorate and the change in turnout between 2014 and 2017

Electorate	Turnout 2017 (%)	Change from 2014 (%)
Te Tai Tokerau	70.5	+2.9
Tāmaki Makaurau	64.0	+0.8
Hauraki-Waikato	67.3	+3.2
Waiariki	68.9	+4.2
Te Tai Hauāuru	69.5	+3.9
Ikaroa-Rāwhiti	67.6	+2.3
Te Tai Tonga	71.3	+5.6
Total	68.5	+3.3

Source: Electoral Commission (2017).

Campaigns were conducted before the election to increase Māori voter turnout. In the 2016 budget, the government committed NZ$5 million over four years to Te Puni Kōkiri (the Ministry of Māori Development) to increase Māori electoral participation and awareness across the 2017 and 2020 elections and to advertise the 2018 Māori electoral roll option (Māori Party, 2016; Treasury, 2016). A NZ$2 million campaign by Te Puni Kōkiri, 'For Future's Sake vote' (#FFSVOTE), was aimed primarily at the

18–29 age group (Te Puni Kōkiri, 2018), reflecting the fact that Māori are a relatively young population (32 per cent of Māori are aged 18–29); crucially, young people are less likely to vote. The slogan, reportedly tested on focus groups, was a play on the commonly used text-talk abbreviation where the 'F' represents an expletive. The campaign mostly used social media (Facebook, Twitter and Snapchat) and skits by comedian William Waiirua (Tahana, 2018). A similar campaign was mounted by RockEnrol; although it was not specifically targeted at Māori (given their younger average age than non-Māori), it may have had an effect. RockEnrol began in the 2014 election, through crowdfunding, led by 'four ambitious and idealistic twenty-somethings' with links to community campaigning organisations (RockEnrol, 2016). RockEnrol used a three Ps approach—Pledge, Party, Polls—wherein young people were asked to pledge to vote or express an interest in voting, were then given tickets to concerts and were later reminded to vote by volunteers.

Although these campaigns have been credited with increasing the youth vote in 2017, and despite Te Puni Kōkiri's confident claims that the campaign was a success (Strongman, 2017), Bargh (2017) noted that more robust analysis is required regarding the efficacy of the #FFSVOTE campaign. She noted significant variations in voter turnout both among and within Māori electorates (Bargh, 2017). It is also unclear what #FFSVOTE may have added above and beyond RockEnrol's three Ps evidence-based approach (O'Connell Rapira, 2016).

Institutional barriers may also have suppressed Māori voter turnout. Controversy arose during the 2017 campaign when Massey University lecturer Veronica Tawhai (2017) reported that Māori had complained to her that polling booth staff lacked knowledge of the Māori roll and the electoral system, which led to some Māori having their voting rights violated. Some Māori on the Māori roll were told they were not registered; others were given incorrect information about enrolling and were handed incorrect voting forms. Tawhai's claims are supported by evidence suggesting that a lack of knowledge on the part of electoral staff is a structural barrier to Māori voting (Galicki, 2018). The Electoral Commission (2017) received 40 complaints from Māori voters, many echoing Tawhai's concerns. Following Tawhai's press statement, the Electoral Commission issued a memo to polling booth staff in an attempt to rectify these concerns (Robinson, 2017).

There are many reasons that Māori might not vote. First, Māori tend to be a younger population and, generally, younger people are less likely to vote than older cohorts (Statistics New Zealand, 2013; Vowles, 2014). Other likely contributing factors relate to socio-economic variables such as home ownership, income, education and employment (Chapple, 2000; Humpage, 2005). Second, many Māori may view the voting system as a colonial Pākehā construct and have no desire to participate. Indeed, under early colonial governments, Māori political participation formed a key goal of assimilation; therefore, voting could be interpreted as an endorsement of this colonial system (Walker, 2004). Indigenous peoples, and ethnic minorities generally, tend to have lower levels of trust in government and elected officials and lower political efficacy (Banducci, Donovan & Karp, 2004; Clymer & Falk, 2004; Evans, 2014; Fitzgerald, Stevenson & Tapiata, 2007; Hill & Alport, 2010; Rahn & Rudolph, 2005).

Further, voter turnout is only one indicator of political participation; Māori and non-Māori may participate in politics in different ways (Bargh, 2013; Greaves et al., 2018; McVey & Vowles, 2005). Māori have a long tradition of notable hīkoi (protest marches), such as the 2004 Foreshore and Seabed hīkoi and the 1975 Māori Land March. Recognising this variety, we examined a range of types of Māori political participation in addition to voter turnout (including collective or online action), to provide the full picture of Māori political engagement in the 2017 general election and over the past five years. This examination revealed an interesting pattern of differences, as illustrated in Table 7.3.

The non-Māori sample had higher participation than Māori in only one area; they were more likely to engage in financial activities such as boycotting products or contributing monetary donations to a campaign. However, Māori on the Māori roll were more likely to have participated in social activities such as talking to someone about how they would vote and attending a political meeting or hīkoi/protest. The difference was significant—20.3 per cent of Māori on the Māori roll in the past five years indicated this type of engagement compared to 8.3 per cent of non-Māori. There also existed differences between Māori and non-Māori engagement with media and social media: Māori on the Māori roll watched an election debate at higher rates than non-Māori (70.2 per cent versus 63.7 per cent) and Māori on both rolls reported promoting issues on social media at higher rates than non-Māori. Māori were more likely to have signed a petition and were slightly more likely to have phoned talkback.

Table 7.3: The frequency of engaging in various political activities by descent and roll type

	Māori on Māori roll % (n)	Māori on General roll % (n)	Non-Māori % (n)
This election			
Contributed money	4.2 (9)	3.3 (7)	**4.7 (129)**
Put up a sign/poster	**4.8 (10)**	0 (0)	1.5 (40)
Watched an election debate	**70.2 (165)**	61.8 (141)	63.7 (1,838)
Attended a political meeting	**9.5 (20)**	1.9 (4)	5.0 (134)
Talked to someone about how they should vote	77.8 (182)	**86.0 (191)**	71.5 (2,045)
Last five years			
Signed petition	**40.8 (98)**	40.7 (92)	35.6 (1,007)
Select or Royal Committee submission	**4.5 (11)**	3.9 (9)	3.8 (113)
Consultation with government	**10.1 (24)**	9.3 (29)	9.3 (261)
Written to a newspaper	5.5 (13)	**5.7 (13)**	5.4 (153)
Protest/march/hīkoi	**20.3 (48)**	13.7 (31)	8.3 (232)
Phoned talkback	4.7 (11)	**5.2 (12)**	3.4 (94)
Boycotted product	20.2 (48)	26.5 (60)	**28.2 (795)**
Promoted issue on social media	26.1 (62)	**27.4 (62)**	22.8 (639)
Contacted politician/official	18.4 (44)	**21.1 (48)**	18.4 (516)

Note: The first segment of questions asked participants if they had performed the activities during the election campaign; the second segment asked if participants had performed any of the following activities in the past five years. Bold represents the highest value across the three groups.

Source: New Zealand Election Study (2017).

It is important to note that the NZES did not include measures of participation in politics at other levels significant to Māori, such as iwi, hapū or marae politics. These are essential indicators of Māori political participation and engagement, which are worthy of future investigation (Bargh, 2013; Greaves et al., 2018). Further, future research could investigate patterns of Māori political participation over the rich history of the NZES. In summary, Māori voter turnout increased in 2017 due to multiple factors, in the context of a long history of non-electoral political participation by Māori that has been significant in a range of ways, not least in the birth of the Māori Party.

Populism, Authoritarianism, Māori Voters and the Māori 'Seats'

The New Zealand First party leader, Winston Peters, is Māori and is also commonly referred to as a populist leader (as discussed in Chapter 1). Are these two characteristics somehow related? Exploring populism within minority groups has rarely, if ever, been attempted because minorities are commonly targeted by populists. New Zealand provides an excellent context for such a study, given that Māori are a sizeable and vocal numerical minority and are also tangata whenua (i.e. they have differential status to other ethnic minority groups due to their indigeneity). We might expect Māori to be more populist, given the popularity of Winston Peters and New Zealand First with Māori (Greaves, Robertson, et al., 2017; Vowles et al., 2017). In 1996, New Zealand First became the first political party to break the Labour party's stronghold on the Māori electorates, winning all five Māori electorates. Further, Māori have good reasons to be anti-elite, given their experiences with colonisation and assimilation. It may be predicted that Māori would score lower on populism, which has been theorised as a reaction to growing diversity, which relates to the desire to return to the 'good old days' or some kind of mythical past existence (Taggart, 2000). Originally, goodwill existed between populists and elites, but this has been eroded; for Māori, however, sustained trust has never existed between Māori and (largely Pākehā) elites throughout New Zealand's colonial history. Further, in Western nations, populism is typically associated with those of European descent (Frank, 2007).

In this discussion, we approach the question of Māori and populism from two perspectives: (1) the extent to which Māori themselves are populist and (2) the extent to which the general population's attitudes towards the Māori electorates might be associated with populism. First, to explore differences between Māori and non-Māori in terms of populism, we test the populism and authoritarianism scales across Māori on the Māori roll, Māori on the general roll and non-Māori. As discussed in Chapter 2, populism can be measured in various ways. We use the populism and authoritarianism scales, where populism taps into attitudes that elites are 'out of touch' and corrupt and authoritarianism is associated with the desire for a strong leader, majoritarianism (with minorities adapting to majority will) and a belief in discipline (e.g. the death penalty and parental discipline).

Second, opposition to the Māori electorates is often interpreted as one way that populism manifests in the New Zealand context (as discussed in Chapter 1). As tangata whenua, Māori have strong claims to the national identity in relation to Pākehā New Zealanders (and more recent immigrants). The populist response, seeking to undermine Māori identity claims, would be to create a superordinate 'New Zealander' category that obscures ethnic group differences to hold a true nativist-style identity in relation to recent immigrants to New Zealand. Consequently, the Māori electorates are often targeted by politicians who position their existence as an 'us versus them' issue and promote the idea that abolition of the Māori electorates creates true equality among 'us' (Māori and Pākehā) as true 'New Zealanders' (Brash, 2004).

Māori Voters, Populism and Authoritarianism

In relation to the question of how 'populist' Māori themselves are, NZES data reveal that Māori on the Māori roll were more populist than non-Māori; Māori on the general roll typically fall somewhere between the two. The average scores across groups for populism are presented in Figure 7.4, which shows that Māori on the Māori roll had the highest average score (0.66), while Māori on the general roll scored 0.53 and non-Māori scored the lowest with 0.47. Is this driven by a high level of agreement for Māori on certain questions or do Māori on the Māori roll score higher on populism across all questions?

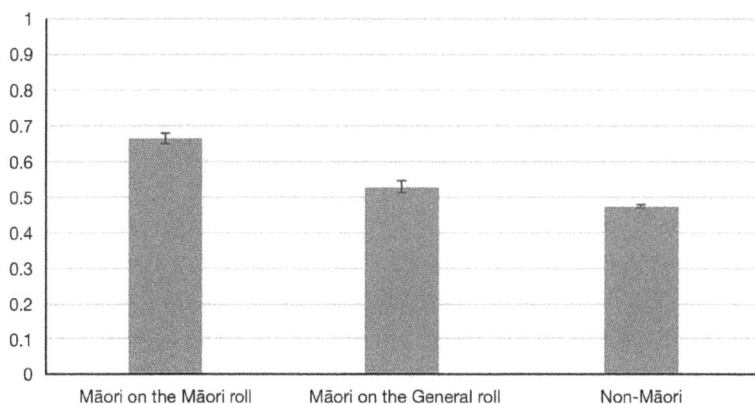

Figure 7.4: Average populism scores for Māori on the Māori roll, Māori on the general roll and non-Māori.
Source: New Zealand Election Study (2017).

We can break this down further by examining the statements presented in the NZES and the percentage of people from each group agreeing with those statements. This reveals that Māori on the Māori roll scored highest of all groups on all statements:

1. *The people, and not politicians, should make our most important policy decisions:* 65 per cent of Māori on the Māori roll agreed or strongly agreed with this statement, compared with 57 per cent of Māori on the general roll and 52 per cent of non-Māori.

2. *Most politicians care only about the interests of the rich and powerful:* 62 per cent of Māori on the Māori roll agreed or strongly agreed, compared to 48 per cent of Māori on the general roll and 34 per cent of non-Māori.

3. *How widespread or unusual do you think corruption such as bribe-taking is among politicians and public servants in New Zealand? Would you say it is very widespread, quite widespread, quite unusual, or very unusual?:* 60 percent of Māori on the Māori roll selected 'very' or 'quite widespread', as did 26 percent of Māori on the general roll and 25 percent of non-Māori.

4. *The New Zealand government is largely run by a few big interests:* 65 per cent of Māori on the Māori roll strongly or somewhat agreed, as did 52 per cent of Māori on the general roll and 45 per cent of non-Māori.

5. *Where 1 means government should listen more to experts and 5 means government should listen more to the public, where would you put your view?:* 60 per cent of Māori on the Māori roll selected 4 or 5 (suggesting that the public rather than experts should be listened to), as did 51 per cent of Māori on the general roll and 41 per cent of non-Māori.

6. *What people call compromise in politics is really just selling out on one's principles:* 60 per cent of Māori on the Māori roll agreed or strongly agreed, compared to 44 per cent of Māori on the general roll and 42 per cent of non-Māori.

Māori, particularly those on the Māori roll, appear more populist than other groups. This makes sense in the New Zealand context: New Zealand First is typically called New Zealand's populist party and is (as noted above) a party that has always had a Māori leader (Winston Peters) and, in 1996, won all five Māori electorates. However, the picture is more complex than this; it may be that populism as measured here is linked to the measure of external political efficacy (a voter's belief that they can influence politics). Therefore, we investigated external efficacy across

Māori on the Māori roll, Māori on the general roll and non-Māori. Māori on the general roll had the highest score on efficacy (an average of 0.82), which is significantly higher than both Māori on the Māori roll (0.80) and non-Māori (0.76). The difference between Māori on the Māori roll and the other groups was not statistically significant; however, the difference was significant between Māori on the general roll and non-Māori.

This suggests that Māori on the general roll score slightly higher on efficacy than others on the general roll, at least in terms of beliefs that voting and those in office can make a difference. By contrast, the populism questions listed earlier probe issues relating to trust in government and elites, in response to concerns that trust has recently been in decline among the majority culture. However, a minority indigenous culture may never have had a high level of trust in government and elites. As noted above, indigenous peoples have lower trust in government within the context of colonisation; thus, lower regard among Māori for political elites could be reasonably expected (Banducci et al., 2004; Clymer & Falk, 2004; Evans, 2014; Fitzgerald et al., 2007; Hill & Alport, 2010; Rahn & Rudolph, 2005). Additionally, one of the largest effects was the difference in reported corruption (60 per cent of Māori on the Māori roll, compared with 25 per cent of non-Māori). It may be the case that Māori believe that corruption is widespread because they actually experience corruption more than Pākehā. For example, analysis of the 2016 International Social Survey Programme question 'In the last five years, how often have you come across a public official who hinted/asked for a bribe or favour in return for service' has shown that 8.6 per cent of Pākehā had experienced this kind of corruption, compared to 20.8 per cent of Māori (Milne, Humpage & Greaves, 2016). Therefore, it remains problematic to generalise regarding the explanations for high populism scores across Māori and non-Māori in response to the survey questions. Perhaps Māori have always viewed the elites in this way.

Populism, Authoritarianism and Attitudes towards the Māori Electorates

In 1986, the Royal Commission recommended that New Zealand adopt a form of mixed member proportional (MMP) system that did not have a Māori roll or Māori electorates (Royal Commission on the Electoral System, 1986). As discussed earlier, this recommendation was not upheld—the electorates and roll were both retained and, indeed, strengthened. The *Electoral Act* was amended so that the numbers on the Māori roll were used to determine the number of Māori electorates in the same ratio as the general electorates. Following the first MMP election, Māori representation in parliament increased and has since been consistently at or above the proportion of Māori in the population.

Since the introduction of MMP, public debates regarding Māori representation have focused on the increasing number of Māori in parliament; calls have arisen to abolish the seats because they are no longer necessary to increase numbers of Māori in parliament (Joseph, 2008). Calls to abolish the Māori seats to reduce Māori representation in parliament overlook the fact that non-Māori can stand for election in those seats; therefore, Māori representation is not guaranteed. Nevertheless, appeals to abolish the seats have resonated with some voters (as discussed below). Most notably, in 2004, National Party leader Don Brash delivered his infamous 'Orewa speech' in which he called for the abolition of the Māori seats (Brash, 2004). In 2008, despite longstanding National Party policy to abolish the seats, party leader John Key refused to do so, suggesting there would be 'hīkois from hell' if he did so (Young, 2014). Since the 2017 election, New Zealand First has called for a referendum on the seats, despite dropping its demand for their abolition when the party formed a coalition government with Labour (New Zealand First, 2018). More recently, the ACT Party has reaffirmed its policy for the abolition of the seats (Radio New Zealand, 2018).

The NZES has asked a question on the abolition of the Māori electorates for several elections; this forms a useful proxy for testing this New Zealand–specific style of populism. To determine whether opposition to the Māori electorates relates to an underlying dislike of ethnicity-based outgroups, we use the anti-out-group questions from the Comparative Study of Electoral Systems (CSES). Most of these questions examine attitudes towards immigrants and what it takes to be a 'true New Zealander'. In summary, we investigate populism, authoritarianism and in- and out-group attitudes across Māori and non-Māori in relation to how supportive people are of the Māori electorates.

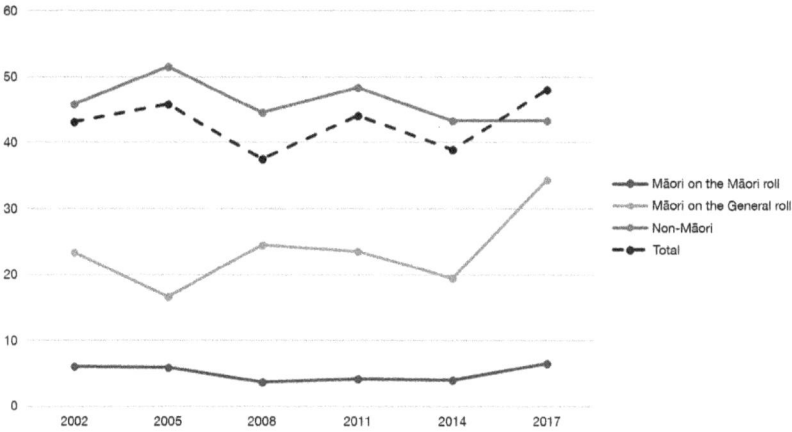

Figure 7.5: The percentage of people opposed to the Māori seats/ electorates.

Note: The NZES question wording changed in 2017—a 'fewer seats' option was added. This response has been combined with the 'abolish' responses in this figure.

Source: New Zealand Election Study (2017).

Figure 7.5 shows the percentage of people opposed to the Māori electorates from 2002 to 2017. These results indicate two general trends. First, support for the Māori electorates increased after 2002, reduced in 2011 and has since been increasing again. Overall, since 2002, there has been more support for keeping or increasing the number of electorates than for abolishing them. There may be various reasons for this; as discussed above, the Māori Party's support of the National-led government from 2008 onward was unpopular with Māori voters. The Māori Party candidates were elected from the Māori electorates; this association may have driven down support for the Māori electorates themselves among disgruntled Māori voters (although this support returned over time).

Second, unsurprisingly, support for the electorates has always been significantly higher among Māori on the Māori roll than any other group. Māori on the general roll have been less opposed to the electorates than non-Māori. It may seem that opposition to the electorates among Māori on the general roll rose sharply between 2014 and 2017; however, this is likely because the wording of the NZES question changed. The 2017 NZES added the response option of 'fewer', whereas previous surveys only allowed for a choice between abolition, keeping the electorates as they are or adding more electorates. For Māori on the general roll, this 'fewer' option may better reflect their preferences, because their choice to enrol to vote on the general roll effectively means there will be fewer electorates. To compare across elections, we have treated both the 'fewer' and 'abolish' categories as opposition. Non-Māori are generally the most opposed to the Māori electorates; only once, in 2014, did that opposition exceed 50 per cent of those surveyed—the opposition declined again in 2017. Overall, NZES data show that, despite the consistent engagement of political parties in debates regarding the future of the Māori electorates, the public generally support retention of the Māori electorates and such support is increasing over time.

How do attitudes towards the Māori electorates intersect with populist attitudes? Because so few Māori opposed the Māori electorates, to obtain more reliable estimates for these analyses we have split people into two categories: Māori (the Māori on the Māori roll and Māori on the general roll categories together) and Pākehā. Because the theory and literature currently address populism as a majority European phenomenon, Pākehā are the group of most interest here. Small subsamples for other tauiwi—those without iwi, such as Pasifika and Asians—preclude separate analysis here.

The first panel of Figure 7.6[2] demonstrates a clear pattern—the higher Māori score on populism, the more they tend to support the Māori electorates. This may mean that many Māori, compared to Pākehā, interpret the populism questions differently, reflecting a longstanding distrust in what they perceive to be settler colonial government, underscored by Māori perceptions of corruption (Banducci et al., 2004; Fitzgerald et al., 2007). Conversely, these results also suggest that Māori may see the Māori electorates as an expression of Māori self-determination that cannot be achieved through general electorate representation. Indeed, past research has shown that those who believe their identity as Māori is both positive and important and those who stand up for Māori political rights and believe in the continued importance of Te Tiriti o Waitangi are more likely to be on the Māori roll (Greaves, Osborne, Houkamau & Sibley, 2017).

---

2   Figure 7.6 is drawn from a regression model in the Appendix (see Table A7.1). In line with the models laid out in Chapter 3, we examined whether people wish to abolish the Māori electorates against our composite NZES variables representing populism and authoritarianism, and three other sets of attitudes, which reflect the original CSES 'attitudes to out-groups'. These include cultural conformity, nativism and anti-immigration attitudes. Our model also includes ethnic identity and a control for external efficacy. We interacted ethnicity with populism, authoritarianism, nativism, cultural conformity and anti-immigration attitudes to draw out probability estimates for Māori and Pākehā.

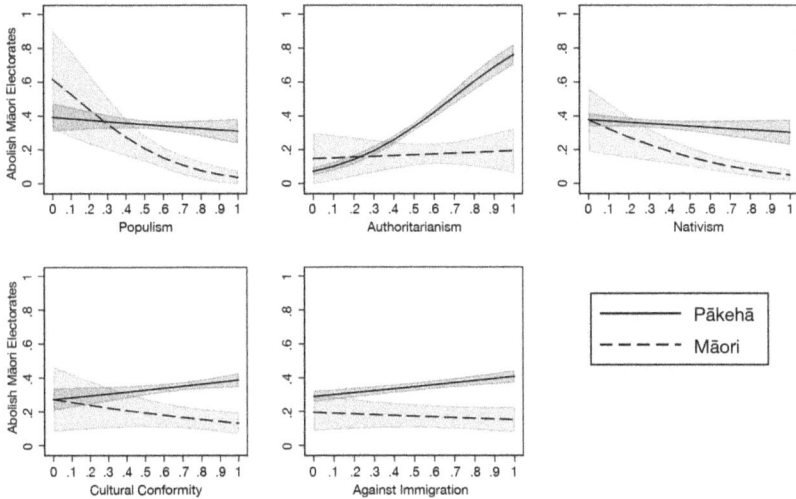

Figure 7.6: Attitudes towards the abolition of the Māori electorates.

Note: 'Cultural conformity' combines importance of language and importance of customs to be a true New Zealander; 'nativist' includes importance of being born in New Zealand, having grandparents born in New Zealand and Māori ancestry; and 'anti-immigration' refers to immigrants' effects on economy, crime and culture.

Source: New Zealand Election Study (2017).

All else being equal, populism has little or no impact on whether Pākehā support or oppose the Māori electorates; the slope is only marginally negative, within confidence intervals. Our analysis indicates that a high level of populism is associated with Pākehā supporting more Māori electorates and a lower level wishing for the number to stay the same; however, these are not large differences. We can only speculate as to the causes of this effect: perhaps these participants represent left-wing populists who are dissatisfied with the system and how elites have treated Māori? Or perhaps those who distrust elites also think that Māori do not currently hold a fair number of Māori electorates?

The top middle panel of Figure 7.6 shows that, for Māori, being more or being less authoritarian does not relate to support for, or opposition to, the Māori electorates. However, for Pākehā, the difference is dramatic— authoritarianism is the greatest motivation for their opposition to the Māori electorates. These questions index an individual's desire for a strong leader, majoritarianism and belief in discipline. In this context, these responses make sense; more authoritative leaders such as Winston Peters and Don Brash have been vocally opposed to the Māori electorates/seats (Brash, 2004; One News, 2018). Further, Māori are a numerical ethnic minority in Aotearoa New Zealand; therefore, people who endorse these views are perhaps more likely to believe that Māori should not have any 'special rights', reflecting 'Māori privilege' discourse (Barnes et al., 2012).

The top right panel indicates that those who think being born in New Zealand and/or being of Māori descent are important for being a New Zealander are, if anything, less likely to oppose the Māori electorates. The relationship is weak for Pākehā but matters more for Māori. The results for cultural conformity in the bottom left panel are entirely predictable—for Māori, the importance of their language and customs makes them less likely to oppose the existence of the Māori electorates; however, this relationship is relatively weak and falls within confidence intervals. For Pākehā, belief that their culture and customs are important is associated with increased desire to abolish the Māori electorates. For Māori, attitudes to immigration have no bearing on their opinions regarding the Māori electorates; for non-Māori, being opposed to immigration is somewhat associated with being more likely to oppose the Māori electorates.

Conclusions

This chapter has used NZES data to investigate the Māori Party, Māori participation and aspects of populism. The discussion has revealed that the decline of the Māori Party was predictable when the trends over time are considered. However, the popularity of Labour leader Jacinda Ardern likely hastened the party's departure from parliament. Regarding participation, while Māori voter turnout improved in 2017, it remains low compared to non-Māori. However, turnout is one of the few areas where non-Māori participate more than Māori. We found much higher participation by Māori in a significant range of other political activities.

Finally, Māori score higher on the populism scale than non-Māori. However, this finding should be treated with caution because some of these questions define populism as a low estimation of the majority population's trust and satisfaction with elites and government. For historical reasons, Māori (as an indigenous minority) have probably never exhibited high levels of trust in government elites. Therefore, it would be problematic to interpret Māori lack of trust as a 'populist' trend, in relation to broader international concerns regarding increasing 'nativism'. However, even if it is motivated in part by alienation from Pākehā-dominated elites, there is reason to believe that Māori populism is, at least in part, an expression of a desire for collective self-determination.

Most importantly, opposition to the Māori electorates among non-Māori is not based in populism. The main source of opposition to the Māori electorates is authoritarianism among non-Māori who strongly value cultural conformity and oppose immigration. Non-Māori who exhibit high authoritarian tendencies, who desire conformity to their values and who oppose immigration, tend also to oppose the Māori electorates. These electorates symbolise Māori identity and claims to indigenous rights and put into institutional practice the idea of a New Zealand identity that acknowledges pluralism and biculturalism. However, it is necessary to emphasise that this opposition to the Māori electorates is not a majority view; rather, our results indicate that a question of abolition of the Māori electorates would probably lose in a national referendum.

References

Banducci, S. A., Donovan, T. & Karp, J. A. (2004). Minority representation, empowerment and participation. *The Journal of Politics, 66*(2), 534–556. doi.org/10.1111/j.1468-2508.2004.00163.x

Bargh, M. (2013). Multiple sites of Maori political participation. *Australian Journal of Political Science, 48*(4), 445–455. doi.org/10.1080/10361146.2013.841123

Bargh, M. (2017). Ma pango, ma whero … Māori campaigning and voting in the 2017 general election. *Māori Law Review*. Retrieved from maorilawreview.co.nz/2017/11/ma-pango-ma-whero-maori-campaigning-and-voting-in-the-2017-general-election/

Barnes, A. M., Borell, B. McCreanor, T., Nairn, R., Rankine, J. & Taiapa, K. (2012). Anti-Māori themes in New Zealand journalism—Toward alternative practice. *Pacific Journalism Review: Te Koakoa, 18*(1), 195–216. doi.org/10.24135/pjr.v18i1.296

Blais, A. (2000). *To vote or not to vote?: The merits and limits of rational choice theory.* Pittsburgh, PA: University of Pittsburgh Press. doi.org/10.2307/j.ctt5hjrrf

Bracewell-Worrall, A. (2017). It's all on—Polling for three Māori electorates released. *Newshub*. Retrieved from www.newshub.co.nz/home/election/2017/08/it-s-all-on-polling-for-three-maori-electorates-released.html

Brash, D. (2004). Orewa speech. *Scoop*. Retrieved from www.scoop.co.nz/stories/PA0401/S00220.htm

Carter, K. N., Hayward, M., Blakely, T. & Shaw, C. (2009). How much and for whom does self-identified ethnicity change over time in New Zealand? Results from a longitudinal study. *Social Policy Journal of New Zealand, 36*, 32–45.

Chapple, S. (2000). Maori socio-economic disparity. *Political Science, 52*(2), 10115. doi.org/10.1177/003231870005200201

Clymer, A. & Falk, E. (2004). *A polling microscope: The national Annenberg election survey measures opinions of groups too small for any other poll to see clearly (Asians, Native Americans and sub-groups of Latinos)*. Paper presented at the Annual Meeting of the American Political Science Association, Chicago. Retrieved from citation.allacademic.com/meta/p_mla_apa_research_citation/0/6/0/8/1/pages60813/p60813-1.php

Curia. (2017a). *ONE News Colmar Brunton Poll late July 2017*. Retrieved from www.curia.co.nz/2017/07/one-news-colmar-brunton-poll-late-july-2017/

Curia. (2017b). *ONE News Colmar Brunton Poll 20 September 2017*. Retrieved from www.curia.co.nz/2017/09/one-news-colmar-brunton-poll-20-september-2017/

Davidson, I. (2017). Green Party co-leader Metiria Turei resigns. *New Zealand Herald*. Retrieved from www.nzherald.co.nz/nz/news/article.cfm?c_id=1&objectid=11901089

Durie, M. (1998). *Te mana, te kawanatanga: The politics of Māori self-determination*. Victoria, Australia: Oxford University Press.

Electoral Act. (1993). Retrieved from www.legislation.govt.nz/act/public/1993/0087/latest/DLM307519.html

Electoral Commission. (2013). *Results—Māori electoral option 2013*. Retrieved from www.elections.org.nz/events/Māori-electoral-option-2013/results

Electoral Commission. (2017). *General election results 2017*. Retrieved from www.electionresults.govt.nz/electionresults_2017/

Evans, L. E. (2014). Tribal-state relations in the Anglosphere. *Annual Review of Political Science, 17*, 273–289. doi.org/10.1146/annurev-polisci-073012-112513

Fitzgerald, E., Stevenson, B. & Tapiata, J. (2007). Māori electoral participation: A report produced for the Electoral Commission. New Zealand: School of Māori Studies, Massey University. Retrieved from www.academia.edu/1559198/Māori_Electoral_Participation

Forbes, M. (2017). Māori King backs Rahui Papa for Hauraki-Waikato. *Radio New Zealand*. Retrieved from www.radionz.co.nz/news/te-manu-korihi/326229/Māori-king-backs-rahui-papa-for-hauraki-waikato

Frank, T. (2007). *What's the matter with Kansas? How conservatives won the heart of America*. New York: Henry Holt/Metropolitan Books.

Galicki, C. (2018). Barriers to voting and the cost of voting among low socioeconomic, young and migrant voters in New Zealand. *Political Science, 70*(1), 41–57. doi.org/10.1080/00323187.2018.1473014

Geddis, A. (2006). A dual track democracy? The symbolic role of the Māori seats in New Zealand's electoral system. *Election Law Journal, 5*(4), 347–371. doi.org/10.1089/elj.2006.5.347

Geys, B. (2006). Explaining voter turnout: A review of aggregate-level research. *Electoral Studies, 25*(4), 637–663. doi.org/10.1016/j.electstud.2005.09.002

Godfery, M. (2015). The Māori party. In J. Hayward (Ed.), *New Zealand government and politics* (pp. 240–250). Melbourne, Australia: Oxford University Press.

Godfery, M. (2017a). The end of 'neither left nor right, but Māori'. *The Spinoff*. Retrieved from www.thespinoff.co.nz/politics/30-09-2017/the-end-of-neither-left-nor-right-but-Maori/

Godfery, M. (2017b). Please don't tell Don Brash, but the Māori Party could decide the next government. *The Spinoff*. Retrieved from www.thespinoff.co.nz/politics/03-09-2017/please-dont-tell-don-brash-but-the-Maori-Party-could-decide-the-next-government/

Godfery, M. (2018). Did the Māori electorates decide the 2017 general election? *E-Tangata*. Retrieved from www.e-tangata.co.nz/comment-and-analysis/did-the-maori-electorates-decide-the-2017-election/

Gower, P. & Barraclough, B. (2017). Newshub poll: Winston Peters cements position as kingmaker. *Newshub*. www.newshub.co.nz/home/election/2017/07/newshub-poll-winston-peters-cements-position-as-kingmaker.html

Greaves, L. M., Robertson, A., Cowie, L. J., Osborne, D., Houkamau, C. A. & Sibley, C. G. (2017). Predicting party vote sentiment: Identifying the demographic and psychological correlates of party preference in two large datasets. *New Zealand Journal of Psychology, 46*(3), 164–175.

Greaves, L. M., Osborne, D., Houkamau, C. A. & Sibley, C. G. (2017). Identity and demographics predict voter enrolment on the Maori electoral roll. *MAI Journal, 6*(1), 3–16. doi.org/10.20507/MAIJournal.2017.6.1.1

Greaves, L. M., Sengupta, N. K., Townrow, C. S., Osborne, D., Houkamau, C. A. & Sibley, C. G. (2018). Māori, a politicised identity: Indigenous identity, voter turnout, protest and political party support in Aotearoa New Zealand. *International Perspectives in Psychology: Research, Practice, Consultation, 7*(3), 155–173. doi.org/10.1037/ipp0000089

Hill, L. & Alport, K. (2010). Voting attitudes and behaviour among Aboriginal peoples: Reports from Anangu women. *Australian Journal of Politics & History, 56*(2), 242–258. doi.org/10.1111/j.1467-8497.2010.01552.x

Humpage, L. (2005). *Tackling indigenous disadvantage in the twenty-first century: 'Social inclusion' and Maori in New Zealand.* London, United Kingdom: Zed Books.

Irons Magallanes, C. J. (2005). Indigenous political representation: Identified parliamentary seats as a form of indigenous self-determination. In B. A. Hocking (Ed.), *Unfinished constitutional business? Rethinking indigenous self-determination* (pp. 106–117). Canberra, Australia: Aboriginal Studies Press.

Joseph, P. (2008). *The Maori seats in Parliament* (Working Paper 2) (Te Oranga o te Iwi Maori: A study of Maori economic and social progress). Retrieved from www.nzcpr.com/wp-content/uploads/2014/08/TheMaoriSeatsInParliament.pdf

Koti, T. (2017). Who are our Māori members of parliament now? *Te Ao.* Retrieved from www.māoritelevision.com/news/politics/who-are-our-Māori-members-parliament-now

Māori Party. (2016). *$5m to promote Māori voter participation* [Press release]. Retrieved from www.māoriparty.org/_5m_to_promote_Māori_voter_participation

Māori Party. (2017). *Our Kaupapa.* Retrieved from www.māoriparty.org/our_kaupapa

Māori Television. (2017). Māori have 'gone back like a beaten wife to the abuser', defiant Marama Fox says. *Stuff.* Retrieved from www.stuff.co.nz/national/politics/97179049/mori-have-gone-back-like-a-beaten-wife-to-the-abuser-defiant-marama-fox-says

McVey, A. & Vowles, J. (2005). Virtuous circle or cul de sac? Social capital and political participation in New Zealand. *Political Science, 57*(1), 5–20. doi.org/10.1177/003231870505700102

Miller, R. (2015). *Democracy in New Zealand*. Auckland, New Zealand: Auckland University Press.

Mills, S. (2018). Survey findings and the 2017 election. In S. Levine (Ed.), *Stardust and substance: The New Zealand general election of 2017* (pp. 365–378). Wellington, New Zealand: Victoria University Press.

Milne, B. J., Humpage, L. & Greaves, L. (2016). *ISSP 2016 role of government dataset*. Retrieved from www.auckland.figshare.com/articles/ISSP2016_Role_of_Government_V/4747405

Moir, J. (2017). Andrew Little: Māori King is 'abusing his office' by endorsing Rahui Papa for the Māori Party. *Stuff*. Retrieved from www.stuff.co.nz/national/politics/90342952/andrew-little-Māori-king-is-abusing-his-office-by-endorsing-rahui-papa-for-the-Māori-party

New Zealand Election Study. (2017). *New Zealand Election Study* [dataset]. Retrieved from www.nzes.org/exec/show/data

New Zealand First. (2018). *Binding referendum on Maori seats to be debated*. Retrieved from www.nzfirst.org.nz/binding_referendum_on_maori_seats_to_be_debated

Newshub. (2017, 12 September). Bill English NZ's preferred PM on latest Newshub poll. *Newshub*. Retrieved from www.newshub.co.nz/home/election/2017/09/bill-english-nz-s-preferred-pm-on-latest-newshub-poll.html

O'Connell Rapira, L. (2016). How grassroots innovation turned around the youth vote after decades of decline. *Te Punaha Matatini*. Retrieved from www.tepunahamatatini.ac.nz/2016/08/03/how-grassroots-innovation-turned-around-the-youth-vote-after-decades-of-decline/#_edn3

One News. (2018). Winston Peters renews his push for referendum on future of Māori seats. *One News*. Retrieved from www.tvnz.co.nz/one-news/new-zealand/winston-peters-renews-his-push-referendum-future-m-ori-seats-in-parliament?variant=tb_v_1

Parliamentary Library. (2003). *The origins of the Māori seats*. Retrieved from www.parliament.nz/resource/en-NZ/00PLLawRP03141/e27e432e971eb1f60ea75b00c987a39e4b2e62ce

Radio New Zealand. (2017). Labour MPs opt for Māori electorate do-or-die. *Radio New Zealand*. www.radionz.co.nz/news/political/327115/labour-mps-opt-for-Māori-electorate-do-or-die

Radio New Zealand. (2018). Seymour wants Māori seats abolished. *Radio New Zealand*. Retrieved from www.rnz.co.nz/news/political/363899/seymour-wants-maori-seats-abolished

Rahn, W. M. & Rudolph, T. J. (2005). A tale of political trust in American cities. *Public Opinion Quarterly, 69*(4), 530–560. doi.org/10.1093/poq/nfi056

Robins, A. (2017). Acclaim for Jacinda Ardern. *The Standard*. Retrieved from thestandard.org.nz/acclaim-for-jacinda-ardern/

Robinson A. J. (2017). Complaints laid against election staff. *Newshub*. Retrieved from www.newshub.co.nz/home/election/2017/09/complaints-laid-against-election-staff.html

RockEnrol. (2016). *About us—RockEnrol*. Retrieved from www.rockenrol.org.nz/aboutus.html

Royal Commission on the Electoral System. (1986). *Report of the Royal Commission on the electoral system: Towards a better democracy*. Wellington, New Zealand: Government Printer.

Statistics New Zealand. (2013). *2013 Census quickStats about Māori*. Retrieved from www.stats.govt.nz/Census/2013-census/profile-and-summary-reports/quickstats-about-Māori-english/population.aspx

Strongman, S. (2017). Youth voter turnout gets a big bump. *Radio New Zealand*. Retrieved from thewireless.co.nz/articles/youth-voter-turnout-gets-a-big-bump

Sullivan, A., von Randow, M. & Matiu, A. (2014). Māori voters, public policy and privatisation. In J. Vowles (Ed.), *The new electoral politics in New Zealand: The significance of the 2011 election* (pp. 141–160). Wellington, New Zealand: Institute for Governance and Policy Studies.

Taggart, P. (2000). *Populism: Concepts in the social sciences*. Philadelphia, PA: Open University Press.

Tahana, Y. (2018). Māori media and the campaign. In S. Levine (Ed.), *Stardust and substance: The New Zealand general election of 2017* (pp. 132–136). Wellington, New Zealand: Victoria University Press.

Tarrant, A. (2017). Election 2017 could be decided by the Māori seats. *Interest*. Retrieved from www.interest.co.nz/opinion/86964/election-2017-could-be-decided-Māori-seats-alex-tarrant-writes-while-national-clearly

Tawhai, V. (2017). Electoral Commission undermining of Māori rights. *Scoop*. Retrieved from www.scoop.co.nz/stories/PO1709/S00303/electoral-commission-undermining-of-Maori-rights.htm

Te Puni Kōkiri. (2018). *Questions and answers*. Retrieved from www.tpk.govt.nz/en/whakamahia/Maori-electoral-participation/questions-and-answers

Treasury. (2016). *Vote Māori development. The estimates of appropriations 2016/2017.* Wellington, New Zealand: New Zealand Treasury. Retrieved from www.treasury.govt.nz/budget/2016/estimates/v8/est16-v8-maodev.pdf

Vowles, J. (2010). Electoral system change, generations, competitiveness and turnout in New Zealand, 1963–2005. *British Journal of Political Science, 40*(4), 875–895. doi.org/10.1017/S0007123409990342

Vowles, J. (2015). Voter turnout. In J Hayward (Ed.), *Government and politics in New Zealand* (pp. 287–299). Melbourne, Australia: Oxford University Press.

Vowles, J., Coffé, H. & Curtin, J. (2017). *A bark but no bite: Inequality and the 2014 New Zealand General Election.* Canberra, Australia: ANU Press. doi.org/10.22459/BBNB.08.2017

Walker, R. (2004). *Ka whawhai tonu matou: Struggle without end* (2nd ed.). Auckland, New Zealand: Penguin Books.

Young, A. (2014). John Key: Dropping Māori seats would mean hikois from hell. *New Zealand Herald.* Retrieved from www.nzherald.co.nz/nz/news/article.cfm?c_id=1&objectid=11312498

Appendix

Table A7.1: Abolish Māori electorates (logistic regression)

Abolish Māori electorates (logistic regression)	1	2	3	4	5	6
Efficacy	0.079	0.105	0.101	0.112	0.069	0.099
	(0.287)	(0.284)	(0.286)	(0.286)	(0.288)	(0.283)
Authoritarianism	3.397***	3.791***	3.429***	3.365***	3.378***	3.400***
	(0.322)	(0.333)	(0.322)	(0.323)	(0.325)	(0.325)
Populist	−0.636*	−0.601*	−0.410	−0.636*	−0.626*	−0.643*
	(0.356)	(0.363)	(0.378)	(0.358)	(0.355)	(0.357)
Nativism	−0.738***	−0.729***	−0.688***	−0.376	−0.675**	−0.723***
	(0.261)	(0.257)	(0.261)	(0.273)	(0.262)	(0.258)
Cultural conformity (CC)	0.470**	0.460**	0.475**	0.495**	0.575**	0.451**
	(0.230)	(0.231)	(0.229)	(0.229)	(0.248)	(0.229)
Anti-immigration	0.467***	0.465***	0.469***	0.456***	0.459***	0.573***
	(0.113)	(0.114)	(0.113)	(0.113)	(0.114)	(0.121)

Abolish Māori electorates (logistic regression)	1	2	3	4	5	6
Māori	−1.094***	0.810	1.038	−0.004	0.003	−0.566
	(0.280)	(0.659)	(0.726)	(0.475)	(0.572)	(0.400)
Pasifika	−1.113**	3.637***	0.885	−0.851	−0.433	−0.569
	(0.503)	(1.052)	(1.415)	(0.588)	(0.918)	(0.598)
Asian	−1.142***	−1.502	−2.050**	−0.625*	−1.674**	−0.775**
	(0.275)	(1.331)	(0.879)	(0.376)	(0.813)	(0.343)
Other	−1.921**	−74.414***	−2.596	−0.270	−5.314**	−13.502***
	(0.893)	(4.020)	(1.842)	(0.777)	(2.664)	(0.365)
Māori * populist		−3.684***				
		(1.232)				
Pasifika * populist		−3.622				
		(2.430)				
Asian * populist		1.663				
		(1.595)				
Other * populist		1.055				
		(3.218)				
Māori * authoritarian			−3.456***			
			(1.020)			
Pasifika * authoritarian			−8.352***			
			(1.828)			
Asian * authoritarian			0.574			
			(2.138)			
Other * authoritarian			90.610***			
			(4.882)			
Māori * nativist				−2.248***		
				(0.735)		
Pasifika * nativist				−0.726		
				(1.501)		
Asian * nativist				−2.951*		
				(1.730)		
Other * nativist				0.000		
				(0.000)		
Māori * CC					−1.563**	
					(0.672)	
Pasifika * CC					−0.959	
					(1.269)	

Abolish Māori electorates (logistic regression)	1	2	3	4	5	6
Asian * CC					0.804	
					(1.095)	
Other * CC					4.303	
					(3.016)	
Māori * anti-immigrant						−0.897*
						(0.493)
Pasifika * anti-immigrant						−0.951
						(0.955)
Asian * anti-immigrant						−0.841
						(0.542)
Other * anti-immigrant						12.120***
						(1.197)
Constant	−2.426***	−2.669***	−2.594***	−2.559***	−2.501***	−2.488***
	(0.307)	(0.305)	(0.309)	(0.298)	(0.311)	(0.300)
Pseudo-R-squared	0.100	0.110	0.110	0.110	0.110	0.110
observations	3,455.000	3,455.000	3,455.000	3,446.000	3,455.000	3,455.000

Source: New Zealand Election Study (2017).

8

THE UNEXPECTED COALITION – CHALLENGING THE NORMS OF GOVERNMENT FORMATION

Jack Vowles

As established in previous chapters, populism and authoritarianism have strong roots in New Zealand political culture and public opinion. Combined, these two attitudinal dimensions are associated with vote choices for New Zealand First, widely recognised as a populist party. However, populism is also associated with vote choice for Labour and is more strongly aligned with left-wing rather than right-wing opinion. Following the 2017 election, the outcome of government-formation negotiations was momentous and surprising: National, the party with the most votes, was excluded from government. A coalition government was formed but its largest party had failed to gain a vote plurality. This presented a potential challenge to both populist and authoritarian values, raising the question of a legitimacy crisis. Therefore, deeper inquiry is required into the normative foundations of the new government's claim to take office.

This chapter begins with a discussion of the normative principles used to justify and defend government formation and goes on to test their consistency with voters' preferences for the party to lead the government, voters' general evaluations of the parties, leadership preferences, evaluations of leaders, issue and policy positions and how these apparently aligned with the positions of the actual and alternative government coalitions that might have formed. A higher-level norm was also called into question by the 2017 outcome: the justification for coalition rather than single-party government, a key objective of electoral system reform in the 1990s. According to standard theory, both populists and authoritarians should be opposed to the principle and practice of coalition government—authoritarians because they prefer strong leaders and populists because they are claimed to be anti-pluralist. One might also expect overall support for coalition government to fall, particularly among National voters. Satisfaction with democracy may also be affected, which would assist to provide some additional detail regarding the minor decline reported in Chapter 3.

Norms and Legitimacy

In political theory and political science, the concept of legitimacy is both confused and complex (Marquez, 2015). Healthy democracies operate on foundations of congruence between norms and outcomes, elite and mass perceptions of which can be loosely characterised as defining legitimacy or its absence. In electoral politics, there exist winners and losers. When the norms associated with winning and losing are confused or contested, public confidence in the democratic process may waver. Losers must accept that they have lost; if they fail to do so, democracy may be at risk (Anderson et al., 2005). Conflict over norms may open the door to authoritarian populism.

Powell (2000) has identified two normative models of democracy: majoritarian and proportional. Most countries' institutions and practices fall comfortably within one or the other model. When applied to a parliamentary democracy, the majoritarian model identifies the winner as whoever gains a plurality of votes and a majority of seats in the legislature—the winner is also assumed to be a single party. In a proportional system, a single party is unlikely to win a majority of votes alone and must seek the consent of other parties to govern, either by forming a majority coalition with a subset of those parties or negotiating a minority government of some kind. In a random draw of possible outcomes in a proportional system, with all else being equal, a party that is the plurality winner is still more likely than other contenders to form a government. However, there are many scenarios in which the plurality winner may be excluded from office by a coalition of other parties. In this way, plurality 'losers' may become government 'winners'. Here, the norms underlying majoritarian and proportional systems conflict with one another.

New Zealand's first election under the mixed member proportional (MMP) system occurred in 1996. Between 1996 and 2014, in seven elections, the party who won a vote plurality was able to form a government. In 2017, this run of plurality winners forming governments ceased. The National Party, in power since 2008, was thrust out of office despite winning by far the largest share of the votes. Instead, the Labour Party formed a government in coalition with the New Zealand First Party, giving that party four of 20 Cabinet positions, and with support from the Green Party on confidence and supply. The Greens also took three ministerial positions outside Cabinet.

This is a situation ripe for conflict between norms. In 2017, many New Zealanders still remembered the old single-member plurality (SMP) system. In that year, a little less than two-thirds of people on the electoral rolls were still old enough to have been eligible to vote under the old system. In fact, many still favoured the SMP system over MMP. Populism has long been identified as a central component of New Zealand's 20th century political culture, as has authoritarianism; these values have affected people's electoral system preferences and expectations of government in the recent past (Lamare & Vowles, 1996; Vowles, 2011). Authoritarian attitudes lay behind 1996 preferences to retain the SMP system and 2011 preferences to return to it. Meanwhile, contrary to claims of anti-pluralism in populist thinking, populist attitudes can be identified in the arguments for electoral system change. Rather than aspiring towards consensus-based government, reformers were seeking rule by absolute majorities, rather than narrowly based pluralities, and wished to see governments become more likely to keep their promises and heed public opinion (Katz, 1997; Nagel, 1998, p. 265).

It may be that values are changing, particularly among young New Zealanders, who tend to be less authoritarian in their values than the old (Vowles, 2011, p. 141; see Chapter 3). A majority voted to retain the MMP system at a referendum in 2011, in which younger people with no experience of voting under the old rules were significantly more in favour of the new status quo (Karp, 2014). Despite the continued prevalence of plurality winners forming government until 2017, the norms underlying the MMP electoral system are well understood, particularly among the political elite, most members of which have accepted proportional norms.

On election night in 2017, National Party leader and Prime Minster Bill English did claim the 'moral authority' to have the first chance to form a government. Given the six-point vote gap between the two major parties, most observers expected that New Zealand First would form a coalition with National, as it had in 1996 (see e.g. Milne, 2017). Nonetheless, Winston Peters, leader of the New Zealand First Party, announced that he would conduct parallel negotiations with both major parties, as he had also done in 1996. Meanwhile, at the special vote count, released two weeks after the election, National lost two seats to the benefit of the Labour and Green parties, adding to the potential majority for the Labour, New Zealand First and Green parties, if they were able to form a government. It was Peters himself, on 19 October, who made the announcement. Bill English's acceptance of the outcome was clear—he noted that the result was unusual, given his party's high vote share (44 per cent), but added that he accepted the results (Radio New Zealand, 2017). He went on to congratulate Labour leader Jacinda Ardern on her success.

However, not all on the right and centre-right were so generous. An incoming National Party member of parliament posted on Facebook that 'MMP was never intended to deny the party that polled highest by far, the win'—a post that was subsequently deleted (MacDonald, 2017). Former ACT party leader Richard Prebble described the new government as 'a coalition of losers' and alleged that there had been a 'coup'. He went on to say that:

> The political scientists can tell us it's legal but the fact remains—it is undemocratic. For the first time in our history, who governs us is not the result of an election but the decision of one man. Jacinda Ardern is Prime Minister in name only. (Prebble, 2017)

Right-wing shock jock radio host and commentator Mike Hosking declared 'that's the madness of MMP' (2017). This theme was also taken up in Australia (NZ shock, 2017).

Nonetheless, the prevailing tone of media commentary ran against this current of criticism. It was conceded that there had been an attitude shift among voters towards a government of change; therefore, Winston Peters and New Zealand First had made a wise decision. National Party pollster David Farrar even expressed relief that his party had not formed a government with New Zealand First, because such a government had the potential to damage National (Farrar, 2017). Bill English graciously accepted the outcome: 'we all know the rules, we play by them. This is the result … we certainly accept it' (Radio New Zealand, 2017). The excitement associated with a change of government and the appointment of a new, relatively young female prime minister added to the mood. Many voices within the intellectual community and the commentariat articulated a normative defence of the result. Perhaps the most accessible, in popular terms, was Eva Allan (on Facebook):

> Allow me to explain MMP: There's one mince and cheese pie left in the shop—it costs $5. Bill has $4.50. Jacinda has $3.70. Winston has 70c. James has 60c and David has 5c. No one has enough money to buy the pie by themselves but Jacinda, Winston and James put their money together and buy the pie. Bill gets no pie because he needed 50c but didn't have any friends to help him pay for the pie. I hope this helps explain things. (cited in Edwards, 2017)

Voter Preferences and the Government Outcome

Except for a few episodes of anecdotal *vox pop* coverage in the commercial media, the public response, seemingly positive, cannot be estimated, certainly not in any depth. Admittedly, post-election polls indicated a minor further shift to Labour (see Chapter 9) and a further upward boost in the new year following the announcement that Jacinda Ardern was expecting a baby. On first sight, the New Zealand Election Study (NZES) lacks an instrument to directly assess the normative reception of the change of government. However, because the return of questionnaires took place over several weeks, the data available can indirectly compare how people responded before and after the change of government.

Figure 8.1 displays responses to a particularly pointed question with obvious implications for the legitimacy and acceptability of the outcome: 'On election day 2017, between National and Labour, which one did you most want to be in government?' Across the whole period of sampling, from just after the election until the end of February, 48 per cent of those who responded to the question in the weighted sample wished to see a National-led government, compared to 42 per cent who preferred Labour. Upon digging deeper into the data, 44 per cent of those voting for the pivotal New Zealand First Party preferred National, compared to 34 per cent who preferred Labour. These numbers should, of course, be treated with caution. For an unweighted number of 235 New Zealand First voters, the confidence interval is plus or minus 6.4 per cent.

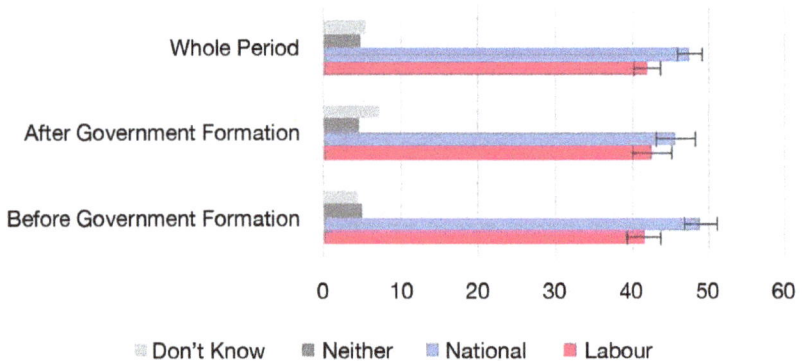

Figure 8.1: Preferences for a National- or Labour-led government.

Note: The data were re-weighted on party vote to standardise report of vote across pre- and post-government announcements.

Source: New Zealand Election Study (2017).

Even if the confidence intervals were disregarded, these numbers cannot be taken wholly on face value. Cueing effects should be tested for by breaking the data down more deeply, comparing those responding before and after the announcement of the government outcome. That is, we may investigate whether perceptions of the government outcome affected the responses of voters with weak preferences regarding the two main parties, cueing them towards the winner. This cueing could be operative, not only after the announcement but also before it, exaggerating both early preferences for a National-led government and the later preferences for one led by Labour.

Initial investigation, using the standard weight applied to make the sample representative in terms of demography and voting patterns, indicated a 'flip', with a Labour-led government leading after the announcement— an apparently significant cueing effect. However, further inquiry leads us to conclude that it is more likely that the formation of the Labour-led government cued National voters in another way, discouraging those who had not yet responded to the survey questionnaire from doing so. Meanwhile, the non-voters in the sample, who tended to prefer a National-led government, were much more likely to respond after 19 October; those responding later still favoured National but were more likely to choose Labour than those responding earlier. Therefore, the dataset had to be weighted further, to adjust for differential response rates among National voters and non-voters between the two periods, including adjustment for the exaggerated effect of cueing on non-voters following 19 October.

Having applied the new weight, Figure 8.1 shows that, after the government announcement, preference for a National-led government remained ahead, but the gap with Labour was no longer statistically significant. While the specific numbers are only indicative, due to even wider confidence intervals, New Zealand First voters may have flipped. They opted 51 to 26 per cent for National before the announcement of the government on 19 October (a difference outside even a wide confidence interval) and 48 to 33 per cent to Labour afterward (a difference just within confidence intervals). However, non-voters, a much larger population group, also shifted towards Labour after 19 October; even then, they still gave National an edge: 46 to 25 for National against Labour, prior to government formation, and 35 to 33 to National, post government formation. These relatively minor cueing effects among non-voters and New Zealand First voters mostly account for the differences before and after 19 October. However, these conclusions rely on a critical assumption—that respondents were reporting their party vote choices correctly (both before and after 19 October). This assumption is reasonable, given that the main source of error in reported votes is non-voters who claim to have voted; however, these errors are already corrected in our data (see Figure A8.1). Therefore, the government outcome presents a legitimacy issue, particularly from the point of view of at least some constructions of populist attitudes. Admittedly, the gap is a narrow one, and the overall distribution is also influenced by the somewhat greater proportion of pre-announcement respondents, as compared to post-announcement responses in the dataset.

Various other questions in the survey provide more relevant data. When asked which political party they 'liked the most' on election day, as with the votes cast, the combination of Labour, Green and New Zealand First narrowly edged out the combined preferences of the parties in the previous government—National, ACT, Māori and United Future—however, by less than 1 percentage point, which is well within the error margin. When asked 'which party if any best represents your views?', nearly 40 per cent indicated the parties of the new government, compared to just over 37 per cent choosing the parties of the old: again, this difference is well within sampling error. After being asked to indicate the most important issue in the election, respondents were asked 'which party would be best at dealing with that issue?' Across the sample, just over 42 per cent indicated a new government party and just under 35 per cent indicated an old government party. However, this question is also likely to be strongly cued by whether the designated party was expected to be in government and, therefore, have the opportunity to 'deal'. Before 19 October, with the government formation weight applied, the two sets of parties were level, with the Labour-led parties only marginally ahead, at approximately the 40 per cent mark: after 29 October, the new government's parties moved decisively ahead at 46 to 30.

Another approach is to calculate the distance between the alternative sets of government parties, the average and the median voter. For this, as shown in Figure 8.2, one relies on the 0–10 left–right scale, where respondents placed themselves and the parties, respectively. From this, we can calculate the perceived left–right position of the government, weighting respondents' left–right perceptions of the parties by the parties' vote shares. To include all respondents, missing values and 'don't knows' must be set at the midpoint of 5. Parallel analysis that drops those cases loses many who could not place the smaller parties; however, when the numbers are recalculated on this basis, the gaps stay relatively in proportion. Coding the missing values as 5 pulls all parties towards the centre—the more so the more values that are missing. Figure 8.2 displays these data with the missing values coded as 5. An alternative figure without missing values makes no difference to the findings in Figure 8.2.

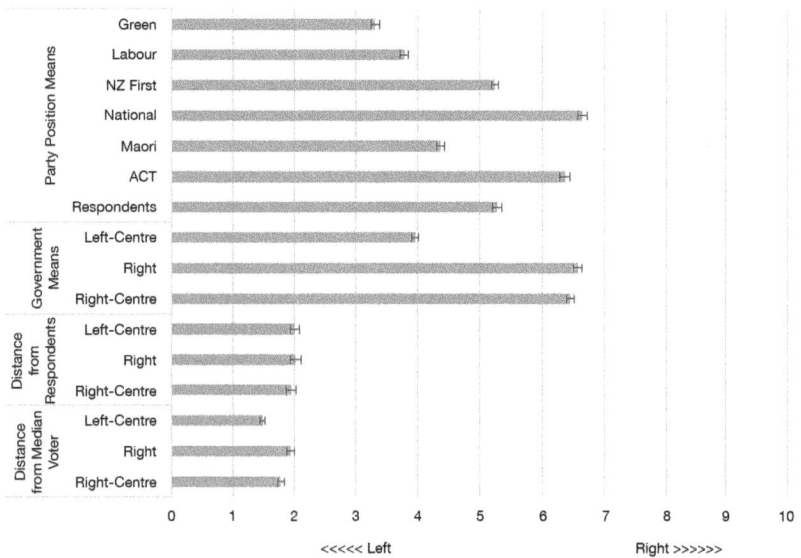

Figure 8.2: Party, alternative government and respondent right–left positioning and distance from the average and median voters.
Source: New Zealand Election Study (2017).

In this figure, most left is 0 and most right is 10. For the most part, when averaged across respondents, perceptions of party positions accord with expert assessments. The exception is ACT—it scores as less to the right than National. This is because only two-thirds of the sample rated ACT on the scale. Without missing and 'don't know' values set at 5, ACT scores 7.24, only slightly further to the right than National (7.15), also without missing values. The average respondent scores 5.28 (without missing values, only slightly higher at 5.35). The median respondent is 5.

In the government mean and distance rows, left-centre represents the Labour–New Zealand First–Green combination and right represents National, ACT and Māori. Former National support party United Future was not scored on the left–right scale and could not be included, although the party received a microscopic vote in 2017. Right–centre represents a hypothetical National–New Zealand First coalition. The government mean scores put the current left-centre government at just below 4. Right or right-centre differ little, with New Zealand First potentially pulling a right-led government marginally towards the centre. Distances from respondents measure the average difference between respondents' self-positioning and where they placed the three alternative governments—a more finely grained comparison than that based on the average party positions displayed in the top two sections of the figure. The three alternative governments are almost indistinguishable on this distance estimate. The difference emerges when respondents' left–right assessments of the three alternative governments are compared with the position of the median voter (at 5). On this basis, the current Labour–New Zealand First–Green grouping is significantly closer to the median. This remains true when missing and 'don't know' values are dropped from the calculations.

On policy and attitudinal grounds, a case can be made that the parties of the new government had a slight edge in terms of public preferences. On grounds of incumbency and perceptions of competence, preferences were more likely to favour the National-led grouping. However, regarding preferred prime minister, less than 2 percentage points gave the edge to preferences for National, ACT and Māori Party leaders against those for Labour, Green and New Zealand First. On ratings of competence and trust, as applied to the two major party leaders, translated into a scale from 0 to 4, the gap is similarly narrow. We have already seen this data broken down by gender (see Chapter 6, Figure 6.2). Across both genders, Figure 8.3 shows that, while English was perceived as significantly more competent, Ardern out-rated him by a somewhat greater margin on trust. Ardern had the advantage of being a new leader, whereas English's long record as a politician was bound to generate distrust, particularly among his opponents. In Ardern's case, respondents might have selected 'don't know', again scored as a mid-point in the scale along with missing values, more frequently; however, she was ahead of English, even in the positive responses to the trust question.

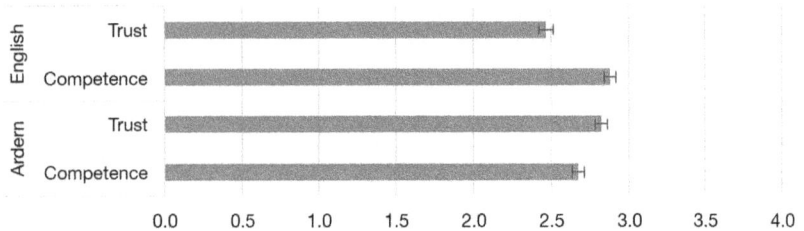

Figure 8.3: Jacinda Ardern and Bill English—how trust and competence can be used to describe them.
Source: New Zealand Election Study (2017).

On other questions, though, the competence factor weighs in. Regarding the general performance of the previous government, more than two-thirds of respondents thought it had done a very good or fairly good job, with most (54 per cent) selecting the 'fairly good' option.

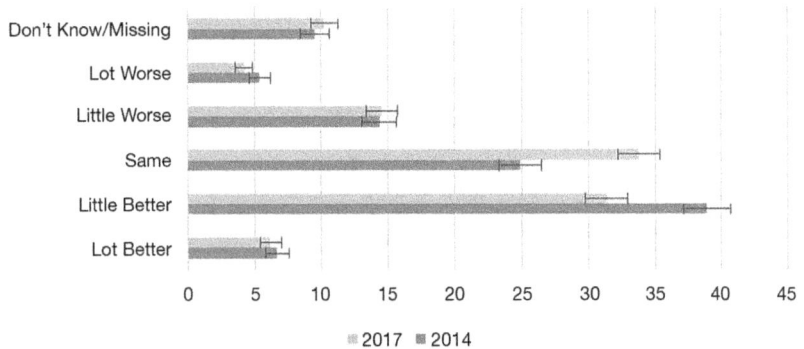

Figure 8.4: The state of the economy over the last 12 months prior to the 2014 and 2017 elections.
Source: New Zealand Election Study (2017).

Turning to the economy, Figure 8.4 shows that those expecting things to improve a little were a smaller group in 2017 than 2014, matched by a proportionately larger group in the 'stay the same' category in 2014.

The outrightly negative groups were equivalent in size in both election years, most likely prompted more by their partisan choices than objective assessment. However, some of the shine of the National-led government's reputation for 'good' economic outcomes was missing when compared to 2014.

On the balance of assessments, one can understand the response of the National Party and its allies to the formation of the Labour, New Zealand First and Green–backed government and give due respect to National's moderate and gracious acknowledgment of defeat. On election day, by a near margin, a plurality of voters might have preferred, and most expected, that a National-led government would prevail. A similarly small plurality preferred a National Party prime minister. By a significant margin, the electorate rated the National-led government's performance as positive, and had confidence in the state of economy, albeit with slightly less enthusiasm than in 2014. Equally marginally, it seems that pluralities of voters preferred the issue positions of the new government's parties to those of its predecessor. Of perhaps greater significance, perceptions of the new government's position on the left–right dimension put that government significantly closer to the median voter than would have been the case under the parties of the previous government, or even a hypothetical National–New Zealand First coalition. However, this leaves the debate regarding 'legitimacy' virtually where it begins, surrounding a very close election and an unexpected outcome that is still questioned by many.

Attitudes towards Coalitions

In a situation where those of the losing side come to question an election result, trust in the political process and in democracy may be damaged. Scepticism regarding the normative basis of coalition governments compared to those of single parties may also increase. Such a situation could encourage authoritarians and populists to further intensify their disdain regarding the values of political compromise and minority positions. If so, how the government outcome affected more fundamental attitudes to New Zealand democracy is a crucial question to address.

One of the key elements of a proportional electoral system is its tendency to encourage coalition rather than single-party governments. Indeed, a preference for coalition rather than single-party government underpinned many New Zealanders' selection of the MMP system in

1993 (Lamare & Vowles, 1996) and again in 2011 (Karp, 2014). Since 1993, over nine elections up to 2017, the NZES has asked a question with four components, as follows: 'Generally speaking, do you think that a government formed by one party, or formed by more than one party, is better at doing the following things: providing stability, making tough decisions, keeping promises, and doing what the people want?' Respondents answer the question for each of its components by indicating 'one party best', 'more than one party best', 'both about the same' or 'don't know'.

The data extracted from these questions indicate that most respondents find it easy to distinguish between the advantages and disadvantages of various aspects of performance when comparing multi-party and single-party governments (see Table A8.1). The broad patterns of responses have become relatively consistent, particularly from 2002 onward, as experience has accumulated. Pluralities, and sometimes outright majorities, believe single-party governments to be more stable, although support for each type of government was evenly split in 2014. In 1999, a plurality found single-party governments better at making tough decisions than coalitions. In 2002, there was equal support for both forms of government in terms of being tough. From 2005, pluralities found single-party governments tougher until 2011; however, in both 2014 and 2017, the judgment shifted to coalitions. There is consistent plurality support for coalitions being better than one-party governments at keeping promises and consistent majority support for coalitions being more responsive to public opinion than single-party governments. On balance, and assuming all four aspects of government performance are equally weighted, preferences for coalition government consistently win out over single-party government (Vowles, 2011).

However, there is a complication—popular understandings of coalition are not consistent with the formal definition. Strictly speaking, a coalition government is one in which two or more parties have ministerial positions in Cabinet, the central decision-making body in the executive. All members of Cabinet are bound by collective Cabinet responsibility and are held accountable for all government decisions. In terms of Cabinet composition, coalition governments were formed after the 1996, 1999, 2002, 2005 and 2017 elections. However, following the 2008, 2011 and 2014 elections, the National Party formed single-party Cabinets. Technically speaking, all New Zealand governments since 1998 have also been minority governments who relied for their majorities on confidence and supply agreements with other parties. From 2005 onwards, confidence and supply agreements have been underpinned by support parties usually taking ministerial positions outside Cabinet. Those ministers are responsible for government policy within their own portfolios but are not required to defend or support policy in other areas unless they agree or have committed to do so by agreement. The popular understanding of coalition in New Zealand encompasses this type of government; support parties are considered part of the government, as indeed they are, particularly if their leaders hold significant ministerial portfolios.

The key point is this, New Zealand's post-MMP experience of coalition government has tended to be shaped by the continued dominance of one large party within a coalition. At times, coalition partners with Cabinet seats have been significant players—from 1996 to 1998, National with New Zealand First, and from 1999 to 2002, Labour with the Alliance. Following 2002 and until 2008, the Labour-led government was in a commanding position. Between 2008 and 2017, a National-led government was in an even stronger position, with three small support partners, not all required for a majority. New Zealanders quite reasonably understand such governments to be coalitions because the core party cannot command a majority on its own and has to negotiate with its partners to achieve its aims, sometimes failing to achieve all that it wants, but usually prevailing. The reappearance of coalition government in its more precise definition in 2017 could therefore shift perceptions, as constraints on the largest party have clearly increased. Indeed, as argued above, the very formation of the Labour–New Zealand First Cabinet provoked challenges to its legitimacy.

To probe the data more deeply, the first step is to deconstruct general attitudes towards coalitions versus single-party government across the populist, authoritarian and left–right attitudinal dimensions in multivariate analysis—the latter to control for the effects of the left-leaning tendencies of most New Zealand populists. For good measure, a control for political efficacy may be added (see Table A8.2). Derived from this model, Figure 8.5 confirms that populists are significantly more likely to be in favour of coalition government in New Zealand than non-populists, even after controlling for left–right position and political efficacy. An alternative model adds age, which is non-significant (whether estimated continuously, or in cohorts). This throws further doubt on any claim that New Zealand populists might be significantly 'anti-pluralist'— this is despite the retention of an 'anti-pluralist' question in the populist scale, indicating opposition to political compromise. Meanwhile, authoritarians are more in favour of single-party government, as expected, and in confirmation of previous findings, with the left being more in favour of coalitions and the right more likely to be against them.

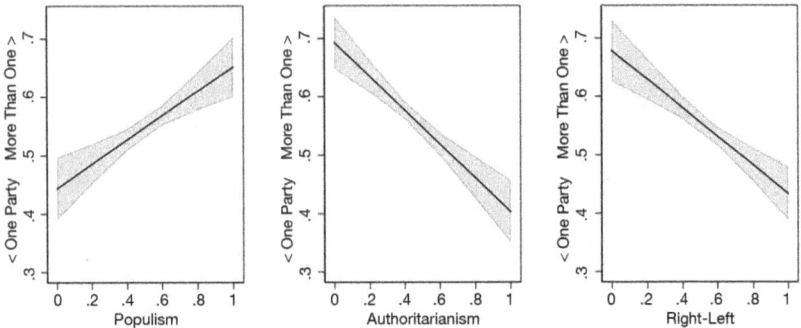

Figure 8.5: Associations between populism, authoritarianism and left–right position on preferences for single party or multi-party governments.

Note: The model also controls for political efficacy. Preferences for one-party–multi-party government range between 0 (strongest preferences for single-party) and 1 (strongest preferences for multi-party).

Source: New Zealand Election Study (2017) (see Table A8.2).

Turning to the potential short-term effects of the unexpected coalition, Figure 8.6 shows that support for coalition government drops between 2014 and the immediate post-election period, and again after the formation of the coalition government, while remaining just in positive territory. Meanwhile, Figure 8.7 shows that, measured as a five-point scale between 0 and 1, satisfaction with democracy remained at the same level as in 2014 (before government formation in 2017) and only dropped marginally thereafter. If the unexpected formation of the government had any effects on overall satisfaction with democracy, these were very minor.

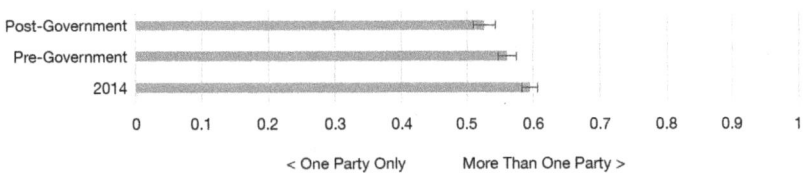

Figure 8.6: Coalition versus one-party government summary scale (2014–2017).

Source: New Zealand Election Study (2017).

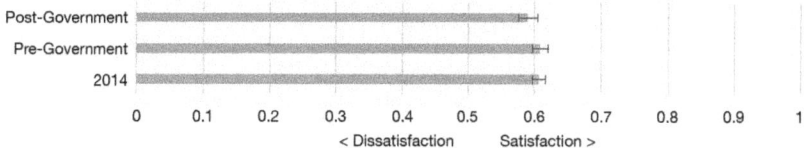

Figure 8.7: Satisfaction with democracy (2014–2017).
Source: New Zealand Election Study (2014, 2017).

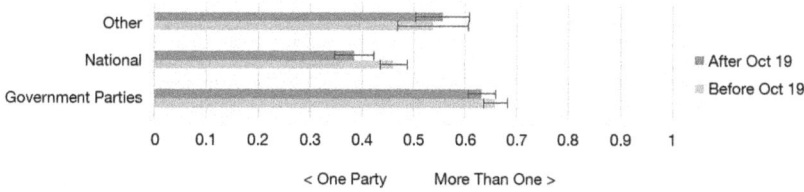

Figure 8.8: One-party versus multi-party government and party votes.
Source: New Zealand Election Study (2017) (see Table A8.4 [Model 1]).

The drop in support for coalition government merits the most attention. One would expect the effect to be found mainly among National party voters—and, indeed, it is. A further regression model included response pre- or post-government formation and three voting categories: those for the three government parties, those for National and those for non-voters and the rest (weighted to correct for response rate bias between the two periods, as explained earlier). With their key effects in the background, the two variables were interacted. Even among government party voters, support for coalition goes down marginally, but remains well within confidence intervals. As Figure 8.8 shows, National party voters drop eight points (from 46 to 38 on the coalition/one-party government scale), just outside confidence intervals.

An age cohort effect was also to be expected. Support for MMP and for coalitions is stronger among those who never voted under the old system and weaker among those who voted under the old SMP system (Karp, 2014). Figure 8.9 displays the results of post-estimation from a regression model with an interaction between government formation and pre- and post-MMP generations, in addition to their key effects. It shows that the pre-MMP cohort drop significantly in their support for coalitions; however, the post-MMP age cohort appears unaffected by the formation of an unexpected government.

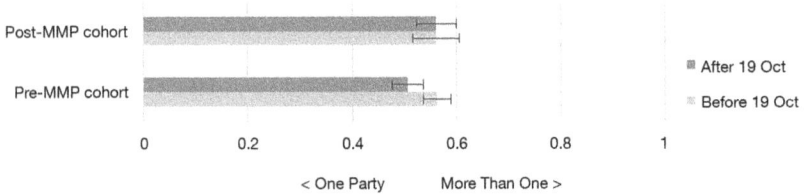

Figure 8.9: Coalition/one-party government preferences and age cohorts.
Source: New Zealand Election Study (2017) (see Table A8.4 [Model 2]).

In the short term, the intensification of coalition-style politics under the Labour–New Zealand First–Green government could be expected to challenge the positive perceptions of coalition governments that have, until now, been exhibited by the majority of New Zealanders. Indeed, preferences and evaluations of multi-party and single-party government alternatives have waxed and waned over the MMP period. When coalition politics became more conflicted or unstable, opinions shifted, first in 1998–1999, when the first MMP coalition government splintered (Karp & Bowler, 2001), and again in 2005 (Vowles, 2008), when New Zealand First became a support partner for Labour following a very close election and Winston Peters took the position of Minister of Foreign Affairs. A minor age-cohort effect is associated with the short-term shift in sentiment against coalitions among the pre-MPP generation, with no effect at all among those who began voting after the MMP system was established. However, over the longer term, age (however it is measured) demonstrates no association with one-party versus multi-party government preferences after populist, authoritarian and left–right attitudes are taken into account. Even dropping political efficacy from the Figure 8.5 and Table A8.2 analyses does not bring age back into contention. However, doubts remain. Other research provides evidence that, following more extreme conditions of government instability and collapse, as in the aftermath of the events of 1998, young people may react both more strongly and more negatively than older people (Vowles, 2011, p. 141). More robust methods of age–period cohort analysis will be required to investigate these questions more thoroughly (to the extent that this is possible, given the fewer questions available for analysis in earlier data).

Conclusions

The unexpected outcome of the government-formation process in 2017 did not pose a serious challenge to the legitimacy of the coalition government or to the election system that made it possible. On the margins, when they were voting, more people probably preferred the outcome of a National-led to a Labour-led government; however, these margins were thin and flexible—some, at least, adjusted their preferences after the government was announced. The strongest reason to choose National was perceptions of the party's positive performance in office, whereas the strongest reason to choose Labour or one of its partners was the party's policy positions. When measured in terms of perceptions of the left–right positions of alternative governments, Labour, New Zealand First and Green were closer to the median voter than the other National-led alternatives.

Satisfaction with democracy hardly shifted—the downward shift was too minor to provoke concern. Support for the idea of coalition governments fell back on the margins but remained significantly stronger than that for single-party government. Meanwhile, populists emerged as the strongest supporters of multi-party government, bringing the association between populism and anti-pluralism into question, at least in the New Zealand context.

In taking stock, as the 2020 election grows nearer, questions of legitimacy remain on the table. A government that is based on three significant parties presents far greater potential for disagreement, division and potential failure than the New Zealand governments formed since 1996. The very composition of the government is a point of vulnerability at which both the Opposition and critical political commentators continue to probe and poke. Evidence of poor performance and, even more seriously, a government collapse, may bring the legitimacy question to the fore. Alternatively, successful completion of the three-party government's term could cause remaining concerns regarding legitimacy to subside, thus further reducing their relevance in the years to come.

References

Anderson, C. J., Blais, A., Bowler, S., Donovan, T. & Listhaug, O. (2005). *Losers' consent: Elections and democratic legitimacy.* Cambridge, United Kingdom: Cambridge University Press.

Edwards, B. (2017). Political roundup: The legitimacy of the Labour-led government. *New Zealand Herald.* Retrieved from www.nzherald.co.nz/nz/news/article.cfm?c_id=1&objectid=11936270

Farrar, D. (2017). *It's Labour.* Retrieved from www.kiwiblog.co.nz/2017/10/its_labour.html

Hosking, M. (2017). Mike Hosking: Already a mess—We are all in trouble. *New Zealand Herald.* Retrieved from www.nzherald.co.nz/nz/news/article.cfm?c_id=1&objectid=11934989

Karp, J. A. (2014). Generations and the referendum on MMP. In J. Vowles (Ed.), *The new electoral politics in New Zealand* (pp. 187–198). Wellington, New Zealand: Institute for Governance and Policy Studies.

Karp, J. A. & Bowler, S. (2001). Coalition government and satisfaction with democracy: Explaining New Zealand's reaction to proportional representation. *European Journal of Political Research, 40*(1), 57–79. doi.org/10.1111/1475-6765.00589

Katz, R. S. (1997). *Democracy and elections.* New York: Oxford University Press.

Lamare, J. & Vowles, J. (1996). Party interests, public opinion and institutional preferences: Electoral system change in New Zealand. *Australian Journal of Political Science, 31*(3), 321–346. doi.org/10.1080/10361149651085

MacDonald, L. (2017). MMP attacked online after coalition formed. *Newshub.* Retrieved from www.newshub.co.nz/home/election/2017/10/mmp-attacked-online-after-coalition-formed.html

Marquez, X. (2015). The irrelevance of legitimacy. *Political Studies, 64*(1), 19–34. doi.org/10.1111/1467-9248.12202

Milne, J. (2017). Voters cannot, and will not, tolerate Winston abusing his kingmaker position. *Sunday-Star Times.* Retrieved from www.stuff.co.nz/national/politics/96867393/jonathan-milne-voters-cannot-and-will-not-tolerate-winston-abusing-his-kingmaker-position

Nagel, J. (1998). Social choice in a pluralitarian democracy: The politics of market liberalisation in New Zealand. *British Journal of Political Science, 28*(2), 223–267. doi.org/10.1017/S0007123498000155

New Zealand Election Study. (2014). *New Zealand Election Study* [dataset]. Retrieved from www.nzes.org/exec/show/data

New Zealand Election Study. (2017). *New Zealand Election Study* [dataset]. Retrieved from www.nzes.org/exec/show/data

NZ shock: Losers take power. (2017). *The Australian*. Retrieved from www. theaustralian.com.au/nation/world/new-zealand-shock-losers-labour-and-nz-first-take-power/news-story/78dfb678806601e8387b2f6c1be3b3ac

Powell, G. B. (2000). *Elections as instruments of democracy*. New Haven, CT: Yale University Press.

Prebble, R. (2017). Jacinda Ardern will regret this coalition of losers. *New Zealand Herald*. Retrieved from www.nzherald.co.nz/opinion/news/article. cfm?c_id=466&objectid=11935125

Radio New Zealand. (2017). Ardern's rise 'remarkable'—Bill English concedes. *Radio New Zealand*. Retrieved from www.radionz.co.nz/news/ political/341964/ardern-s-rise-remarkable-bill-english-concedes

Vowles, J. (2008). The genie in the bottle: Is New Zealand's MMP system here to stay? In M. Frances & J. Tully (Eds), *In the public interest: Essays in honour of Professor Keith Jackson* (pp. 105–125). Christchurch, New Zealand: University of Canterbury Press.

Vowles, J. (2011). Why voters prefer coalitions: Rationality or norms? *Political Science, 63*, 126–145. doi.org/10.1177/0032318711403917

Appendix

Figure A8.1 reports the vote shares for the four main parties, reported both before and after government formation. Our main concern was the possibility of the misreporting of vote choices among those voting for National and Labour—Labour voters saying they voted National before government formation and National voters saying they voted Labour afterward. On inspection, the figure suggests that the most significant reason for the difference in government outcome preferences lies in the significantly lower number of National Party voters responding to the survey after the announcement. Error in reporting voting choice is less likely an explanation—the difference is too great for this explanation to be credible, except on the margins.

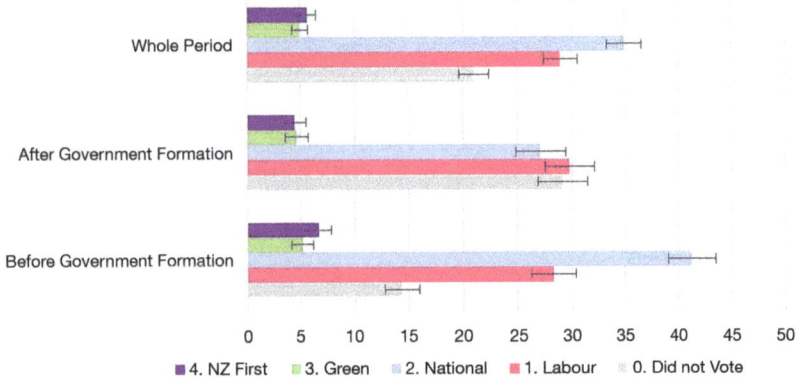

Figure A8.1: Reported and validated votes (before and after government formation).

Note: Standard weight applied.

Source: New Zealand Election Study (2017).

While there is a recorded tendency of survey respondents to incorrectly report voting for the winner in post-election surveys, this is most likely to apply to non-voters who report voting. However, such cases are correctly classified as non-voters in our data. There was a much higher proportion of non-voters responding later in the period, but there is no reason to suspect that this had anything to do with the formation of the government—we might expect non-voters less engaged with the election to respond later, if at all. The same propensity for non-voters to respond late was observed in 2014, although the tendency was somewhat stronger in 2017. Non-voter preferences remained somewhat greater for a National-led government throughout, although the margin narrowed to almost zero post government formation. Green and New Zealand First differences were too minor to be significant.

Therefore, it is reasonable to assume that the differences in prior to and post government formation reported behaviour in the initial analysis relate more to the drop in National voting respondents post government formation and the differential response rate of non-voters prior to and post government formation. Misreporting vote choice is likely to be marginal. However, more robust statistical tests for this assumption could be applied.

Table A8.1: Evaluations of coalition versus single-party governments (1993–2017)

Providing stability	One party best	More than one best	Both same	Don't know	N
1993	45	34	8	13	1,978
1996	46	35	10	10	3,999
1999	57	25	11	8	4,885
2002	56	26	10	8	4,609
2005	61	24	8	7	2,787
2008	48	34	8	10	2,619
2011	47	35	9	10	2,399
2014	39	39	13	8	2,782
2017	46	33	13	9	3,308
Making tough decisions	**One party best**	**More than one best**	**Both same**	**Don't know**	**N**
1993	36	46	8	11	1,959
1996	35	47	9	9	3,961
1999	42	40	11	7	4,851
2002	42	42	10	7	4,594
2005	46	39	8	6	2,767
2008	43	40	8	9	2,606
2011	43	39	9	9	2,374
2014	35	46	13	8	2,882
2017	36	45	11	8	3,298
Keeping promises	**One party best**	**More than one best**	**Both same**	**Don't know**	**N**
1993	17	59	13	11	1,969
1996	20	59	12	10	3,996
1999	30	43	17	9	4,861
2002	29	47	16	9	4,584
2005	38	42	12	8	2,760
2008	35	42	11	10	2,614
2011	31	47	12	10	2,375
2014	26	49	16	9	2,768
2017	33	44	15	9	3,284

Doing what the people want	One party best	More than one best	Both same	Don't know	N
1993	13	64	12	12	1,973
1996	10	63	15	12	3,992
1999	19	51	19	11	4,850
2002	18	56	17	9	4,598
2005	24	53	14	9	2,763
2008	23	54	12	11	2,608
2011	20	55	13	12	2,370
2014	15	56	18	10	2,768
2017	19	54	16	10	3,301

Source: New Zealand Election Study (2017).

Table A8.2: Populism, authoritarianism and coalition/one-party government preferences

	1	2
Authoritarianism	−0.290***	−0.297***
	(0.049)	(0.048)
Populism	0.209***	0.211***
	(0.052)	(0.051)
Right–left position	−0.245***	−0.250***
	(0.049)	(0.051)
Political efficacy	0.087**	0.080**
	(0.039)	(0.039)
Age		0.001
		(0.000)
Constant	0.650***	0.633***
	(0.043)	(0.043)
Observations	3,455.000	3,455.000
R-squared	0.093	0.093

Note: Robust standard errors in parentheses.

*** $p < 0.01$, ** $p < 0.05$, * $p < 0.1$.

Source: New Zealand Election Study (2017).

Table A8.3: Attitudes to single or multi-party government: Vote choice and government formation (Model 1); generations and government formation (Model 2)

	1	2
After = 1; before = 0	−0.026	−0.056***
	(0.018)	(0.021)
Reference: Government party voter		
National voter	−0.198***	
	(0.018)	
Non-voters and other voters	−0.121***	
	(0.037)	
After x national voter	−0.051*	
	(0.029)	
After x non-vote/other	0.044	
	(0.048)	
Post–mixed member proportional (MMP) generation = 1; pre-MMP = 0		−0.002
		(0.026)
Before/after * pre/post-MMP generations		0.057
		(0.036)
Constant	0.659***	0.562***
	(0.011)	(0.014)
Observations	3,455.000	3,352.000
R-squared	0.090	0.005

Note: Robust standard errors in parentheses.

*** p < 0.01, ** p < 0.05, * p < 0.1.

Source: New Zealand Election Study (2017).

9

NEW ZEALAND POPULISM IN THE 2017 ELECTION AND BEYOND

Jennifer Curtin and Jack Vowles

Just over 50 years ago, in 1969, the movement to Halt All Racist Tours (HART) was formed to protest and prevent rugby sporting tours to apartheid South Africa. HART coordinated the activities of anti-racist groups, unions, churches and university students. Most of its members were of the generation that has become known as 'baby boomers'. They were passionate regarding human rights in South Africa and were becoming increasingly aware of unresolved questions regarding the state and status of Māori at home. Their cause, and the protest action that resulted, helped to persuade Labour Prime Minister Norman Kirk to cancel the 1973 All Black rugby tour of South Africa.

This clash of politics and sport divided New Zealanders and, in 1975, authoritarian populist National party leader Robert Muldoon harnessed a cultural backlash in his bid to become prime minister. He referred to the protesters as 'disruptive, anti-establishment, anti-government, anti-everything that we stand for' (cited in Field, 2010). Once elected, Muldoon wholeheartedly endorsed continued sporting contacts with South Africa, ignoring growing international opposition to New Zealand's position and the Gleneagles agreement that had been signed by 26 Commonwealth Heads of State. Muldoon's use of sport as a political instrument to mobilise support for his government continued throughout his nine years in office.

This vignette is a reminder that New Zealand is not immune to authoritarian populism—to the sight of political leaders leveraging anti-elitist, anti-internationalist sentiments, demanding loyalty and being prepared to use the police and security services to repel public protest. As one HART leader has argued, 'the country was Muldoon's playground … he was Trump before Trump' (Wickham, 2019).

As we suggested in our introductory chapter, this experience may have inoculated New Zealand against the authoritarian populist politics witnessed elsewhere over the last decade or more. Winston Peters, leader of New Zealand First, was a member of parliament in the Muldoon government between 1979 and 1981. Peters is on record as not supporting government action to cancel the 1981 Springbok tour, although he made a personal decision not to attend any games (Neas, 2012). Scholars internationally position his party as right-wing populist; however, this oversimplifies New Zealand's contemporary political landscape. Rather, as the chapters in this volume reveal, populism in New Zealand is best viewed as moderate, majoritarian and mainstream (see Chapter 1). Peters and his party combine populism and pluralism. As Peters himself has explained, 'one of the great principles of democratic government is protection of the minority. That's fundamental. That is a critical issue' (cited in Neas, 2012). At times, the discourses employed by New Zealand politicians and parties have been exclusionary; however, at other times, leaders such as Jacinda Ardern have invoked an inclusive notion of the 'people' (see Chapter 6). Anti-pluralist populism, where it exists, is expressed in some prejudice against immigrants; however, it has adopted a more subtle form of exclusion when facing the indigenous minority within 'the people' by failing to accept Māori rights as a Treaty partner (Chapter 7).

Party discourse during the 2017 election campaign was anti-immigration rather than anti-immigrant. As Chapter 5 has demonstrated, those voters who were concerned regarding net migration were most likely to choose New Zealand First. While Labour also committed to reducing levels of immigration, their proposed cuts in numbers were lower than those of New Zealand First and were framed in terms of the need to reduce pressure on infrastructure, social services and housing. More generally, our results have demonstrated that concern regarding immigration is low and there is little evidence of a cultural backlash by social conservatives against social liberals (see Chapter 2). As Kate McMillan and Matthew Gibbons demonstrated, populism did feed a desire to reduce immigration but explained very little of that preference. Half of the populist effect occurred through prejudice against immigrants; however, the other half was channelled through support for unions, the need for income redistribution and greater availability of housing—economic and social inequities partly generated by historically high immigration levels. Meanwhile, authoritarian attitudes did not affect immigration policy in any way. Anti-immigrant prejudice had direct effects, though not necessarily functioning via populism, as did preferences for cultural conformity. At various times over the course of Labour's time in opposition, while commentators had been keen to claim Labour was at electoral risk by associating itself too closely with 'identity politics', our analysis of voters' opinions suggests otherwise. The economy, housing, health and inequality were the issues that mattered in 2014 (Vowles, Coffé & Curtin, 2017) and these were again important in 2017.

Nor has New Zealand been witnessing declining levels of political trust, which are often deemed to be a core element in the rise of populist parties. As discussed in Chapter 4, democratic satisfaction has remained steady at approximately 65 per cent—which, while not outstanding in comparison to most Scandinavian countries, is somewhat better than average among developed democracies. Further, while there has been a long-term trend of decreasing turnout, somewhat more among younger generations (and within this group, among younger men), turnout marginally increased both at the 2014 and 2017 elections, albeit from a historical low point.

We have provided a theoretical and empirical critique of the theory and the literature that have too widely stretched the concept of populism. The concept of populism has been applied to parties that entrench, rather than challenge, the power of elites by dividing rather than uniting the public. Nothing could be further from the intentions of traditional and contemporary populists, who seek to unite an overwhelming majority. We concede that many parties of the authoritarian right use populist discourse and framing. However, this does not necessarily make them populist in their objectives or ideology. We define populism as a normative democratic theory, in opposition to an elitist or liberal theory of democracy. Populist rhetoric provides a frame that all political actors may use from time to time; however, this does not make them populist. Our sense of what lies behind the current critique of populism leads us to speculate (if not conclude) that, because elitist democratic theory denies the possibility and legitimacy of majoritarian democracy, it provides the key normative foundation of 'anti-populism'. As argued in Chapter 1, this anti-populism concedes too much normative territory to those it seeks to oppose. We define populism as a continuum of norms and discourses, of more or less populism, rather than categorising parties or attitudes in terms of their fit to an ideal-typical definition. Distinguishing between exclusionary and inclusive forms of populism has more analytical veracity. Exclusionary forms are associated with authoritarianism and anti-pluralism; however, in contrast to most of the literature, we argue that inclusive forms of populism are consistent with the acceptance of pluralism. Exclusionary forms use populist rhetoric but fail to measure up to the goals of traditional populism in their restrictive notions of 'the people'. Historically, New Zealand exhibits examples both of authoritarian, exclusionary populism and its inclusionary alternative.

As mentioned above, the National Party government of Robert Muldoon (1975–1984) constituted the country's closest meeting with authoritarian populism. By contrast, prime ministers Seddon, Savage and Kirk embodied a 'heresthetic' or strategic leadership style to advance an inclusive populist approach that sought to invoke a wider understanding of who constituted the 'people'. In Chapter 6, Jennifer Curtin and Lara Greaves analysed Ardern's version of inclusive rhetoric being 'kindness', 'hope' and optimism', and the extent to which this resonated with voters. Certainly, support for Labour among women voters increased significantly with Ardern as leader compared to recent past elections. Ardern's explicitly feminist leanings did not lead to a cultural backlash. She was popular with populists, both men and women; however, authoritarians were stubbornly resistant to Ardern's inclusive messages.

Thus, while authoritarian populism might be on the rise globally, there is little to suggest that an upsurge occurred in New Zealand in 2017. Jacinda Ardern's ascension aside, the issues that mattered most to voters represented 'politics as normal'. Material wellbeing—the economy, health and housing—concerned voters from both the left and the right. Inequality and poverty were not far behind. Ardern referred to climate change as New Zealand's 'nuclear-free moment' and New Zealanders rated the environment as highly as immigration among their issues of concern. Although the Key and English governments were deemed to be competent economic managers in the wake of the global financial crisis, they were increasingly subject to a narrative of years of neglect under National's 'austerity-lite' policies. Yet, New Zealand's politics were stable. The moderate multi-party system showed little sign of fragmentation. Votes shifted more in 2017 than at the two previous elections but there were no strong signs of dealignment or realignment. The dominant cleavage remained that of urban versus rural, and political choices between the left and right continued in predictable fashion. The 2017 election demonstrated that there was little appetite for a populist revolution.

Our book operationalised populism in two forms: at the level of discourse and rhetoric and as an underlying dimension in public attitudes. We first analysed populist attitudes by way of the instruments provided by the Comparative Study of Electoral Systems (CSES) (Module 5) and included in the 2017 New Zealand Election Study (NZES). We identified several problems with those instruments. Following Norris and Inglehart (2019), to assist in making the distinction between exclusionary and inclusionary populism, a separation between populist and authoritarian attitudes was required. The CSES questions generated five dimensions, rather than the expected three. The two additional dimensions were (1) associated with questions often used to measure external political efficacy (antipathy to elites) and (2) seemingly measuring majoritarianism (attitudes to representative democracy). Attitudes to out-groups formed the third underlying factor expected in the CSES framework; however, in the New Zealand context, this dimension split into three: anti-immigrant attitudes, in-group exclusivity or 'nativism', and cultural conformity. As New Zealand society comprises a significant indigenous minority, followed by successive waves of immigrants—at first predominantly European, but more recently diverse—this separation was not unexpected.

By retaining some but dropping other CSES instruments, and adding appropriate questions from the NZES, Greaves and Vowles constructed more theoretically appropriate populist and authoritarian scales. However, both may be subject to criticism. Estimates of authoritarian attitudes vary considerably; further, our mix of instruments, while acceptable, is not ideal. The populist scale still contains items usually associated with estimating external political efficacy. However, an independent estimate of external efficacy could also be drawn from other items in the dataset to provide a corrective. Exploring the correlates of populism and authoritarianism in social structure, demographics and among generational cohorts, we found that populists tend to be younger (except for the youngest generation defined), Māori and Pasifika, and are more likely to have no assets, low incomes and lower education. Authoritarians tend to be older, male, from Pasifika and Asian communities, religious and to be less educated.

Identification of populist rhetoric in party discourses finds, as expected, that New Zealand First provides the most examples. However, this has varied over time, reaching a peak in 2011, after a period during which New Zealand First had been excluded from parliament and sought successfully to return. In 2017, populist signifiers could be found in other party platforms. In New Zealand, populists tend to the left, authoritarians to the right, both in terms of left–right orientations and in party choice. New Zealand First voters are alone in tending both towards populism and authoritarianism, confirming that, in the eyes of many of its voters, New Zealand First is a party, like its leader, in the Muldoon tradition. It was possible that Labour and left populism might be shaped by low efficacy, resulting from the party's several years in opposition. Even after controlling for efficacy, once they knew their party was in government, Labour voters became only marginally less populist, while the strength of the association remained.

Populist and authoritarian attitudes partly shape satisfaction and support for democracy. Because they have greater expectations than non-populists that governments should be responsive to majority opinion, populists tend to be much less satisfied with democracy than non-populists. They show a slight tendency to become less supportive of democracy as populist attitudes grow stronger. Authoritarians are marginally less satisfied with democracy; however, authoritarianism does not play into lack of support for democracy. These are unexpected findings. An explanation may lie in New Zealand's simple unitary state that concentrates political authority in central government—the lack of fundamental constitutional law and, thus, the existence of near-absolute parliamentary supremacy and a consequently powerful executive. This provides political elites with the opportunity to exert the strong leadership valued by authoritarians; however, such strong leadership may not always accord with majority opinion, leading populists to be less satisfied and more critical. Chapter 4 also addressed claims that younger generations have become less supportive of democracy. Comparing the same age cohorts in 2002 and 2017, it seems more likely that these age differences are the result of life cycle rather than generational effects—as people age, they become more supportive of democracy.

After the 2017 election, a legitimacy crisis was possible, following the exclusion from government of the party that won the vote plurality. NZES data throw this into an even harsher light by finding that, when asked to choose between National- and Labour-led governments, people somewhat preferred National over Labour. If anything, New Zealand First voters and non-voters leaned towards National; however, they became less likely to do so after government formation, suggesting some cueing both from the election result (earlier) and government formation (later). New Zealanders marginally favoured National due to its reputation for more competent leadership and stewardship over the economy, although the economic gloss had waned somewhat when compared to the previous election. However, on matters of policy preferences, voters also marginally tended towards Labour and centre-left positions. When comparing the left–right policy positions of the various parties, as perceived by voters themselves and weighted by the vote shares of the actual and hypothetical coalitions of the available and feasible options, the coalition that formed was the one closest to the median voter.

The government outcome marginally depressed satisfaction with democracy and support for coalitions among National voters. More broadly, though, support for the principle and practice of coalition government was strongest among populists and weakest among authoritarians—the latter was expected but the former less so, at least from the standpoint of populist scholarship outside New Zealand. However, this is consistent with strong populist elements in the campaign for proportional representation and continued perceptions among New Zealanders that multi-party government is more responsive to majority public opinion than single-party government. Given this, expectations that New Zealand populism should be anti-pluralist, in this sense at least, are not borne out by the evidence.

The presence of a significant indigenous minority complicates the picture in a society originally based on colonial settlement, particularly given that Māori have their own segment of the electoral system, in the form of the Māori seats. Lara Greaves and Janine Hayward confirmed a series of previous findings showing that, while turning out to vote less than Pākehā, Māori tend to take part in more active forms of participation than other ethnic groups (Chapter 7). Greaves and Hayward broke new ground by finding a relatively high level of populism among Māori and suggested two explanations. Historically marginalised and denied their rights for over a century of colonisation, Māori have low levels of trust in Pākehā-dominated governments and low expectations that governments will respond to their needs. Therefore, it is not surprising that they score high on anti-elitism. Conversely, populism is strongest among Māori on the Māori roll, indicating that this group may perceive the Māori electorates as a means by which they can express their preferences as a people.

Across the entire voting population, support or opposition to the Māori electorates plays strongly into a potentially deep cleavage in New Zealand politics—the extent to which the Māori self-determination promised in the Treaty can be accommodated within the political process. Greaves and Hayward tracked opinion among Māori and non-Māori over time, concluding that a referendum on the Māori seats, were it ever to be held, might affirm rather than reject them. Populism among Māori strongly affects their support for the Māori electorates. When partitioning out Pākehā, populism evidences no relationship with opinion about the Māori electorates—the main source of opposition is authoritarianism. Pākehā populists may turn in either direction. Some presumably respect the democratic choice of Māori to maintain their own means of representation, whereas others may regard dedicated Māori representation as either no longer needed or against principles of liberal individualism that focus on equal citizenship. A belief in a New Zealand identity based on birth and ancestry has no significant relationship with opinion about the Māori seats among Pākehā; if anything, this makes support for the Māori electorates slightly stronger. Meanwhile, 'nativism', in this sense, strongly affects Māori support for their electorates.

Our analysis uncovers the nature of populism in New Zealand in the early 21st century. It aligns to the left rather than the right and is dissatisfied with the current performance of representative democracy. A marginal populist tilt towards giving up on democracy entirely is accounted for by younger populists, who tend to become more supportive of democracy as they grow older. Populism has no relationship to attitudes regarding indigenous Māori rights and, indeed, Māori tend to be slightly more populist than other ethnic groups. Populism only marginally shapes the attitudes people hold about immigration; concern regarding the social and economic consequences of high rates of new arrivals is the more important factor. While the history of New Zealand contains evidence of authoritarian populism, populism (as it exists in public opinion in the early 21st century) prefers multi-party over single-party government, showing little evidence of anti-pluralism. Jacinda Ardern's leadership style is inclusive but only marginally populist. She has stronger support among populists than non-populists; however, this is mainly accounted for by higher levels of populism among the demographic groups that favour Labour. The New Zealand First party does attract support from authoritarian populists but its vote share remains relatively low. Its role as a government coalition partner since 2017 could be the subject of a book in its own right; however, most commentators would concede that it has acted more as a block against left-leaning policy than as a promoter of its conservative values.

Where to in 2020?

In 2017, when Winston Peters announced he would support Labour in forming a coalition government, he asserted that there was need for capitalism to become more humane and responsible. Peters has described neoliberalism as 'a failed experiment' (Moir, 2017). Jacinda Ardern campaigned on the need for politics and policy to be kinder and caring regarding all New Zealanders, particularly those in poverty. Consequently, New Zealand has witnessed an incremental shift in the way budgets are delivered, with a focus on wellbeing, and the way policy is delivered, with a focus on reducing child poverty. While transformation was promised on issues such as climate change, housing affordability, mental health and inequality, progress has been measured, in part due to two factors: the realities of the need for consensus building when in coalition government and the Labour government's desire to demonstrate their capability and expertise in managing the economy. In fiscal terms, since 2016, New Zealand has retained a relatively strong position, with healthy government budget surpluses and relatively low government debt (New Zealand Treasury, 2019; Trading Economics, 2019). Exports have grown (Statistics New Zealand, 2019a) and the unemployment rate as of November 2019 was 4.3 per cent (Statistics New Zealand, 2019b).

As 2019 wore on, there was increasing scepticism that this would be the government's 'year of delivery'. In the 2019 Mood of the Boardroom survey, Jacinda Ardern's level of competence was ranked only fifth in her Cabinet and the government was accused of 'failing to execute its policies in a timely manner' (Parker, 2019). Quarterly business surveys reported low levels of confidence in the economy, but with signs of an upturn at the end of 2019, although the October 2019 survey reported a level of gloom not experienced since 2009. While inconsistent with the data available on current conditions, these perceptions were partly rooted in expectations and possible behaviour shaped by clouds on the international horizon and also by uncertainty regarding government policy (Flaws, 2019). Consequently, economists and commentators expected the Reserve Bank of New Zealand to drop the official cash rate affecting interest rates from 1 to 0.5 per cent in November 2019. However, it did not, suggesting a degree of scepticism regarding the extent of the pessimism. All else equal, including the 'objective economy', business confidence tends to be lower under Labour than National governments, indicating the political bias of businesses (Hickey, 2017). Business pessimism regarding their own immediate futures is more telling but may still be overstated.

Early in 2020, as Figure 9.1 shows, opinion polling indicated that the margin between vote intentions for the two main parties was continuing to wax and wane. Labour's apparent defeat at the 2017 election drove down its polling immediately after; however, following the announcement that it would lead the government on 17 October, Labour rose to 40 per cent—three points above its election vote—and has remained at or above that level since. Meanwhile, despite its consignment to opposition, post-election vote intentions for the National Party remained firm. There were signs of National decline, combined with a Labour surge on the back of Jacinda Ardern's powerful, empathetic and inclusive response to the Christchurch terror attack on Islamic worshippers in March 2019. However, this trend was arrested in mid-2019 and National's support remained firm until April 2020. Since 2017, while National has outpolled Labour over a longer period than Labour over National, intentions to vote for the Green Party have usually remained above the 5 per cent threshold. The crucial margin is between Labour/Green and National—this moves back and forth. Early 2020 polling displayed either a tight race or a wider National margin over Labour/Green, depending on polling organisation.[1] To the disgust of Winston Peters, who regularly chastises pollsters, New Zealand First has fared less well, usually sitting just below the threshold— albeit at a somewhat higher level than at the same stage in previous years (Miller & Curtin, 2011).

---

1   By early 2018, regular publicly released political polling in New Zealand had shrunk to being from only two organisations: Reid Research, who poll for TV3, and Colmar-Brunton, who poll for One News. YouGov entered the field in November 2019, polling for the Stuff/Fairfax media. Polling over the same periods, there are significant differences, with Colmar-Brunton tending to give higher estimates to National, and lower to Labour, and Reid Research and YouGov reporting tighter margins between the two major parties.

This situation facilitates a National Party strategy to keep New Zealand First vote intentions down by appealing to its potential voters who lean towards authoritarian populism—an attempt to rekindle the old Muldoon constituency for National. National also hopes that the Green Party will fall below the 5 per cent party vote threshold for representation in 2020 and has encouraged the development of an apparently centrist alternative green party, Sustainable New Zealand, hoping it will attract enough votes to push the Green Party below the threshold. However, this party has been slow in development and shows little sign of support. Meanwhile, in government, the Green Party has, in the words of its male co-leader, James Shaw, been obliged to 'swallow some dead rats'. The Greens have given ground on a number of policy issues, including to take an incremental approach to including methane emissions in their signature Zero Carbon Bill. As a result, the party has faced criticism from its left regarding succumbing to excessive moderation (Trevett, 2018). In the early months of 2020, Green Party polling was tracking only just above the 5 per cent threshold.

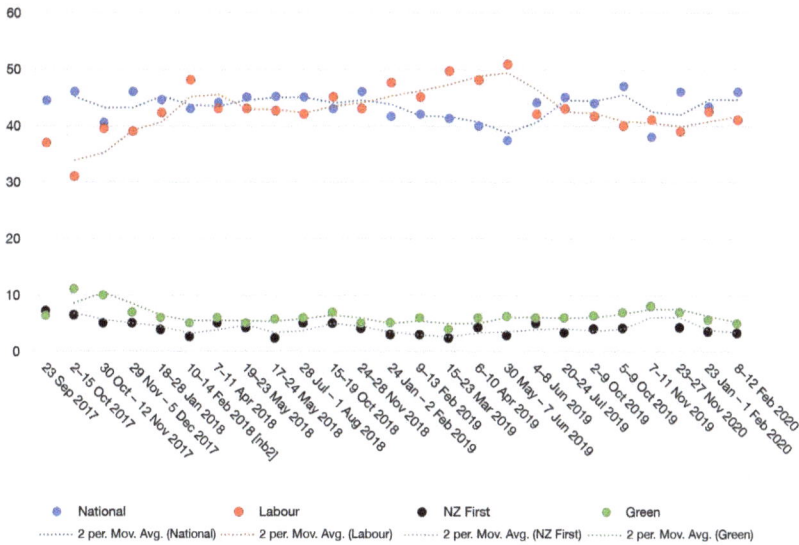

Figure 9.1: Public opinion polling and party vote intentions (2017–2020).

Source: Cooke (2019); Curia (2019a–c). Includes Colmar Brunton, Reid Research, Roy Morgan (ceased in November 2017) and YouGov polls (one poll so far from 7–11 November 2019).

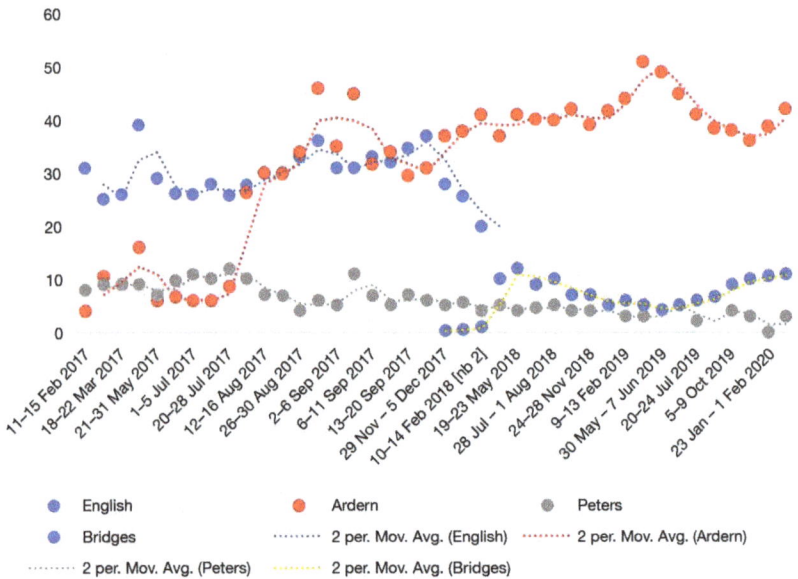

Figure 9.2: Public opinion polling regarding preferred prime minister (2017–2019).

Source: Curia (2019a–c).

Figure 9.2 also tracks the polling for preferred prime minister, beginning when Bill English took over the leadership of the National Party and position of prime minister. Ardern may be internationally popular; however, her popularity among New Zealand voters has waxed and waned. Before she became Labour leader, as Curtin and Greaves have reported, Ardern was already registering as preferred prime minister, at a popularity level almost as high as then Labour Party leader Andrew Little. On taking the Labour leadership on 1 August 2017, Ardern rivalled and, at times, exceeded English's popularity (see Chapter 6). Simon Bridges, who succeeded English as National Party leader following the election, has failed to make a significant mark. Winston Peters continues to register at a low level of preference that closely matches that of his party. Since the 2017 election, Ardern's preferred prime minister average is approximately 41 per cent. By contrast, over his first term of government (2008–2011), former National Party prime minister John Key averaged 51 per cent. Ardern has been a powerful force behind Labour's resurgence since 2017; however, John Key provided an even stronger foundation for National Party success between 2008 and 2016. Indeed, his legacy may underpin National's continued high polling. Early in 2020, preferences for Ardern as preferred prime minister were tracking upward again. Less steeply, and at a much lower level, Opposition leader Simon Bridges was also making some headway.

The government faced criticism, not only from the expected directions but also from its own supporters and sympathetic commentators. At the end of 2019, expectations of rough economic weather may have been pessimistic; however, there was enough international uncertainty to cause concern. Until December, the government had been continuing to cleave to fiscal policy objectives set by the Labour and Green parties, which promise budget surpluses over a five-year economic cycle, government core spending at no more than 30 per cent of GDP and government debt at or below 20 per cent. Many economists, including those unsympathetic to the government, were calling for a fiscal stimulus, taking advantage of very low interest rates for sovereign debt. In early December, Finance Minister Grant Robertson at last began to follow that advice, announcing a NZ$12 million boost in infrastructure expenditure (Daalder & Sachdeva, 2019).

Meanwhile, key government policies promising affordable housing for first home buyers and a light rail network for Auckland have failed to meet their objectives or have been delayed. The government commissioned a review on a Capital Gains Tax but, lacking support from New Zealand First, backed away from its recommendations, entirely removing the proposal from the political agenda. A new legislative and regulatory framework to address climate change was a key objective signalled by Ardern following becoming Labour Party leader. The Zero Carbon Bill was passed in November 2019 with the support of all but one minor political party, but required considerable compromise to gain such broad approval, including a further postponement for its application to farmers. Strong support for Labour among Māori has been challenged by a stand-off over ownership of former Māori land at Ihumātao, near Auckland International Airport. The land was confiscated following the New Zealand Wars of the 1860s and has significant archaeological and heritage value.

However, there have been some significant wins. The government has achieved a marginal reduction of prisoner numbers; however, the problems underlying high rates of imprisonment are not amenable to a 'quick fix'. Restoring prisoners' voting rights has been the subject of recent debate in the wake of a Waitangi Tribunal Report that ruled that the relevant provision in the *Electoral Act* is inconsistent with the Treaty of Waitangi. After much political wrangling the government was able to pass legislation to partially remove a blanket ban on prisoner voting rights. State and social housing construction have significantly increased but provision remains well below demand. Mental health has received a huge boost in funding. Some punitive aspects of social welfare benefits administration have been relaxed, but many recommendations from a Welfare Advisory Group report released in March 2019 have yet to be addressed, despite the Prime Minister also being the Minister for Child Poverty Reduction.

Thus, although Labour's campaign messaging under Ardern during the 2017 election was one of hope and transformation, at the beginning of 2020 there was some dissatisfaction with the pace of change. It seemed that the 2020 election campaign would look considerably different to that of 2017. Ardern's popularity on the international stage is recognised as valuable by some and inconsequential by others. She was more experienced but less exciting, until the advent of COVID-19. Labour will need to run on its 'record', which, as briefly outlined above, has been inconsistent in its successes. Meanwhile, various scandals have beset New Zealand First, putting it at risk in terms of reaching the 5 per cent threshold. Therefore, it is likely to be a tough and bruising campaign.

There is early evidence to suggest that the National Party may choose a similar strategy to that of Australian Prime Minister Scott Morrison, whose success was underpinned by a range of negative campaigning through both social and traditional media (Gauja, Sawer & Simms, 2020). Law and order and a return to hard-line policies on welfare beneficiaries will form strong National Party policies and talking points. National will target New Zealand First voters, perhaps mobilising populist rhetoric to do so. If New Zealand First were to fail to win seats, as National hopes, continued Green Party representation could be enough to return a Labour-led government that would be far less constrained in its ability to deliver policies on which both parties agree.

All of the above discussion assumes 'normal politics'. As elsewhere, by March 2020 it was becoming clear that the emergence of the COVID-19 virus would present a serious 'shock' to New Zealand's society, economy and politics. Likely recession makes the task of re-election more difficult, but if Labour and its government partners continue to handle the crisis well, they could maintain or even gain ground, much as the Key National government did in the aftermath of the major earthquake that hit Christchurch in 2011 (at much the same time in the electoral cycle). As at April 2020, the Ardern-led government response to the COVID-19 crisis comprised a four-week national lockdown, border closures and considerable additional expenditure to support wage subsidies, beneficiaries and businesses. Voters' initial response to these drastic measures was very positive—the measures were exceptionally well received, with 83 per cent approval (Brain, 2020). Labour is likely to receive an electoral boost due to effective crisis management. However, National may have an advantage, due to its reputation as a sound economic manager that may be better able to bring the country out of recession (Curtin, 2020). The outcome of the 2020 election already appeared unclear at the end of 2019—it has now become even more difficult to predict.

References

Brain, D. (2020). Exclusive: New poll shows rising support for government handling of Covid-19. *Spinoff*. Retrieved from thespinoff.co.nz/society/12-04-2020/exclusive-new-survey-shows-enormous-support-for-govt-handling-of-covid-19/

Cooke, H. (2019). Labour ahead while National dips below 40 in new Stuff poll. *Stuff*. Retrieved from www.stuff.co.nz/national/politics/117662933/labour-ahead-while-national-dips-below-40-in-new-stuff-poll

Curia. (2019a). *Archives Colmar Brunton*. Retrieved from www.curia.co.nz/company/colmar-brunton/page/1/

Curia. (2019b). *Archives Reid Research*. Retrieved from www.curia.co.nz/company/reid-research/page/1/

Curia. (2019c). *Archives Roy Morgan*. Retrieved from www.curia.co.nz/company/roy-morgan/

Curtin, J. (2020). The politics of the Covid-19 relief package. *Newsroom*. Retrieved from www.newsroom.co.nz/ideasroom/2020/03/18/1087930/the-politics-of-the-covid-19-relief-package

Daalder, M. & Sachdeva, S. (2019). Robertson reveals $12b infrastructure boost. *Newsroom*. Retrieved from www.newsroom.co.nz/2019/12/11/943952/robertson-reveals-12b-infrastructure-boost

Field, C. (2010). Have you heard from Johannesburg? Fair play. *Clarity Films*. Retrieved from vod.clarityfilms.org/

Flaws, B. (2019). Business confidence at lowest level since 2009: NZIER. *Stuff*. Retrieved from www.stuff.co.nz/business/116225611/business-confidence-at-lowest-level-since-2009-nzier

Gauja, A., Sawer, M. & Simms, M. (Eds). (2020). *Morrison's miracle: The 2019 Australian federal election*. Canberra, Australia: ANU Press. doi.org/10.22459/MM.2020

Hickey, B. (2017). Politically-biased business confidence. *Newsroom*. Retrieved from www.newsroom.co.nz/2017/11/17/61626/politically-biased-business-confidence

Miller, R., & Curtin, J. C. (2011). Counting the costs of coalition: The case of New Zealand's small parties. *Political Science, 63*(1), 106–125. doi.org/10.1177/0032318711407294

Moir, J. (2017). Winston Peters dismisses 'irresponsible capitalism' of other parties with new economic policy. *Stuff*. Retrieved from www.stuff.co.nz/national/politics/94770147/winston-peters-dismisses-irresponsible-capitalism-of-other-parties-with-new-economic-policy

Neas, O. (2012). Winston Peters: The full interview. *Salient*. Retrieved from www.salient.org.nz/2012/10/winston-peters-the-full-interview/

New Zealand Treasury. (2019). *Budget 2019: The Treasury's economic and fiscal forecasts*. Retrieved from www.budget.govt.nz/budget/2019/wellbeing/economic-fiscal-data/economic-fiscal-forecasts-07.htm

Norris, P. & Inglehart, R. (2019). *Cultural backlash: Trump, Brexit and authoritarian populism*. Cambridge, United Kingdom: Cambridge University Press. doi.org/10.1017/9781108595841

Parker, T. (2019). Mood of the boardroom: How business rates the government. *New Zealand Herald*. Retrieved from www.nzherald.co.nz/business/news/article.cfm?c_id=3&objectid=12270089

Statistics New Zealand. (2019a). *Imports and exports*. Retrieved from www.stats.govt.nz/topics/imports-and-exports

Statistics New Zealand. (2019b). *Unemployment rate*. Retrieved from www.stats.govt.nz/indicators/unemployment-rate?gclid=Cj0KCQiAk7TuBRDQARIsAMRrfUbU89sh_Mvitxf7jwMt1oR3m8UVovpFxBR2MGNjuacuRnHGKfj80ocaAgisEALw_wcB

Trading Economics. (2019). *New Zealand government budget*. Retrieved from www.tradingeconomics.com/new-zealand/government-budget

Trevett, C. (2018). Green leader James Shaw tells supporters compromise needed to achieve goals. *New Zealand Herald*. Retrieved from www.nzherald.co.nz/nz/news/article.cfm?c_id=1&objectid=11981886

Vowles, J., Coffé, H. & Curtin, J. (2017). *A bark but no bite: Inequality and the 2014 New Zealand general election*. Canberra, Australia: ANU Press. doi.org/10.22459/BBNB.08.2017

Wickham, D. (2019). *1969–1985: Sixteen years of protest that changed New Zealand*. Retrieved from www.media.auckland.ac.nz/fms/alumni/audio/salon-hart.mp3

www.ingramcontent.com/pod-product-compliance
Lightning Source LLC
Chambersburg PA
CBHW040154270326
41929CB00041B/3406